GW01403249

English in Context
Phrasal Verbs

Betty Kirkpatrick MA

LEARNERS
PUBLISHING

© 2001 Learners Publishing Pte Ltd

First published 2001 by
Learners Publishing Pte Ltd
222 Tagore Lane
#03-01 TG Building
Singapore 787603

Email: learnpub@learners.com.sg
Website: http://www.learners.com.sg

Reprinted 2001(twice), 2002 (twice), 2003

All rights reserved. No part of this book shall be reproduced, or
transmitted by any means, electronic or mechanical, including
photocopying, recording, or by any information storage and
retrieval system, without written permission from the publisher.

ISBN 981 4070 88 2

Printed by Seng Lee Press Pte Ltd, Singapore

**Please remember that
unauthorized photocopying of
this book is illegal.**

Preface

The purpose of this *English in Context* series is, as the title indicates, to show students how various aspects of English, such as idioms and phrasal verbs, are actually used. The passages, which have been specially written for the series, bring to students a very clear idea of how these various aspects are used in context. The use of passages, rather than a single example sentence of the kind found in most dictionaries, demonstrates in a lively and graphic way just how words and sentences relate to each other and how English is actually put together.

Phrasal verbs consist of a verb followed by a preposition, a verb followed by an adverb, or a verb followed by both an adverb and a preposition. They do not look difficult, but they can cause major problems for those learning English.

The meaning of a phrasal verb is not necessarily simply the literal meanings of the verb and adverb or preposition put together. Thus, to **come up with** means something more than the meaning of these three words put together. It means to think of an idea and suggest it, as in '**come up with** a plan'.

Sometimes an object can come between the verb and preposition and sometimes it cannot. Sometimes the positioning of the object depends on whether the object is a noun or pronoun. The best way to master this aspect of phrasal verbs is to see them in context, as they are in this book.

Each section of the text includes: a specially written passage containing ten phrasal verbs, a list of phrasal verbs used, together with clear definitions and example sentences, and a set of questions to test the student's understanding of what has been learnt.

Please note that phrasal verbs can have more than one meaning. Only the meaning dealt with in the passage is defined.

Contents

Phrasal Verbs
in Use

1 A Missing Passport

Phrasal Verbs in Use

Jane could not find her passport. She **had gone through** all her private papers, but it was not among them. Where could it be? Usually she was very careful about **putting** things **away**. However, her passport was definitely not in its proper place. She tried to remember when she had last seen it, but she had not needed it for some time. The last time she had been overseas had been three years ago and she **had** not **looked for** it since. Now she simply had to find it. She and two other students in her course had been fortunate enough to win a scholarship to study English in London and the university **had asked** them **for** their passports so that travel arrangements could be made. Although the others **had handed in** their documents right away, Jane **had put off** doing so. Yesterday she had been told that her documents must be at the university office by the end of the week or her study trip **would be called off**. She kept hoping that the passport **would turn up** but so far it remained missing. Finally, she decided to **talk** the matter **over with** her mother in case she had any idea where it could be. At first the line was engaged but, when she eventually heard her mother's voice, Jane was greatly relieved. 'Don't you remember? You **left** your passport **behind** with me after your last holiday in case you lost it.'

Know the Meaning

go through to examine (something) carefully, sometimes in order to search for (something): *Mary went through her friend's entire wardrobe looking for something to wear to the party. There is no error in the company books — the accountant has gone through them twice.*

put away to put (something) tidily in its proper place, sometimes where it cannot be seen: *Their mother told the children to put their toys away in the cupboard before going to bed. The cookery books were lying on the kitchen table but I put them away on the shelf.*

look for to try to find (something), to search for (something): *Jack has mislaid his notebook and is looking for it. The visitors are looking for an inexpensive hotel.*

ask for to say (to someone) that you would like to have (something), to request (something) from (someone): *Fred has gone to the bank to ask for a loan. If you want some water ask the waitress for it.*

hand in to give (something) to (someone) or take (something) to (somewhere) so it can be dealt with: *Joe has gone to the office to hand in his job application. How can the teacher mark your essay if you do not hand it in?*

put off to delay or postpone (something): *Because of illness we have decided to put off the meeting until next week. The club has put the match off until the end of the season. Jill hates cleaning the house and so she puts it off as long as possible.*

call off to cancel (something that has been arranged): *The organizers had to call off the fete because of bad weather. We called the jumble sale off because of lack of support. Sue's engagement to Tom lasted for two years, but then she suddenly called it off.*

turn up to be found or to appear, sometimes after being thought to be lost or to be unavailable: *The family thought that their cat was dead, but it turned up in the next village alive and well. Liz is unemployed but she's sure that the right job will turn up soon.*

talk over (with) to discuss (something) with (someone): *We had a meeting to talk over our various experiences. The students were advised to talk their problems over with their teachers. We all have different ideas about the new sports centre — let's meet and talk them over.*

leave behind not to take (something or someone) with you, sometimes accidentally, sometimes deliberately: *Tina left her jacket behind at the restaurant. I can't find my briefcase — I must have left it behind at the office. Mark has gone to work overseas, leaving his wife and children behind until he finds accommodation.*

Do it Yourself

1 Complete the sentence: *The burglar had _____ all the papers on my desk, looking for money.*

2 Complete the phrasal verb: *The secretary was asked to **put** the documents _____ in the filing cabinet.*

3 Replace the underlined words with a phrasal verb: *The police are trying to find the murder weapon.*

4 Replace the underlined word with a phrasal verb: *The student requested more time to finish his essay.*

5 Complete the phrasal verb: *We have to **hand** _____ the money for the college outing today.*

6 Replace the underlined word with a phrasal verb: *Some people are off ill and so we are delaying the meeting until tomorrow.*

7 Replace the underlined word with a phrasal verb: *The theatre trip has been cancelled — not enough people wanted to go.*

8 Complete the phrasal verb: *We thought Don had left the area but he suddenly **turned** _____ in the pub last night.*

9 Replace the phrasal verb with a suitable verb: *I would like to **talk over** my career plans **with** my parents.*

10 Complete the phrasal verb: *It had started to rain and Alice **had left** her umbrella _____ on the bus.*

2 A Street Accident

Phrasal Verbs in Use

A group of students from the drama college were sitting anxiously in the casualty department of the local hospital. Becky, one of their fellow students, **had been run over** by a van and the doctor was examining her in one of the cubicles. When the van hit her she **had** fallen heavily and **been knocked out**. Although it had not taken her long to **come round**, the doctor told her friends that at this stage he **could** not **rule out** the possibility of head injuries. What made things worse was that Becky's parents were working overseas and could not be contacted. However, the students had got in touch with Becky's aunt and uncle who **were acting as** guardians and they were on their way to the hospital. Fortunately, her uncle was a lawyer because the van-driver **was making out** that the accident was Becky's fault. He **had brushed aside** the students' claims that he was speeding, but luckily there were other eyewitnesses who **agreed with** Becky's friends. By the time her relatives reached the hospital Becky had been told that she had no major injuries. The hospital staff, however, **were keeping** her **in** overnight just as a precaution because she had been unconscious for a time. Becky was very relieved that there was nothing seriously wrong. She was playing the lead in the college end-of-term play and had been worried in case she would have to **pull out of** the part because of her injuries.

Know the Meaning

run over *(of a vehicle or of the driver of a vehicle)* to knock down and possibly drive over (someone or something), often causing injury or damage: *We nearly ran over a cat as we drove off. The dog dashed out onto the road and a car ran it over. Watch you don't get run over as you cross the road!*

knock out to cause (someone) to become unconscious: *The fierce blow knocked out Mr Smart. The attacker hit the old man on the head and knocked him out. The burglar lifted a baseball bat and knocked the shopkeeper out with it.*

come round to become conscious again, to regain consciousness: *The pregnant woman fainted in the heat but soon came round.*

rule out not to consider (something) because it is regarded as being impossible or extremely unlikely: *The police have ruled out robbery as a motive for the murder. Suicide has been ruled out as a cause of death. The fire may have been a result of arson — the fire inspector has not ruled it out.*

act as to carry out the work or duties of (someone or something): *The assistant manager acts as head of department when the manager is away. This sofa acts as a bed as well as something to sit on.*

make out to claim or pretend that (something is true): *He made out that he was a millionaire, but, in fact, he had very little money.*

brush aside to pay no attention to (something), to take no notice of (something). *The boss always brushed aside any suggestions made by the workers. The boss brushed our complaints aside very rudely. We tried to make a protest to the council, but they brushed it aside.*

agree with to say the same as (someone or something), to have the same opinion as (someone): *I agree with you that something must be done. The information which Jack gave to the police agreed with that given by Bill.*

keep in not to let (someone) leave (somewhere): *Mary is keeping her child in bed until his cold's better. Jack is not home yet — the doctor is keeping him in hospital.*

pull out of not to continue with (something), to stop taking part in (something): *Our team has had to pull out of the football competition because of illness. There are not many competitors in the race — several people pulled out of it at the last minute.*

Do it Yourself

1 Complete the phrasal verb: *The delivery lorry ____ **over** the little girl when she ran in front of it.*

2 Complete the phrasal verb: *The burglar hit the old man on the head with a vase and ____ him **out**.*

3 Replace the underlined words with a phrasal verb: *Tara regained consciousness in hospital after the attack on her.*

4 Replace the underlined words with a phrasal verb: *We did not consider failure.*

5 Fill in the missing phrasal verb: *Mr Jackson is off ill and Mrs Cook is going to ____ team coach until he recovers.*

6 Replace the underlined words with a phrasal verb: *Tessa was only a student but she pretended that she was an experienced teacher.*

7 Complete the phrasal verb: *The referee **brushed** ____ my protest and went on with the game.*

8 Replace the underlined words with a phrasal verb: *Mike's account of the accident says the same as that of the other driver.*

9 Complete the phrasal verb: *We always ____ the children **in** their playroom if it is raining heavily.*

10 Replace the underlined words with a phrasal verb: *The leading actor has a sore throat and has decided not to continue with the performance.*

3 The Missing Directions

Phrasal Verbs in Use

There were only a few days of the summer vacation left and neither Jim nor his friends had been on holiday. He decided to call them and try to **fix** one **up**. 'Why don't we go camping?' he suggested. 'My brother has two large tents and I'm sure he'll let us borrow them.' None of them had been camping before, but Jim was very persuasive and soon **talked** them **round**. 'I'll hire a mini-van and **pick** you all **up** at 8 o'clock tomorrow morning at the town hall.' 'Where are we going?' asked Pete as they **set off**. 'My brother's given me directions to a superb campsite in the mountains,' replied Jim. 'He goes there often.' After they had been driving for what seemed a long time Jock **called out** from the back of the van, 'It's time we **looked up** your brother's directions. I think we might be lost.' Jim opened his rucksack to **search for** them and then confessed, 'I think I left them on the kitchen table.' 'That's all right,' said Jock hopefully. 'I heard your brother telling you how to get there.' 'He did,' said Jim, 'but I **did**n't **take** it **in**. I thought we'd have the written instructions.' By now it was getting very dark and they weren't very sure how to **put up** a tent, even if they found a campsite. 'We'll just have to **make do with** sleeping in the van,' said Mark. 'Not what I'd call the perfect holiday!'

Know the Meaning

fix up to arrange (something): *We have fixed up a meeting of the club for next week. Have you had time to fix the next game up? We're going on a cruise next year but we haven't fixed it up yet.*

talk round to persuade (someone): *It's easy to talk my mother round — she's now agreed to lend us the car. Jane's father said at first that she couldn't go on the college trip, but she eventually talked him round.*

pick up *(of a vehicle or the driver of a vehicle)* to stop and let (someone) into a vehicle in order to take the person somewhere: *The bus will stop at the college gates to pick up all the students. I have to drive over to the next village to pick a friend up. Dad says that he'll pick us up outside the cinema.*

set off to begin a journey: *The family had to set off at dawn to get to the airport in time for their flight.*

call out to say (something) loudly, to shout: *Anne called out from the back of the bus that she was cold.'Watch! You're driving too fast!' called out Lou. Their neighbour called out a greeting as he passed.*

look up to look at (a reference book, set of instructions, etc) to try to find some information: *We looked up a dictionary to find out what the word meant. I'll have to look up the instructions to find out how the machine works.*

search for to try to find (someone or something), to look for (someone or something): *The police are out searching for the missing child. We must start searching for somewhere to stay the night. I mislaid my notebook and spent hours searching for it.*

take in to understand and remember (something that is read, heard, etc): *I was too tired to take the information in properly. The pupils were restless and didn't take in what the teacher said. The lecturer gave an excellent description of the Middle Ages but few of the students took it in.*

put up to assemble (the parts of something), to build (something), to erect (something): *They're putting up a new block of flats near our house. They put the new supermarket up in record time. The builders have finished the house — they put it up very quickly.*

make do with to have to use (something) instead of something else which is more suitable, desirable etc, to have to use a less acceptable, often inadequate substitute or alternative: *I really need cream for this recipe, but I'll just have to make do with milk. The family had to make do with much less money after their father lost his job.*

Do it Yourself

1 Replace the underlined word with a phrasal verb: *We haven't had time to <u>arrange</u> the annual meeting of the club yet.*

2 Replace the phrasal verb with a suitable verb: *Bert eventually **talked** his father **round** and he was allowed to borrow the family car.*

3 Complete the phrasal verb: *Jock has hired a minibus to take us to the football match and is going to _____ us **up** at the college gates.*

4 Replace the underlined words with a phrasal verb: *We <u>began the journey</u> at dawn.*

5 Replace the underlined word with a phrasal verb: *'We've taken the wrong road,' <u>shouted</u> Carol.*

6 Fill in the missing phrasal verb: *I wanted to find out exactly where Sydney was and so I _____ an atlas.*

7 Complete the phrasal verb: *We had to stop **searching** _____ the missing child when night fell.*

8 Replace the underlined words with a phrasal verb: *We simply cannot <u>understand and remember</u> all the information that the teacher gives in one lecture.*

9 Replace the underlined word with a phrasal verb: *My new desk arrived in a flat pack and I cannot <u>assemble</u> it.*

10 Write the missing phrasal verb in the space provided: *Mike had to take a reduction in salary when he moved jobs and now he has to _____ a poorer standard of living.*

4 Childminding

Phrasal Verbs in Use

It was Saturday morning and Val **had got up** late. She was now feeling bored and decided to phone her friend Dee and ask if she wanted to go shopping. 'I can't,' said Dee. '**I'm looking after** my niece and nephew today. My sister, May, has had to go into the office today. She has a nanny for the children, but she's off-duty this weekend and I offered to **stand in for** her.' 'Why don't I come and help?' said Val. 'Good idea!' replied Dee. 'Some adult company **will keep** me **from** going mad. I love the children very much, but they can be exhausting. I just don't know how the nanny **puts up with** it.' Val soon saw that Dee was absolutely right. The children — Colin who was 6 years old and Anya who was 4 — were charming but full of energy and mischief. 'This **is turning into** a nightmare,' cried Dee trying to get the children to eat lunch. Anya would not eat anything but ice cream and then **threw up** all over the carpet. Dee went off to find a bucket and cloth and came back to **wipe up** the mess. Meanwhile Val was regretting offering to help and wondering if she could **last out** until May came home. Just then they heard the front door open and May **burst into** the room. 'Are the children all right?' she asked anxiously. 'They're fine,' said Dee. 'But we have to go now.'

Know the Meaning

get up to get out of bed, to rise: *We have to get up very early to catch the first bus.*

look after to take care of (someone), to attend to the needs of (someone): *Their grandmother looks after the children during the school holidays when their parents are at work. Jan's parents are both elderly and she has given up work to look after them.*

stand in for to carry out the work or duties of (someone), to take (someone's) place temporarily: *Fred is standing in for the firm's accountant who is on holiday. The history lecturer is on maternity leave and Mr Jones is standing in for her.*

keep from to stop oneself from (doing something), but with difficulty: *Jill was organizing a surprise party for Jo's return home, but she was so excited that she could scarcely keep from telling everyone about it. Tim is so conceited that he cannot keep from admiring himself in every mirror.*

put up with to tolerate (someone or something), to have to accept (someone or something) unpleasant or difficult: *The Millers can't put up with their noisy neighbours any longer and so they're moving house. Patsy hates the canteen food but she has to put up with it because it's cheap.*

turn into to become (someone or something different): *It was a sunny morning but it turned into a stormy day. Nick was a charming child, but he turned into a really nasty young man.*

threw up (*informal*) to vomit, to be sick: *The child got car sick and threw up all over the coats in the back seat.*

wipe up to remove (something such as dirt, liquid, etc) from a surface with a cloth, to clean (something) up: *The children were making dough on the kitchen table and it took a while to wipe up the mess. Please wipe up all that mess before you leave the kitchen. There's mud all over the carpet — I'll have to wipe it up.*

last out to survive, to continue to exist or function in a difficult situation: *The travellers were cold and hungry and just hoped that they could last out until help arrive. Jim is supposed to have stopped smoking, but he won't last out until tonight without a cigarette.*

burst into to enter (somewhere) suddenly and sometimes violently: *The couple were watching television when the burglar burst into the room and pointed a gun at them.*

Do it Yourself

1 Replace the underlined words with a phrasal verb: *Paul had been to a late-night party the night before and did not want to <u>get out of bed</u>.*

2 Replace the underlined words with a phrasal verb: *The childminder is paid to <u>take care of</u> three young children.*

3 Replace the underlined words with a phrasal verb: *The head of department is on study leave and her deputy is <u>taking her place temporarily</u>.*

4 Complete the phrasal verb: *I was so tired that I could hardly **keep** _____ falling asleep.*

5 Replace the phrasal verb with a suitable verb: *Liz said that she divorced Alex because she could not **put up with** his laziness.*

6 Complete the phrasal verb: *It was a dull, wet morning but it _____ **into** a beautiful day.*

7 Replace the underlined word with a phrasal verb: *Fred drank too much beer at the party and <u>vomited</u> on the steps of the house.*

8 Replace the phrasal verb with a similar phrasal verb: *The waitress **cleaned up** the spilt coffee.*

9 Complete the phrasal verb: *The patient is losing a lot of blood — she may not _____ **out** until the ambulance gets here.*

10 Complete the phrasal verb: *The police **burst** _____ the nightclub to search for drugs.*

5 A Change of Subject

Phrasal Verbs in Use

Peter **was heading for** his tutor's office. Mrs Wood was always very understanding and he wanted some advice on his university career. At the moment he was studying biology and he wanted to **give** it **up**. Peter was a hard-working student and he hadn't **got behind with** his work. Indeed all his course lecturers said that he was doing very well. Furthermore he loved student life and he certainly did not intend to **drop out of** university. The problem was that he did not find science very interesting and wanted to study English. Since he had excellent university entrance qualifications and since he was only in his first term, he would probably have no difficulty in **going over to** the arts faculty. However, his father had persuaded him to **take up** science, saying that there were far more job opportunities in the science field. Now Peter regretted this but he didn't seem to be able to **get through to** his father how miserable he was. He **put** his son's unhappiness **down to** difficulty in making the adjustment from school to university and this was a problem for many new students. When Peter reached Mrs Wood's office he found that she had already met his father and talked about the possible change of course. To Peter's surprise she **had won** him **over** to Peter's way of thinking. He was able to change courses and **put** all his unhappiness **behind** him.

Know the Meaning

head for to go or move towards (something), to move in the direction of (something): *We're heading for London but we're staying overnight in York. With poor sales figures like these the firm is heading for disaster.*

give up to stop doing or taking (something), because one is no longer interested in it, because it is bad for one, etc: *Giles keeps getting chest infections and has been advised to stop smoking. Tess used to play tennis, but she had to give it up when she injured her arm.*

get behind with to be late or slow in (doing something), not to make as much progress with (something) as might be expected: *Molly is studying in the library all day because she has got behind with her vacation reading list. The students are given so many essays to write that most of them get behind with them.*

drop out of to stop being involved in or taking part in (something), to withdraw from (something): *Alan dropped out of university because he found the work too hard. The group dropped out of society and went to live in a commune on a remote island. It was a boring course and several students dropped out of it.*

go over to to change to a different system, organization, set of beliefs, etc: *Paula's parents are dissatisfied with state education and have gone over to the private system. There's a new youth club in the village and many of our members have gone over to it.*

take up to start doing (something): *Jenny has decided to take up nursing as a career. In order to be good at ballet you really have to take it up when you are very young.*

get through to to make (someone) understand (something): *They just cannot get through to their daughter that hitchhiking can be dangerous. How can we get the importance of eating healthily through to them?*

put down to to regard (something) as being caused by (something), to believe that (something) is a result of (something): *It is difficult to put the two burglaries down to coincidence. Jeff keeps getting headaches and his doctor puts them down to stress.*

win over to persuade (someone) to support or agree with one or one's point of view: *Paul tried to win his friends over to his way of thinking but failed. Val eventually got a new bike — she's good at winning her father over. At first Tina supported the rival candidate, but we eventually won her over to our side.*

put behind (one) to try to forget about (something) and not let it affect one any more: *Sara hopes to put her unhappy divorce behind her and make a new life for herself. Jake was involved in petty crime when he was young, but fortunately he has put it behind him now.*

Do it Yourself

1 Replace the underlined words with a phrasal verb: *The children were going towards the school when we met them.*

2 Replace the underlined words with a phrasal verb: *Patrick has been advised to stop doing his present job as it is too stressful for him.*

3 Complete the phrasal verb: *I have got _____ with my ironing and all my clothes are creased.*

4 Replace the underlined words with a phrasal verb: *Jo was a singer but he stopped being involved in pop music some years ago.*

5 Replace the underlined words with a phrasal verb: *Amy was a member of the Labour Party, but she changed to the Green Party some months ago.*

6 Complete the phrasal verb: *Jack felt in need of a hobby and so he took _____ chess.*

7 Write down a phrasal verb which means 'to make someone understand something'.

8 Replace the underlined word with a phrasal verb: *We attributed her absence to illness.*

9 Complete the phrasal verb: *They didn't want to vote for us at first but we eventually won them _____.*

10 If you **put** an event in your life **behind you** do you try to think about it a lot?

6 Waiting for a Job

Phrasal Verbs in Use

Jock **had run into** Pam on the way home from college and she had told him that Mr Cook, the father of Ron, a mutual friend of theirs, **was starting up** a new computer software firm. Pam thought that Mr Cook might be needing students to work in the factory for the summer and suggested that Jock apply, since he wanted to make as much money as possible in the vacation. Jock **had acted on** her suggestion immediately and **had put in for** a job as a programmer. He was now waiting to hear if he had got a job. Up till this year he would have been able to **fall back on** a job in his brother-in-law's paint factory if nothing else was available. However, his brother-in-law had had to **shut down** the factory earlier in the year because the business was losing money at an alarming rate. It was financially essential for Jock to work during the vacations and he **was banking on** getting a job from Mr Cook. He had tried several local firms for work, but they **had** all **passed** him **over**. Jock was reluctant to contact Mr Cook and try to **pin** him **down** about the job, but he needed to know as soon as possible. He had just decided that he would ring Mr Cook the following day when he received a letter saying that he was prepared to **take** him **on** as soon as term ended. Naturally, he was extremely relieved.

Know the Meaning

run into to meet (someone) unexpectedly: *The other day I ran into an old friend from my schooldays. We ran into each other when we were shopping.*

start up to begin to operate or to establish (a new business, etc): *They're planning to start up a new chess club. The business is quite old — my grandfather started it up.*

act on to act according to (what someone has advised, suggested, etc): *Paddy refused to act on my advice. I made various suggestions, but the committee did not act on any of them.*

put in for to apply for (a job, competition, etc): *Jim has put in for a job in a different department. Several jobs were advertised and hundreds of applicants put in for them.*

fall back on to use (something) or seek help from (someone) that you know that you can rely on when everything else has failed: *We have an open fire which we can fall back on if the central heating system fails. Sheila does some temporary work for us — we can always fall back on her.*

shut down to close (a business, etc) completely so that it no longer operates: *The old man had to shut down his business when he became ill. The firm has decided to shut all their country branches down. The firm was losing money and the owners had to shut it down.*

bank on to rely on (something), to hope and believe that (something will happen): *Phil is banking on getting a loan from his parents. I hope that Muriel gets a good mark in her exam because she's banking on it.*

pass over to ignore or reject (someone): *The boss passed June over again and promoted her assistant. Jill applied for a job in another department, but she was passed over and was not even given an interview. Jack said that he wished to be considered for the post of deputy manager, but the directors passed him over.*

pin down to make (someone) give a definite answer or opinion: *I have been trying to pin Fred down, but all he would say is that he will be here some time next week. The shop-owner spoke vaguely about offering me some work some time, but I couldn't pin him down about an exact date.*

take on to begin to employ (someone): *The business is expanding and we have taken on new staff. The firm takes fewer people on in the winter months. We can't take you on just now as we have no vacancies.*

Do it Yourself

1 Complete the phrasal verb: *Last night at the theatre I **ran** _____ my friend Bill.*

2 Complete the phrasal verb: *John is going to ask the bank manager for a loan so that he can **start** _____ a sandwich bar.*

3 Complete the phrasal verb: *Julie decided that it was best to _____ **on** her uncle's advice and get a mechanic to check the car before she bought it.*

4 Replace the underlined words with a phrasal verb: *Kevin got really good marks in his exams and he is going to start <u>applying for</u> a better job straight away.*

5 Complete the phrasal verb: *I'm glad that I know how to type because it's something that I can always **fall** _____ **on** if I cannot find other work.*

6 Replace the phrasal verb with a suitable verb: *Ian was very upset when he realized that he would have to **shut down** his shop because it was not making any money.*

7 Replace the underlined words with a phrasal verb: *Helen has already bought a car so she is <u>relying on</u> passing her driving test.*

8 Complete the sentence: *Joe was devastated when he was _____ for promotion.*

9 Complete the phrasal verb: *I tried to **pin** Jack _____ for an exact date for the wedding but he did not give me one.*

10 Complete the phrasal verb: *Carol was amazed that the bank agreed to **take** her _____ even though she had failed her exams.*

7 Sunbathing Interrupted

Phrasal Verbs in Use

Ted went round to Ralph's house to visit him and Ralph's sister **asked** him **in**. In fact, Ralph was not in the house but in the garden. There he **had stretched** himself **out** on a deck-chair and **was soaking up** the sun. A bottle of wine stood close by and Ted nearly **knocked** it **over**. 'It's time to stop sunbathing,' said Ted to Ralph. 'We agreed to book our holiday overseas today. The travel agent in the high street has a bargain deal to Europe, but she said that other people are sure to **snap** it **up** if we don't book quickly.' Ralph replied sleepily, 'Travel agents always say things like that. I hope you didn't let her **talk** you **into** anything too expensive. I'll just **drink** my wine **up** and **put** the deck-chair **away** and then we'll go.' Ralph's sister appeared in time to hear this and said, 'You'd better **throw on** some clothes as well — those shorts you're wearing are rather short to wear in the high street.' When Ralph was dressed, he and Ted went to the travel agent. Ralph agreed that the suggested holiday package was a good deal and they confirmed the booking and paid a deposit. 'Now all we have to do is to **save up** our money to pay for the rest of the fare and for our living expenses,' said Ted. 'It's just as well that we have a few months to do that!' replied Ralph.

Know the Meaning

ask in to invite (someone) to go into a house: *Jill's mother told her to ask the visitors in. I knocked at the door but Mr Brown did not ask me in.*

stretch out to lay (oneself or someone) out straight: *Frank was tired and stretched himself out on the sofa. The nurses stretched the patient out on the bed.*

soak up to absorb (something), to lie or sit for a long time in (sunshine): *The blotting paper soaked up the ink. The girls lay on the beach and soaked up the hot sunshine. It's a pity to waste all this sunshine — let's go out and soak it up.*

knock over to make (something) fall, often accidentally: *The woman knocked over a valuable vase with her handbag. The child knocked the paint tin over. The bottle was full of wine and the dog knocked it over.*

snap up to buy (something) quickly, often because it is cheap or rare: *At that price that table is a bargain — you should snap it up. The shop is having a sale, but most of the goods were snapped up right away. As soon as the tickets for the pop concert went on sale, the students snapped them up.*

talk into to persuade (someone) to do something: *Harry talked his friends into joining him. We didn't want to go swimming, but Lucy talked us into it.*

drink up to finish (a drink) completely: *Drink up your tea — it's time to leave. The child was told to drink her milk up. The coffee was very hot, but I drank it up.*

put away to return (something) to where it is usually placed or stored: *I've put the Christmas tree away till next year. Could you put away the clean dishes, please? Pat lifted the box and put it away in the attic.*

throw on to put on (clothes) hurriedly and carelessly: *When she realized that she had overslept, Sue threw on jeans and a sweater and ran to catch the bus. It was cold and Jean threw a warm sweater over her summer dress. Look at his clothes — he must have thrown them on.*

save up to keep and collect (money) instead of spending it, often so that it can be spent later on something particular: *The children are saving up their pocket money to buy a present for their mother. We all save a part of our salary each month. Don't spend your extra money — save it up!*

Do it Yourself

1 Complete the phrasal verb: *I thought that it was very rude of Mrs Williams not to **ask** us _____ after we had done all her shopping for her.*

2 Replace the underlined words with a phrasal verb: *The doctor advised Sharon that the best thing to do for her sore back was to <u>lie down flat</u> on the floor.*

3 Replace the underlined words with a phrasal verb: *David is really looking forward to his holiday; he plans to do nothing but <u>lie in</u> the sun for two weeks.*

4 Complete the phrasal verb: *The glass of milk was on the edge of the table and when I stood up I **knocked** it _____.*

5 Complete the phrasal verb: *Daisy is going to make her chocolate cake for the bring-and-buy sale. It is delicious and is bound to get **snapped** _____ straight away.*

6 Complete the phrasal verb: *Fred eventually **talked** Tina _____ going out on a date with him.*

7 Replace the underlined word with a phrasal verb: *The waiter told us to <u>finish</u> our wine and leave the restaurant as it was about to close.*

8 Complete the phrasal verb: *I have to _____ **away** the laundry before I can make the dinner.*

9 Complete the phrasal verb: *I don't take much care over my appearance; I tend to just _____ **on** the first thing that I find in my wardrobe.*

10 Replace the underlined word with a phrasal verb: *George is <u>keeping</u> all his coins in a jar.*

8 Choosing a Present

Phrasal Verbs in Use

Vicky was trying to **find out** what her mother would like as a birthday present. Her mother had replied that she did not know, but that she would **think** it **over**. When Vicky asked her the next evening she said that she still had not decided, but that she would **sleep on** the problem and tell her in the morning. In the morning she said that she would like some make-up or some bath oil and Vicky asked her sister, Jane, to go shopping with her. Jane suggested that they **put off** the shopping trip until the next day. Then she suggested that they could **do away with** the need for a shopping trip completely because she had a friend who was an agent for a cosmetics firm who would bring a selection to the house. They could then **look over** her stock in comfortable surroundings and find something that their mother would like. The two sisters **whiled away** a pleasant evening with Jane's friend, Margo. After they **had tried out** several products from Margo's samples, they chose some body lotion and some bath oil for the sisters' mother. The products were quite expensive and Vicky said that she would ask their brother, Tom, to share the present and to help **pay for** it. Jane was not sure that he would agree to this, but he did and Vicky went off to buy some pretty paper in which she **wrapped up** the present. Their mother was delighted.

Know the Meaning

find out to learn or discover (something): *At last we found out where he was. Now they have found all the facts out. The information is up-to-date — we've just found it out.*

think over to think about (something) carefully before deciding: *Polly needs time to think things over before she decides about the job offer. I'm thinking over one or two ideas. That's the problem — please think it over.*

sleep on to wait until next morning before making a decision about (something): *How to pay for the new car is difficult — I'm going to sleep on the problem. I can't decide where to go on holiday and so I'm going to sleep on it.*

put off to delay or postpone (something): *The groom was taken ill and they had to put the wedding off for a few weeks. Let's put off talking to them until we have more details. We planned a meeting for next week, but we've had to put it off.*

do away with to get rid of (something): *We did away with that old garden shed. The Smiths had an open fire in the study, but they did away with it and put in an electric heater.*

look over to examine or inspect (a piece of property) fairly quickly to see if it is satisfactory and suitable: *The estate agent gave us the keys and we looked over the cottage last night. We looked over several properties. I know the house — we looked over it last month.*

while away to spend (a period of time) without being bored, often because you have nothing else to do or because you are waiting for something: *We had an hour to wait for the bus, but we whiled away the time by walking in the park. You can while a few pleasant hours away watching the boats in the harbour. If you ever have an hour to spare try whiling it away at the local museum.*

try out to test (something) by using it in order to see if it is suitable, reliable, etc: *I'm going to try out a new recipe. The firm is trying a new system out. If you're interested in the exercise bike you should try it out.*

pay for to give (money) for (something): *Joan's parents are paying for the holiday. Rachel would love that coat, but she would never be able to pay for it.*

wrap up to cover (something) by folding paper, etc round it: *I'm just going to wrap up this wedding present. Barbara is just wrapping the gift up now. This is a valuable vase — I'll have to wrap it up carefully.*

Do it Yourself

1 Replace the underlined word with a phrasal verb: *Susan was delighted when she <u>discovered</u> that her old friend had bought a flat in the street that she lived in.*

2 Complete the phrasal verb: *Bob has gone to stay with his parents for a few days so that he can **think** things _____ and decide if he wants to get married or not.*

3 Complete the phrasal verb: *I can't decide if I should accept the job offer — I think the best thing to do is to **sleep** _____ it.*

4 Replace the phrasal verb with a suitable verb: *Wendy had to **put off** her party because she was not well.*

5 Replace the underlined words with a phrasal verb: *Steven was surprised to discover that the school had <u>got rid of</u> exams and now all the students had to do was write essays.*

6 Replace the underlined word with a phrasal verb: *Tracey asked an architect to <u>inspect</u> the flat before she bought it.*

7 Complete the phrasal verb: *On a Sunday Ruth likes to **while** _____ the time feeding the ducks.*

8 Replace the underlined word with a phrasal verb: *Paul is going to <u>test</u> the bike before he decides if he will buy it.*

9 Complete the phrasal verb: *Mary reminded Lisa that she still had to _____ **for** her share of the bill for the meal that they had last week.*

10 Complete the phrasal verb: *I will be ready in a minute — I just need to _____ Andy's present **up**.*

9 Burglary

Phrasal Verbs in Use

Mr Wilson was feeling quite cheerful as he went to **open up** his shop, but that soon changed. As he put his key in the door he realized that something was wrong. The door was open. He immediately realized that someone **had broken into** the shop during the night and felt both angry and afraid. Although the shop had an alarm system, it had not done any good as someone **had switched** it **off**. Furthermore, the burglar **had cut off** the phone and so Mr Wilson had to go a long way down the street to a public phone box in order to **send for** the police. It was quite early in the morning and he did not want to disturb the people in the neighbouring house. The police **arrived at** the shop shortly after the shopkeeper returned and said that they would examine the shop to look for fingerprints and other clues. In the meanwhile they asked Mr Wilson to see if there was any money missing from the till and to **write down** a list of any items that had been taken. The burglar had smashed several of the glass shelves and had broken a window, but the police asked Mr Wilson not to **sweep up** the broken glass until they had finished. By the time the shopkeeper **had carried out** his instructions the police had done all they could and left. Mrs Wilson arrived just then saying, 'Thank goodness the burglar did not **beat** you **up**!'

Know the Meaning

open up to unlock the door to a building so that people can get in: *Mark rarely opens up the office until 9.15 although he should open at 9 o'clock. Mario doesn't open his restaurant up until the evening. There was a queue outside the shop and so we opened it up early.*

break into to enter (a building, etc) illegally and often by using force: *Thieves broke into the jewellers in the high street. The building had an alarm system, but burglars broke into it, nevertheless.*

switch off to stop (an electrical device, etc) from working by pressing a switch: *Myra switched off the television when the programme finished. You can switch the engine off now. That radio's too loud — please switch it off!*

cut off to disconnect (a telephone service): *The engineer accidentally cut off our phone when repairing the line. Bad weather had cut our phones off. The cottage had a telephone connection, but the thieves cut it off.*

send for to ask (someone) to come, often in order to give some form of help: *Dad's ill — send for the doctor! There was nothing the police could do, but Bert still sent for them.*

arrive at to reach (a place): *We arrived at the hotel rather late. The cottage is still a considerable distance away and we won't arrive at it until morning.*

write down to record (something) in writing, using pen or pencil and paper: *I wrote down your telephone number, but I've lost it. She wrote several addresses down. I'll forget your address — please write it down!*

sweep up to remove (something) by sweeping with a broom or brush: *Anne dropped a cup and had to sweep up the pieces. The gardener was sweeping the leaves up from the lawn. There were crumbs all over the floor and the children were asked to sweep them up.*

carry out to act according to (instructions, etc), to put (something) into practice: *The team carried out the captain's orders. The teachers are just carrying government policy out. That was the head teacher's suggestion and we are carrying it out.*

beat up to strike or kick (someone) very badly: *The youths beat up the stranger, but they did not steal his wallet. The same gang have beaten several people up. Whenever they see a pupil from another school they beat him up.*

Do it Yourself

1 Complete the phrasal verb: *Claire asked if I could* **open** _____ *the coffee shop in the morning as she had an appointment at the dentist.*

2 Complete the phrasal verb: *Janice was very upset after the thieves* **broke** _____ *her house and stole her jewellery.*

3 Complete the phrasal verb: *I had to* **switch** _____ *the computer because looking at the screen was giving me a sore head.*

4 Replace the phrasal verb with one word: *James had his phone* **cut off** *because he had forgotten to pay his bill.*

5 Complete the phrasal verb: *The teacher* **sent** _____ *George's parents because he had missed a lot of classes when he had been ill.*

6 Replace the phrasal verb with one word: *The flight was delayed and it was after midnight before we* **arrived at** *the holiday resort.*

7 Replace the underlined word with a phrasal verb: *I had better <u>record</u> this information in the files.*

8 Complete the phrasal verb: *It took David a long time to* **sweep** _____ *the food that had been dropped on the floor at the party.*

9 Complete the phrasal verb: *Carol did not agree with the manager's decision, but she felt that she had to* _____ **out** *his instructions.*

10 Replace the underlined word with a phrasal verb: *Peter was scared to go out at night after he had been <u>assaulted</u> by a complete stranger.*

10 Dieting

Phrasal Verbs in Use

It was just after Christmas and Jill, realizing that she had put on weight because of all of the treats which she had eaten, decided to go on a diet. She was going to **give up** chocolate and pastries and all the other sweet things which she loved. Instead she was going to try to **live on** salads although she could not really **work up** much enthusiasm for this idea. Going to restaurants or to dinner with friends, when she couldn't eat what she would really like to, would be the worst part of it. She knew that she would have to **get out of** some arrangements which she **had** already **set up**, or she was afraid that she simply would not **stick to** her diet. The trouble was that, if she cancelled social engagements which involved eating, she would sit at home and be inclined to eat the very sweet things which she had vowed to **do without**. Jill decided that the best thing to do was to keep busy and began to **clear out** the attic. She **had stored up** a great many things there that she no longer needed. This was an extremely good idea because making decisions about all her old things meant that she was able to **keep** her mind **off** food for long periods of time. At the end of a few weeks she was delighted to discover that she had lost quite a bit of weight.

Know the Meaning

give up to stop using or doing (something): *Bill has given up cigarettes. Mike gave smoking and drinking up at the same time. I don't take sugar in tea — I gave it up.*

live on to eat (something) as one's only type of food: *Very young children live on milk. I like vegetables, but I would not like to live on them.*

work up gradually to develop (something): *Have you worked up an appetite for dinner? Willie couldn't work up the energy to go for a walk.*

get out of to avoid (something): *I'm trying to get out of tomorrow's meeting. Ella tried to get out of tidying her room. Joan has made a date with Tim, but she's trying to get out of it.*

set up to arrange (something), to fix up (something): *We have set up a committee of enquiry. When did you set the meeting up? An investigation is in progress, but we don't know who set it up.*

stick to to continue with (something), not to abandon (something): *We are going to stick to our original plan. They made a decision and they should stick to it.*

do without to manage or survive without having (something): *Anne finds it difficult to do without sugar. Joe likes meat, but he can do without it.*

clear out to make something tidy by getting rid of what is not needed: *Alice cleared out the kitchen cupboards. We cleared the attic out in one day. The room is now very neat because we cleared it out yesterday.*

store up to keep (something) for possible use in the future: *Granny stores up cans of fruit, but she'll never use them all. My uncle stores old newspapers up, but I don't know why.*

keep off to cause (someone or something) to stay away from: *Try to keep the child's attention off the sweets at the supermarket check-out. The fence is supposed to keep people off the grass. If the young people have a club, it helps to keep them off the streets.*

Do it Yourself

1 Replace the underlined words with a phrasal verb: *Jill has decided to stop going jogging because she finds that it hurts her knees.*

2 Replace the underlined words with a phrasal verb: *When I was on holiday I practically ate nothing but fruit and cheese.*

3 Complete the sentence: *Tracey could not _____ any enthusiasm for her new job.*

4 Complete the phrasal verb: *I hope that I can get _____ of going on holiday with Julie because I can't afford it.*

5 Replace the phrasal verb with one word: *The manager has set up a meeting with the customer who made a complaint.*

6 Replace the underlined words with a phrasal verb: *Robert is very reliable — once he makes a decision he does not abandon it.*

7 Replace the underlined words with a phrasal verb: *Wilma thinks that she will have to manage without her car because she has lost her job and can no longer afford to run it.*

8 Complete the phrasal verb: *We had to spend a long time clearing _____ the house before we could sell it.*

9 Replace the underlined word with a phrasal verb: *Sheila is keeping baby clothes in preparation for the birth of her grandchild.*

10 Write the missing phrasal verb: *The teacher warned the children to _____ the ice on the pond.*

11 Gardening

Phrasal Verbs in Use

Since Spring was just beginning Mike and Linda felt that they should **tidy up** the garden because they had neglected it during the winter. They wanted to plant some new bushes, but there were other tasks to do first. Linda **dug up** some old plants, which were past their best, and took them to the compost heap, while Mike said that he would **chop down** the old apple tree. This was not as easy a task as he had thought it would be, and, after some vain attempts with an axe, he decided to **settle for** removing some of the branches. He went to the shed to fetch his saw and began to **cut off** some of the larger branches. Just then their large black cat, Trixie, appeared. Some birds had been frightened out of the tree by the noise of sawing and were spotted by Trixie who suddenly **pounced on** one of them. Mike tried to stop her, but Trixie quickly **carried off** the wretched bird to the far end of the garden. Fortunately for the bird, Linda **caught up with** Trixie within a very short time and succeeded in rescuing the bird. In fact, it was not injured, although very frightened. Trixie **made for** the house, not looking very pleased at the loss of her prey. Linda knew that it was part of a cat's nature to try to catch birds, but was upset and agreed to **leave off** gardening for that day.

Know the Meaning

tidy up to make (something) neat or neater: *I tidied up this room this morning, but it's in a mess again. Tidy up your desk before you go home. The garden had been neglected, but we tidied it up.*

dig up to remove (something) by digging, to remove (something) from the ground: *We dug up the potatoes and cooked them for dinner. They dug the whole crop up. The rose bushes no longer bloomed and so we dug them up.*

chop down to make (usually a tree) fall to the ground by cutting through it with an axe, etc: *The farmer is going to chop down some fir trees and sell them as Christmas trees. We chopped the older trees down last winter. I wondered where the old oak tree was and was told that the owner had chopped it down.*

settle for to accept (something) although it is not quite what you wanted: *I wanted to go to Europe, but I'll settle for a holiday anywhere.*

cut off to remove by cutting with a knife, scissors, etc: *We cut off some of the dead blooms from the bush. The child cut all her hair off. Some of the branches of the tree were blocking the view and so we cut them off.*

pounce on to jump on (someone or something), to move towards and attack or grab (someone or something): *The cat pounced on the mouse. The school bully pounced on the younger child at the bus stop.*

carry off to get hold of (someone or something) and take (it/him/her) away by carrying: *The robbers carried off the bag of jewels. The soldiers watched the enemy carry their friend off. We tried to save the bird, but the cat carried it off.*

catch up with to come level with and sometimes overtake (someone or something): *We were unlikely to catch up with our friends as they left long before us. The other group of walkers left first, but we caught up with them at lunch-time.*

make for to go towards (somewhere): *We're making for the nearest town. We didn't reach the city although we were making for it.*

leave off to stop doing something: *We had to leave off sunbathing as it began to rain.*

Do it Yourself

1 Write the missing phrasal verb: *Kevin is always moaning at me to _____ the kitchen, but I don't make a mess — it's Fred.*

2 Complete the phrasal verb: *Yvonne was very excited when she _____ **up** a gold coin in her garden.*

3 Fill in the missing phrasal verb: *The local residents were very angry when the builders _____ the woodland to make space for the new houses.*

4 Replace the underlined word with a phrasal verb: *Keith has realized that he will have to <u>accept</u> the place at the local college although he had wanted to go to university.*

5 Complete the phrasal verb: *Tina regretted asking the hairdresser to _____ **off** her long hair.*

6 Replace the underlined word with a phrasal verb: *Wendy got a terrible fright when she was <u>grabbed</u> by a stranger.*

7 Complete the phrasal verb: *The football player had to be **carried** _____ the pitch.*

8 Complete the phrasal verb: *We eventually **caught up** _____ the other cars after we found the right road.*

9 Replace the underlined words with a phrasal verb: *We were <u>going towards</u> the house, where the party was, but it started to snow so we decided to go home instead.*

10 Replace the phrasal verb with one word: *Pauline had to **leave off** baking the cake when she realized that she did not have the right ingredients.*

12 A Shopping Trip

Phrasal Verbs in Use

Winnie and Anne were going shopping because Winnie wanted to **look for** a new dress for the tennis club dance. Her father had driven them to the high street and **dropped** them **off** at their favourite shop. However, he had told them that he couldn't **pick** them **up** there because it was a no-parking area. 'Even if we arranged a particular time, I couldn't guarantee that I would be here,' Winnie's father had said. 'The traffic wardens would most likely **move** me **on**.' The girls had told him not to bother to collect them and that they would see him at home. Then they entered the shop. At first they spent some time just looking, anxious to **nose out** some bargains. After a while they **picked out** several dresses and skirts from the display rails. 'Let's **try** these **on** in the changing-room,' said Winnie. They had to queue, but finally got a cubicle each. Anne **put on** a short red dress and went to Winnie's cubicle to show her. As she opened the curtain, Winnie **covered** herself **up** with her coat, saying, 'Close the curtain, Anne! I'm in my underwear and people will see me!' Anne decided that the dress did not suit her and Winnie agreed. She went back to her cubicle to **take off** the dress and decided that she did not want to shop any more that day. Since Winnie was in agreement with her, they went in search of a cup of tea.

Know the Meaning

look for to try to find (something): *Sally is looking for a new car. Mary has lost a glove and she is looking for it.*

drop off (*of a car-driver, etc*) to let (a passenger) out of a vehicle: *The bus dropped the passengers off at the town hall. We gave Pat a lift and dropped her off at her home.*

pick up (*of a car-driver, etc*) to let a passenger into a vehicle in order to take him/her somewhere: *Alice is going to pick Laura up and take her to work. You could pick up Frances on your way home. The driver saw the hitchhiker, but did not pick him up.*

move on to tell (someone) to move from a particular place: *The police moved the beggars on. The driver had parked his car at a bus stop and the police moved him on.*

nose out (*informal*) to find (something) by searching: *The journalist soon nosed out the scandal involving the politician. It took us a long time but we nosed all the facts out eventually. If there are bargain goods to be had, Harry will nose them out.*

pick out to choose (someone or something): *May picked out a car she liked and took it for a test drive. The captains had to pick eleven people out to be members of their teams. We bought three skirts — Jane had picked them out.*

try on to put on (an article of clothing) to see if it fits or is suitable: *Stella tried on three dresses, but didn't like any of them. Mark tried several pairs of trousers on. That's a lovely jacket — I'd like to try it on.*

put on to place (a piece of clothing) over part of the body and wear it: *It was cold and we all put on warm clothes. Since it was a lovely day, Pam put her best summer dress on. Rona carried a jacket, but did not put it on.*

cover up to place (something) over (someone or something) in order to hide or protect him/her/it: *The thieves covered the stolen bike up with a sheet of tarpaulin. The murderers had covered up the body with a pile of leaves. The baby is getting cold — we had better cover her up with a shawl.*

take off to remove (a piece of clothing) which one has been wearing: *Bill took off his wet clothes and put them on a radiator to dry. The child was told to take all his dirty clothes off and have a bath. Janet's sweater was filthy and so she took it off and washed it.*

Do it Yourself

1 Replace the underlined words with a phrasal verb: *Lesley decided that it was time to try to find a new job.*

2 Fill in the missing phrasal verb: *I asked the driver to _____ me _____ at the stop nearest the station.*

3 Complete the phrasal verb: *The taxi is coming to _____ you _____ at 8pm.*

4 Complete the phrasal verb: *The police asked the protesters to* **move _____.**

5 Replace the underlined words with a phrasal verb: *Fiona will be able to tell me what has been happening while I've been away — she always manages to find out the best gossip.*

6 Replace the phrasal verb with one word: *Colin took Rose to the jewellers and asked her to* **pick out** *an engagement ring.*

7 Fill in the missing phrasal verb: *Anna was upset when she _____ her favourite dress and realized that it did not fit her any longer.*

8 Complete the phrasal verb: *It was very cold outside so the teacher told the children to* **put _____** *their hats and gloves.*

9 Complete the phrasal verb: *Louise* **covered _____** *the stain on the carpet with a rug.*

10 Replace the phrasal verb with one word: *I was too hot and so I* **took off** *my jumper.*

13 A Surprise Test

Phrasal Verbs in Use

'You'll never guess what Mr Fowler **has pinned up** on the notice-board!' said Joe to Simon in the college canteen. 'A notice about a history test tomorrow!' Simon looked worried and replied. 'That's very short notice. We had better **get down to** some work right away. I've had so much biology homework recently that I've **got behind with** history and there's so much to learn.' Joe said that he would go and **pass on** the bad news to their fellow-students. When he told Martha she said that Mr Fowler **had hinted at** a possible surprise test the previous week. 'It was when he **was handing back** our essays,' she said, 'and telling us how bad our work was.' They went to find some of the others and Alice said, 'I suppose that it's not all that surprising. He's always **getting on at** us for not doing enough history work. He forgets that we have several other subjects to study.' Val was reasonably calm about the test because she was an industrious student who **worked away at** her various subjects all through the term. Some of the others played more than they worked and had cause for concern. One of these was Sue and she tried to **play down** the test, remarking, 'It's only a class test, not a final exam. We'll just have to hope that we can **muddle through** it.' Val muttered to herself, 'Somehow I don't think Mr Fowler will like that attitude.'

Know the Meaning

pin up to fix (a notice, poster, etc) to a wall, notice board, etc: *The teenagers pinned up posters of their favourite film stars on their bedroom walls. Could you pin this notice up on the shop wall?* — *it's advertising a charity jumble sale. Sean wrote out an ad for a flat and then pinned it up on the college notice-board.*

get down to to start working hard at (something): *The students had better get down to finding somewhere to live. I have three essays to write* — *I need to get down to them right away.*

get behind with not to have made as much progress with (something) as one should: *I've been working late and have got behind with the housework. The students have several essays to write and some of them have got behind with them.*

pass on to give to or tell (someone) something which was given or told to you: *My mother passed on a few cooking tips to my sister. Beth was chosen to pass the bad news on to the others. That was good advice and I passed it on to my friends.*

hint at to suggest (something) in an indirect way: *My parents hinted at moving house. Anne did not actually say that she was leaving, but she hinted at it.*

hand back to return (something) to someone after having borrowed it or taken it for some reason: *I asked Nora to hand back the books which she had borrowed from me. Nora absolutely refused to hand the books back, saying that I had given them to her as a present. The teacher marked the test papers and handed them back to the students.*

get on at to criticize or scold (someone) continually: *The children would like a teacher who does not get on at them all the time. Terry's parents never praise him* — *they just get on at him.*

work away at to work hard and continuously at (something): *The research team worked away at the problem until they solved it. John must have nearly finished his thesis* — *he's been working away at it for months.*

play down to try to make (something) seem unimportant or less important, to minimize: *The police were trying to play down the danger, in order to keep the crowd calm.*

muddle through to succeed in doing (something), although not very well, despite the fact that one does not know much about it: *Somehow I muddled through the interview test although it was very difficult. I knew very little about the last question in the exam, but I muddled through it.*

Do it Yourself

1 Replace the underlined words with a phrasal verb: *It is a good idea to stick up a list of useful numbers on the wall by the phone.*

2 Replace the underlined words with a phrasal verb: *My boss told me that I had better start working hard at the report.*

3 Complete the phrasal verb: *Yvonne had to speak to the manager because she had got _____ with her work after she had been off ill.*

4 Replace the underlined words with a phrasal verb: *Rachel asked me to give you her congratulations on passing your exams.*

5 Complete the phrasal verb: *The teacher did not tell me that I had passed the exam but she hinted _____ it.*

6 Replace the underlined word with a phrasal verb: *I have to go to the library to return the books I took out last week.*

7 Complete the phrasal verb: *Dave asked his girlfriend not to get _____ at him for not buying her expensive gifts.*

8 Complete the phrasal verb: *Howard and Bob worked _____ at the decorating for hours.*

9 Replace the underlined words with a phrasal verb: *George was embarrassed by all the attention that he received for saving the little girl, and he tried to make what he had done seem unimportant.*

10 Complete the phrasal verb: *Ruth had hardly taken any driving lessons, but somehow she managed to _____ through it.*

14 Organizing a Fete

Phrasal Verbs in Use

A group of residents had gathered in the village hall to **sort out** the details of the summer fete. It was only March, but the committee always met early on to **thrash out** any new ideas and any likely problems. Meanwhile, Bill, who had just been appointed treasurer, **was wrestling with** the fete budget. He had remarked that last year's figures did not make sense and had been told that the previous treasurer had not been very good. Two of the committees were trying to **divide up** the jobs for the actual day of the fete. They had a list of the names of all the people who had helped in previous years, and **had ticked off** those who were likely to be available again. Then they **had pencilled in** some new names of likely volunteers, but that was still not nearly enough. 'We're going to have to **look to** some of the young people, I'm afraid,' said Mary. 'Why don't we ask young Becky Rowland to organize some of them? If she **takes after** her mother, she will be an excellent organizer.' At the same time the committee in charge of publicity were having an argument. Some of them thought that one or two posters would suffice, but others thought that they should not **skimp on** advertising if they wanted a large crowd. 'Talking of crowds,' said Paul, 'we should **tighten up** security. Last year a lot of people came without paying the entrance fee.'

Know the Meaning

sort out to deal with (something) and solve any problems associated with it: *The committee have to sort out who's doing what at the village fete. You need to sort your personal problems out with Reg before you go into business with him.*

thrash out to discuss (something) in detail to try to come to a decision or conclusion: *We have to thrash out the objections to the plans before we can proceed with the building. Government ministers are trying to thrash a new economic policy out.*

wrestle with to try with difficulty to deal with or solve (something), to struggle with (something): *Paul could not sleep because he was wrestling with his financial problems. I finally solved the problem, after having wrestled with it for days.*

divide up to share (something) out among the members of a group: *The children divided the sweets up among them. The burglars divided up the stolen goods. We collected a lot of money, but it has to be divided up among several charities.*

tick off to put (a tick or other mark) beside an item in a list to indicate that the item has been dealt with: *Could you tick off the people who have accepted the invitation? I've made a list of the clothes which I'll need on holiday, and I'm ticking them off as I pack them.*

pencil in to write (something) down in pencil, rather than in ink because it may have to be changed, to write (something) down, knowing that it may have to be changed: *I'll pencil the appointment in for next Thursday and you can confirm or change it by phone. The committee secretary pencilled in a tentative date for the next meeting. We can easily change the date of the lunch, but I've pencilled it in for now.*

look to to rely on (someone) to provide help: *Nigel looked to his parents to pay for his college fees. Mr and Mrs Walters have four children and they all look to them for financial assistance.*

take after to resemble (someone) as regards appearance, character, etc: *Jill takes after her father in being a brilliant pianist. Willie is a lazy fellow and his son takes after him.*

skimp on to use less of (something) than is needed or desirable to make something satisfactory: *People complained that the caterers skimped on the wine for the reception. You will need a lot of material for that ball gown — you mustn't skimp on it.*

tighten up to make (something) tighter or stricter: *They've tightened up the school rules with regard to truancy. It is vital to tighten the security system up. The laws against speeding were rather vague, but they've tightened them up now.*

Do it Yourself

1 Replace the underlined words with a phrasal verb: *Angela and Frank have not been getting on very well recently — I hope that they can deal with their problems.*

2 Complete the phrasal verb: *The directors have been in a meeting all day trying to **thrash** _____ the take-over deal.*

3 Complete the phrasal verb: *Tim finally decided to give up on his essay after he had been **wrestling** _____ it for days.*

4 Replace the underlined words with a phrasal verb: *The flat-mates agreed to share out the work that needed to be done.*

5 Complete the phrasal verb: *If you give me a list of what we need from the supermarket, I can _____ things **off** as I get them.*

6 Complete the phrasal verb: *I phoned the hairdresser and asked him to **pencil** _____ an appointment for me on Tuesday.*

7 Replace the underlined words with a phrasal verb: *The team relied on their captain to come up with a plan to save the game.*

8 Replace the underlined word with a phrasal verb: *Susan is very pretty — she resembles her mother.*

9 Complete the phrasal verb: *Wendy did not think the new restaurant was very good since they **skimped** _____ the portions.*

10 Complete the phrasal verb: *The manager has decided that she is going to _____ **up** the security system after the shop was broken into.*

15 A Dyeing Disaster

Phrasal Verbs in Use

Stella had decided that she really didn't like the colour of her hair, which was mid-brown, and she **was planning on** dyeing it. She had asked her friend, Carol, for help and they had both gone to the shopping centre to find a suitable hair-dye. There was a large selection from which to choose, but Carol said, 'I can **vouch for** this brand. My sister **swears by** it. She always uses it and her hair looks great.' Then it was a question of selecting a colour. Many of the shades had exotic names, but Stella chose one that she thought was auburn. When they reached Stella's house, Carol **read out** the instructions on the box carefully and the dyeing process began. Carol helped Stella to **rub** the rather unpleasant-looking creamy substance **into** her hair and Stella then **put** a plastic cap **over** her hair and scalp. They hadn't **used up** all the dye, and so they put the tube in the box and had a cup of coffee while they waited. It would be 45 minutes before they could **wash** the colorant **out**. The time soon passed and Stella **peeled off** the cap. Her hair was a peculiar colour, but the girls thought it would be all right when they **rinse** the dye **out**. Unfortunately, this was not the case. Stella's hair was bright purple. Something had gone far wrong and she had to visit a hairdresser right away before any of her family saw her hair.

Know the Meaning

plan on to intend to (do something): *We're planning on taking an early holiday. John may end up taking early retirement, but he's not planning on it.*

vouch for to say that you can guarantee that (someone/something) is good, reliable, etc: *Tom is an honest worker — I can vouch for him. Rose said that she could vouch for Pat's skill as a nanny. The information is accurate — we can vouch for it.*

swear by to regard (something) as being very effective, reliable, etc: *Mum swears by this recipe for chocolate cake. This is a herbal remedy for headaches — June swears by it.*

read out to say the words aloud as you read (something): *Could you read out the entry in the guidebook? The student read his whole essay out to the class. Jack received a letter from Freda and read it out.*

rub into to apply something to (something) by rubbing: *The cleaner rubbed the polish into the chair. Put some of the cream on your cheeks and rub it in.*

put over to place (something) so that it covers (something else): *Meg put a raincoat over her dress. She put a hand over his.*

use up to use all of (something), to finish a supply of (something) so that there is none left: *We have used up all the milk — there is none left for tea. They've used most of the meat up, but there are plenty of vegetables left. There's no fuel left — we used it up last winter.*

wash out to remove (something) by washing: *Clive washed the dried mud out of his hair. Nita got paint on her shirt but managed to wash it out.*

peel off to remove (something) by pulling: *Joe peeled off his wet sweater. Sara's hat was covered in snow and she peeled it off.*

rinse out/off to remove (something) by rinsing it with water: *I'm rinsing out the shampoo from my hair. Netta put a mudpack on her face and she's rinsing it off.*

Do it Yourself

1 Complete the phrasal verb: *David and Joanna are **planning** _____ getting married in June, but they have not booked a church yet.*

2 Complete the phrasal verb: *Tracey says that she can **vouch** _____ the new restaurant — she ate there last week and thought it was great.*

3 Replace the underlined words with a phrasal verb: *I'm not sure about acupuncture, but Andy regards it as very effective.*

4 Complete the phrasal verb: *The teacher _____ **out** the list of names of children who had been chosen for the football team.*

5 Complete the phrasal verb: *The doctor told Fred to _____ the cream **into** his skin every morning.*

6 Complete the phrasal verb: *Steven **put** a lid _____ the pot of soup.*

7 Replace the underlined words with a phrasal verb: *The chef wanted to use all of the cream because it would go off if it was left for another day.*

8 Complete the phrasal verb: *Hilda tried to _____ **out** the grass stain, but she had no success.*

9 Complete the phrasal verb: *Jack carefully **peeled** _____ the plaster from his sore finger.*

10 Complete the phrasal verb: *Richard **rinsed** the glass _____ before pouring his drink.*

16 A Trip to the Seaside

Phrasal Verbs in Use

The children from the local nursery school were going on a trip to the seaside. They were all very excited as they waited for the bus which would take them there. The teachers **lined** the children **up** outside the school playground and soon the bus arrived. In the bus the children got more and more excited and the teachers found it difficult to **quieten** them **down**. The teacher in charge of the food was worried that there might not be enough, since more children had come on the trip than were supposed to. 'We'll just have to **eke** it **out**,' said one of the other teachers. 'Some of them will **tuck into** the food, but quite a few will be too excited to eat.' When they **got to** the beach, the children ran to play in the sea and sand immediately. One of the little girls was crying. It was one of the twins and few of the teachers could **tell** the sisters **apart**. It was, in fact, Sonia, and she was crying because she had sand in her eyes. One of the teachers **wiped** the sand **off** her face and **tied back** her hair with a ribbon. Sonia felt much better. Then Sonia's sister, Helen, began to weep because a wasp **had landed on** her sandwich. Fortunately, she had not been stung. 'I'm not sure that I can **summon up** the strength to go back on the bus with them,' said the head teacher.

Know the Meaning

line up to place (people or things) in a row or queue: *The organizers lined the audience up outside the concert hall. Mary lined up the chairs in preparation for the meeting. The teacher moved the desks and lined them up against the wall.*

quieten down to make (someone) less noisy: *The police tried to quieten down the gang of youths. Her parents are trying to quieten the child down — she was over-excited. The children at the party were shouting and it was impossible to quieten them down.*

eke out to make (something) last as long as possible or supply as many people as possible: *The walkers had to eke out their water supply. We're going to have to eke out the fuel supply until the end of the week. Don't put too much butter on the sandwiches — there's not much and we have to eke it out.*

tuck into (informal) to eat (something) with pleasure and enthusiasm: *The diners were tucking into juicy steaks. The children had never seen such food and they tucked into it right away.*

get to to reach, to arrive at (somewhere): *We want to get to the city before nightfall. The coast is still a long way off — I don't think you'll get to it tonight.*

tell apart to identify (which is which of two people or things that look alike) by recognizing the differences between them, to distinguish (someone from someone or something from something similar): *Few people other than their mother can tell the twin brothers apart. The painting and the copy are so similar that only experts can tell them apart.*

wipe off to remove (something) by wiping it with a cloth, one's hand, etc: *You should wipe the sticky mess off the table. Did the cleaning agent wipe off the dirty mark? The child got dirt on her dress, but we wiped it off.*

tie back to fasten (something such as hair) with a ribbon, string, etc so that it stays in place and does not get in one's way: *Amy looks pretty when she ties back her long hair. Jo's hair was getting in her eyes and she tied it back.*

land on to come to rest on (something): *The child jumped and landed on a sand castle. There was a field near by and the helicopter landed on it.*

summon up to try to get together enough (of something, such as strength, energy, etc) to do something: *I just cannot summon up enough enthusiasm to go swimming. Pete was so tired that he could scarcely summon up the strength to go home.*

Do it Yourself

1 Complete the phrasal verb: *The teachers **lined** the children _____ outside the cinema.*

2 Complete the phrasal verb: *The teacher was asked to **quieten** the pupils _____ and get them to behave properly.*

3 Complete the phrasal verb: *There were more guests than they had been expecting at the party, and so they had to **eke** _____ the wine.*

4 Replace the underlined words with a phrasal verb: *Rupert loves desserts and he <u>happily ate</u> the chocolate mousse.*

5 Replace the phrasal verb with one word: *The family were glad to **get to** their hotel after a very long journey.*

6 Complete the phrasal verb: *The sisters look very similar and it is hard to **tell** them _____.*

7 Complete the phrasal verb: *Beverly dropped some butter on the carpet, but was able to _____ it **off**.*

8 Complete the phrasal verb: *I always **tie** my hair _____ before I go swimming.*

9 Replace the underlined words with a phrasal verb: *The helicopter was able to <u>come to rest on</u> the roof of the building.*

10 Replace the words with a phrasal verb: *Peter is trying to <u>get together</u> enough courage to ask Linda out on a date.*

17 A Skiing Trip

Phrasal Verbs in Use

Fred and his friends were getting rather anxious. It was beginning to look as though they might have to **call off** their skiing trip, which had been arranged for the end of the month. They had to have ten of them for the package deal, but both Joe and Alan **had let** them **down** at the last minute. Fortunately, Joe's cousin, Morris, had said that he would **stand in for** him, but they still needed one more person. They had immediately **called on** Eddie for assistance, but he had said that he could not possibly **help** them **out** at such short notice. Fred had said rather cynically that Eddie had refused because he did not want to **part with** any money and, indeed, Eddie had a reputation for being very mean. Someone suggested Bert, but they remembered that he **had been turfed out** of the hotel for drunkenness the last time they had all gone on a trip. He really was not suitable, even if they were desperate. Finally, Fred decided to **turn to** his cousin, Bill. He was not very hopeful since Bill was always busy. However, Bill said that he needed some exercise to **work off** all the food which he **had wolfed down** at Christmas and would be very pleased to join them. He was an excellent skier and good company. They were all pleased that he could go. Most of all, they were pleased that they did not have to cancel their holiday.

Know the Meaning

call off to cancel (an arrangement, event, etc): *We had to call off our plans to move house. Not enough people applied and so the university called the whole conference off. Matt and Katie had arranged their wedding but they called it off.*

let down to fail (someone) in some way, not to help (someone) when he/she is relying on you to do so: *Moira felt that her husband had let the children down by being late for the party. Robert let down his entire family by not coming home for Christmas. Sheila won't let you down — if she promised to accompany you, she will.*

stand in for to take (someone's) place because he/she cannot be there, to act as a substitute for (someone): *Mr Green is marketing director, but he is standing in for the managing director at the conference. The star of the show is ill and her understudy is standing in for her.*

call on to ask or appeal to (someone) for something or to do something: *The minister called on all the villagers to help the poor. The president called on neighbouring countries to assist him against the rebel army. Fiona and Colin are reliable people — you can call on them to help.*

help out to give (someone) some assistance, often temporarily or in an emergency: *I lent Edna the money because I felt that I should help out an old friend. Jane helps her neighbour out by looking after her children occasionally. The driver said that he had run out of petrol and asked us if we could help him out.*

part with to give or hand over (money or something of value) to someone else: *Reg is very rich because he rarely parts with any money. The book is of great sentimental value to Pam and she cannot bear to part with it.*

turf out *(informal)* to throw (someone) out, to force (someone) to leave: *The barman turfed Craig out after he caused a fight. Ron is employed to turf out trouble-makers from the club. Don't let the drunk annoy the customers — turf him out!*

turn to to ask (someone) for help, advice, support, etc: *Sally always turns to her elder brothers for advice. Roger's parents are elderly and poor — he cannot possibly turn to them for financial help.*

work off to get rid of (something), often by doing something energetic: *Mike worked off his weight increase by going to the gym. Ella's brother told her rudely to work some of her fat off by walking to work. Jock has a lot of stress at work and he works it off by swimming.*

wolf down to eat (something) quickly and greedily: *Teenage boys always seem to be starving; Beth's son's friends wolfed down the contents of her fridge. The young man was very hungry and wolfed down a huge plate of food. Take time to enjoy your food — don't just wolf it down.*

Do it Yourself

1 Replace the phrasal verb with one word: *Judy had to **call off** her birthday party because she was not well.*

2 Complete the phrasal verb: *I feel that I've **let** myself _____ by not studying hard enough for my exams.*

3 Replace the underlined words with a phrasal verb: *The teacher had to go home early, and the head teacher said that he would <u>take her place for</u> her.*

4 Complete the phrasal verb: *The police **call** _____ the local residents to come forward with any information that would help them to solve the crime.*

5 Replace the underlined words with a phrasal verb: *Anna had to take her daughter to the hospital and she asked if I could <u>give assistance</u> by looking after the shop while she was gone.*

6 Complete the phrasal verb: *Ian would love to go on holiday, but he feels that it is a lot of money to **part** _____ for two weeks in the sun.*

7 Replace the underlined words with a phrasal verb: *Bobby was <u>thrown out</u> of the club for refusing to pay for his drink.*

8 Replace the underlined words with a phrasal verb: *Lynne is desperate, but she can't think of anyone that she can <u>ask for help</u>.*

9 Complete the phrasal verb: *The family decided to go for a walk to **work** _____ the big meal.*

10 Complete the phrasal verb: *You would get indigestion if you **wolfed** _____ your meal.*

18 The Perfect Cottage

Phrasal Verbs in Use

Angela and Phil had taken a trip into the country for the day. It was a beautiful day and they were hoping to find a pub, where they could have lunch and **idle away** a few pleasant hours. Suddenly Angela stopped the car and pointed to a cottage with a For Sale sign in the garden. 'Mum and dad would like that. They **had decided on** one nearer the city, but someone else offered a higher price. I wonder when they could **see over** this.' Angela's parents wanted to buy a country cottage which they would use for family holidays just now, intending to live there permanently on their retirement. Phil **noted down** the estate agent's address and telephone number and they planned to **ring** him **up** after lunch. They found a pub easily and, after an excellent lunch, they asked the landlord where the estate agent's office was. Since it was very near to the pub, Angela and Phil drove to the office and asked if someone could **show** them **round** the cottage that afternoon. The woman in charge of the office **fished out** the cottage keys and drove to the house. Angela and Phil liked it very much, but the woman **impressed on** them that cottages in that area usually sold very quickly. 'Your parents might have to **beat off** several other prospective buyers, unless they move quickly.' Angela's parents **took** her **up on** the suggestion that they see the cottage immediately and were soon its proud owners.

Know the Meaning

idle away to spend (a period of time) not doing very much: *It was lovely to idle away a few hours sitting in the garden. On holiday we idled whole days away just sitting on the beach. The college term was nearly over and Adam had idled it away.*

decide on to choose (something), often after careful thought: *We looked at various holiday destinations but decided on Paris. My parents spent a long time looking at wallpaper and I'm surprised that they decided on that.*

see over to look at the various parts of (a house, etc): *We have seen over several houses, but didn't put an offer in for any of them. There is a flat to let in this street and I'm just going to see over it.*

note down to write (something) down, sometimes informally: *I'll just note down your address and post the information to you. If you note the details down, the manager will deal with your complaint. Bess noted down Charlie's address on a piece of paper, but she can't find it.*

ring up to telephone (someone): *Jim rang up Lily to apologize. We've rung a few people up to get their opinions. Sara will know the answer — I'll ring her up right now.*

show around/round to go to (somewhere) with someone in order to show him/her the main features of the place: *Bob showed his parents around the university. If you like I can show you round the town this afternoon.*

fish out (informal) to take (something) out of somewhere, often with difficulty or after a search: *The teacher opened a desk drawer and fished out a piece of chalk. Moira searched in her handbag and fished a bar of chocolate out. I have a pen in my bag—I'll just fish it out.*

impress on to make (someone) realize how important something is: *The boss impressed on the staff the need for speed. His parents impressed on him the importance of studying hard. The head teacher impressed it on the pupils that school uniform must be worn.*

beat off to prevent (someone) from defeating or overcoming you: *Geoff beat off several other competitors to win the golf championship. Julia beat her rivals off easily. The opposition was strong but we beat it off.*

take up on to accept (someone's) offer, suggestion: *We decided to take George up on his offer to lend us his holiday cottage. I'll take you up on your offer of a cup of tea.*

Do it Yourself

1 Complete the phrasal verb: *Dennis was surprised to notice that it was getting dark and that he **had idled** the whole day _____.*

2 Replace the underlined word with a phrasal verb: *Trevor spent a long time looking at flats before he bought one, but eventually <u>chose</u> one near his work.*

3 Complete the phrasal verb: *Donna thought that the house was worth the asking price, but she asked her father to **see** _____ it before making an offer.*

4 Replace the underlined words with a phrasal verb: *Julie <u>wrote down</u> the details of some holidays that she saw in the travel agent's window.*

5 Replace the phrasal verb with one word: *I **rang up** Paul and asked him to come to the party but he was not in the mood.*

6 Complete the phrasal verb: *Evelyn made an appointment for the estate agent to **show** her _____ the flat.*

7 Fill in the missing phrasal verb: *Donald searched in his rucksack and eventually _____ his passport.*

8 Complete the phrasal verb: *The police **impressed** _____ the children the dangers of playing on thin ice.*

9 Fill in the missing phrasal verb: *The successful candidate had to _____ a lot of stiff competition to get the job.*

10 Complete the phrasal verb: *Alison decided to **take** Robert _____ his offer of a job at the coffee shop.*

19 An Important Invitation

Phrasal Verbs in Use

Tess decided to **pop into** her neighbour's house for a chat. Her neighbour was called Liz and she **let** Tess **in** as soon as she knocked. She was looking rather miserable as she **poured** the coffee **out**. When Tess asked her what was wrong, she told her about her problem. Liz's husband, Giles, had just rung to say that his boss wanted Liz and Giles to spend the weekend at his house in the country. Liz wanted to **cook up** some excuse for not going, but Giles had insisted that they really could not **duck out of** the invitation. He felt that the weekend would be good for his career prospects. Liz felt that she **was being forced into** something, which she did not want to do, and that there was not enough time to make arrangements. '**Leaving aside** some work which is due on Monday, there are the children. I cannot possibly **foist** them **on** my mother again.' Liz worked as a freelance journalist and she and Giles had a three-year old daughter and a six-year old son. Tess said that she **sided with** Giles on this occasion, but Liz refused to listen, saying that Giles had not taken into consideration either the children or her work. Tess tried to **reason with** her and offered to look after the children. She also pointed out that Liz could write her article before she left. Finally Liz agreed that a weekend break was a good idea.

Know the Meaning

pop into (*informal*) to visit (somewhere) briefly: *I'll just pop into the post office for some stamps. Olive popped into her friend's house for coffee.*

let in to allow (someone) to enter somewhere, often by opening the door: *The doctor's receptionist let the patients in. If you let in all those people the hall will be far too crowded. Open this door and let me in at once!*

pour out to cause (something) to flow from a container, usually into another container, such as a cup or glass: *Would you please pour out some milk for the children? I'll pour the tea out later. The wine is over there — please pour it out.*

cook up to put (something) together falsely or dishonestly: *The children cooked up some story about someone stealing their pocket money, but they spent it. Trust Fred to cook a story up about seeing an alien. Don't believe Ron's excuse — he just cooked it up to avoid going to the meeting.*

duck out of (*informal*) to avoid (something or doing something): *It's raining and some of the pupils are trying to duck out of the hockey match. The next meeting is on Christmas Eve and I think most people will duck out of it.*

force into to make (someone) do something against his/her will: *The kidnappers forced the child into entering the old bar. Val didn't want to sell the house but financial circumstances forced her into it.*

leave aside not to consider (something) at the present time: *Let us leave aside the question of payment until the work has been completed. The committee decided to leave the details aside and concentrate on the general principle. We can talk about expanding the firm later, but let us leave it aside just now.*

foist on to make (someone) take or accept (someone or something) that he/she does not really want: *We don't have room to have people to stay, but our son has foisted his friends on us. Meg doesn't look after the children very often — she usually foists them on her parents.*

side with to have the same opinions as (someone), to support (someone) in an argument: *Victor said that he sided with Dave and thought that the rent for the flat was too high. I disagreed with Clara, but most people seemed to side with her.*

reason with to try to persuade (someone) to act in what one believes to be a sensible, reasonable way: *There's no point in trying to reason with Simon — he's made up his mind and he's very stubborn. Anne behaved far too hastily, although we tried to reason with her.*

Do it Yourself

1 Replace the underlined words with a phrasal verb: *Rachael briefly visited her granny's house on her way home from work.*

2 Complete the phrasal verb: *Simon regretted _____ in the salesman, who refused to go away until he had delivered his entire sales pitch.*

3 Complete the phrasal verb: *The waiter _____ out the wine for the wedding guests.*

4 Replace the underlined word with a phrasal verb: *John concocted some excuse about not being well but I did not believe him.*

5 Replace the underlined word with a phrasal verb: *Philip has not studied for the exam and he is trying to avoid sitting it by saying that he is ill.*

6 Complete the phrasal verb: *William wants Helen to marry him but he realizes that there is no point in trying to force her _____ it.*

7 Complete the phrasal verb: *The couple decided to leave _____ the details of the menu until they knew how many people would be coming.*

8 Fill in the missing phrasal verb: *Roger is upset that his daughter has again _____ her dog _____ him while she goes away on holiday.*

9 Replace the underlined words with a phrasal verb: *The manager agreed with the customer and said that Mary had been in the wrong.*

10 Complete the phrasal verb: *John has decided to leave university — his parents have tried to reason _____ him but he will not change his mind.*

20 A Stress Test

Phrasal Verbs in Use

A group of people **had been herded into** a room in a country house. 'I can't think why our manager sent us here,' said Miriam to her colleague, Colin. He replied, 'I think it's to assess leadership ability and to see how we **bear up** under stress. Some of it is about problem-solving. Our firm doesn't have an in-house training programme which **deals with** that kind of thing. This organization arranges such training weekends regularly. As you can see, there are people from several other local firms here.' Miriam was not impressed and said, 'I'd never **heard of** the idea till last week. Trust our management to **hit on** the idea of making us do this kind of thing at a weekend. It wouldn't be so bad if we were missing work.' Just then a man with a clip-board entered the room and **separated** the group **up** into several smaller groups. He put each one of them in a separate room and **gave out** a number of sheets of paper. Then he said that the groups were each to work as a team and that they would be joined by one of the facilitators. Miriam felt that she did not **fit into** her group very well, partly because the others were considerably older, but she tried to **enter into** the problem-solving willingly. As they **hammered out** solutions to the problems, the facilitator at their table was busily writing. 'I don't really like this kind of assessment,' thought Miriam.

Know the Meaning

herd into to gather (people or animals) together into a group, often in an uncomfortable or not very polite way: *The police herded the protesters into a police van. A huge number of people wanted to hear the concert and the organizers tried to herd them all into far too small a hall.*

bear up to remain cheerful and confident: *Try to bear up — you'll be out of hospital soon. Sally is not bearing up very well under the strain of all this overtime.*

deal with to take action with regard to (someone or something): *That department deals with customers' complaints. Harry has financial problems, but he is dealing with them.*

hear of to get information about (something), to learn about (something): *My doctor says he's never heard of the painkiller that's being advertised. That picture's by Jane's favourite artist — have you ever heard of him?*

hit on to think of (an idea, solution, etc): *The Kellys hit on the idea of letting a room out to make some money. I think I've hit on the answer to our problem.*

separate up to separate (a group or quantity) into smaller groups or quantities: *This is a large class and we are going to separate the pupils up into groups of six. This is too large a group — we are going to have to separate it up.*

give out to distribute (something), to hand out (something): *Please give these leaflets out to all the students. We gave out free sweets to the children on the day of the fete. We had several books, but we gave them out.*

fit into to feel comfortable (in a group, etc) as though one belonged: *Elaine felt that she did not fit into her husband's family. The group consisted of very academic people and Tony did not fit into it.*

enter into to become involved in (something), to take part in (something): *Fay entered into the spirit of the game. We had a discussion about possible holiday destinations, but Malcolm refused to enter into it.*

hammer out to produce (something) after much effort, discussion, etc: *The two firms eventually hammered out an agreement and they merged. Management and unions finally reached a compromise, but it took all night to hammer it out.*

Do it Yourself

1 Replace the underlined words with a phrasal verb: *The students were gathered into a group in the hall and told where to sit for the exam.*

2 Replace the underlined words with a phrasal verb: *Sam is trying to remain cheerful, but he is finding it difficult to cope with his new job.*

3 Fill in the missing phrasal verb: *Walter has told Elaine that it is her responsibility to _____ staff who are late for work.*

4 Complete the phrasal verb: *Sarah says that she has _____ of a new restaurant that is meant to serve excellent food.*

5 Replace the underlined words with a phrasal verb: *Sid thought of the idea of selling coffee outside the new office block.*

6 Fill in the missing phrasal verb: *The children were _____ into three teams for the relay race.*

7 Replace the phrasal verb with one word: *The protesters were **giving out** leaflets outside the nuclear plant.*

8 Complete the phrasal verb: *Karen tried hard to **fit** _____ the flat, but she found her flat-mates annoying.*

9 Replace the underlined words with a phrasal verb: *Lydia was invited to join in the game, but she refused to take part in it.*

10 Complete the phrasal verb: *It took Terry several hours to **hammer** _____ his essay, but he finished it on time.*

21 A Car Accident

Phrasal Verbs in Use

Polly was wondering where her brother, Simon, was. She and some of her friends had arranged to **meet up with** him at a country hotel, but he was not there. He should have arrived first because Polly and her friends **had lagged behind** from the start of the journey. She was a slow driver and had left later than her brother had. Then she discovered that a car accident **had snarled up** the traffic on the motorway and had decided to go by a different, longer route. Just as Polly was getting really anxious, the hotel receptionist told her that there was a phone call for her. It was from her father and, as she **listened to** what he had to say, she looked even more worried. He told her that Simon **had smashed up** his car, having **rammed into** the car in front, which had stopped suddenly without warning. Fortunately, Simon did not seem to be hurt, but he had been taken to a local hospital for a check-up, just in case. The car was too badly damaged to be driven and Simon had had to **leave** the car **behind** at the scene of the accident. The police said that they would **tow** it **away**. Polly was glad that her brother was unhurt, but she knew that he **had ploughed** a lot of money **into** the car and that he **had** not yet **paid off** the bank loan for it.

Know the Meaning

meet up with to meet (someone), often by arrangement, but sometimes by chance: *The plan is to meet up with Ellie and Lucy at the airport. We were introduced to Sally and Mike at Frank's wedding, but we didn't expect to meet up with them again so soon.*

lag behind to move more slowly than (someone) and so be further behind than him/her: *Adam was the best runner in the race, but on that day he lagged behind the winners. Phil walked so fast that the other hill-walkers soon lagged behind him.*

snarl up (of traffic) to be unable to move freely, to have some form of obstruction: *The traffic was snarled up by a major road accident. It was an overturned lorry that snarled up the traffic.*

listen to to pay attention to (someone) and to follow his/her advice: *Rena refused to listen to her parents and married Jack against their wishes. Mark warned Bill that Bob was a rogue, but Bill would not listen to him.*

smash up to damage (something) badly, to break (something) so that it is in pieces: *Vandals have smashed up the bench at the bus stop. The intruders did not steal much, but they smashed all the furniture up. Bert had always disliked the vase, and took pleasure in smashing it up.*

ram into to hit (something) very hard, often at great speed or with great force: *The van behind us was going too fast and rammed into our car as we slowed down. Leo lost his temper and rammed his fist into Dick's face. The gate closed as the lorry approached and it rammed into it.*

leave behind not to take (someone or something) with you, sometimes deliberately, sometimes accidentally: *We had to leave some of our belongings behind as the removal van was too small. I can't find my umbrella — I must have left it behind at the office.*

tow away to move (a vehicle) by attaching it by a rope, etc to another vehicle and pulling it along: *The car had engine trouble and had to be towed away. Did the police tow away the car because they thought that it had been abandoned? The van broke down on the motorway and we had to get someone to tow it away.*

plough into (informal) to spend (a lot of money) on something, sometimes unprofitably: *The government is refusing to plough any more public money into the industry. The business failed despite the fact that all the partners ploughed huge sums of money into it.*

pay off to pay all the money that is owing with regard to a bill, loan, etc so that one is no longer in debt: *Robert's monthly instalments are so low that it will be years before he pays off his car loan. I took out a loan to buy a boat, but I paid it off last year.*

Do it Yourself

1. Replace the underlined words with a phrasal verb: *Trevor plans to arrange to meet some old school friends when he is in town.*

2. Fill in the missing phrasal verb: *Diane set a fast pace in the race and soon the other runners were _____.*

3. Complete the phrasal verb: *The traffic got **snarled** _____ when a flock of sheep wandered onto the road and could not be moved.*

4. Replace the underlined words with a phrasal verb: *Rona wished that she had paid attention to her teacher and studied harder for her exams.*

5. Complete the phrasal verb: *Veronica was so annoyed with her husband that she _____ **up** the set of antique plates which he had given her as a present.*

6. Fill in the missing phrasal verb: *The car skidded on the ice and _____ the wall.*

7. Replace the underlined words with a phrasal verb: *The family decided not to take their dog when they went on holiday.*

8. Complete the phrasal verb: *I had to phone the police and ask them to _____ **away** the car that was blocking my driveway.*

9. Complete the phrasal verb: *The firm **ploughed** a great deal of money _____ the new venture, but it did not work out.*

10. Fill in the missing phrasal verb: *The bank manager suggested that I take out a loan to buy a car, but I don't think that I could afford to _____ it _____.*

22 A Football Camp

Phrasal Verbs in Use

A group of boys from various local schools were attending a football camp where they were to have intensive training. They had been told by the head coach that he **had set down** a number of rules for their stay and that all the boys must **abide by** these rules. 'You are here to play football, not to have a holiday. We have had some very good players here in the past, and I hope that at least some of you will **measure up to** them.' Before the first training session, the older boys tended to **look down on** the younger ones because they thought that they were less experienced players. They felt very superior. However, when training began it was one of the younger boys, Derek, whom the coach **singled out** for praise. Derek was a skilful striker and the most boastful older boy, Ally, **let through** a goal kicked by him. The coach **remarked on** the fact that Derek could not only score goals, but that he could also **fend off** attacks by the opposing team very well. He was a good all-round player. Indeed, he was even a good goalkeeper. The coach said encouragingly to him, '**Keep up** this form and you may well have a career as a professional player.' Ally was so jealous of the younger boy that he deliberately kicked him, when he thought the referee was not looking, and had to be **sent off** the pitch for committing a foul.

Know the Meaning

set down to record officially, to establish (a law, regulation, etc): *The school rules are set down by the head teacher and the school governors. They have broken the laws, which were set down to prevent cruelty to children.*

abide by to act according to (a rule, law, etc): *The players were asked to abide by the referee's decision. Those are the school rules and pupils must abide by them.*

measure up to to reach the standard of (someone or something), to be as good as (someone or something): *Carol's quite a good tennis player, but she does not measure up to the rest of the team. The team coach sets such a high standard that few players measure up to it.*

look down on to regard and treat (someone or something) as being inferior or unimportant: *Fred is very rich and looks down on the other householders in the street. Amy's parents cannot afford expensive toys and the other children look down on her.*

single out to treat (someone or something) differently from the others in a group, to select (someone or something) for special treatment: *Jackie was singled out as the most promising new team member. Sam was no more naughty than the other children in the class, but the teacher singled him out and punished him more.*

let through to allow (someone or something) to pass or enter: *The street was closed off and the police refused to let any more people through. The striker gave the ball a powerful kick and the goalkeeper let it through.*

remark on to say or write something about (something) which shows that you have noticed it for some reason, to comment on (something): *The teacher remarked on the high standard of the students' work. The skill of the player was so great that all the spectators remarked on it.*

fend off to try to prevent, keep away or avoid (someone or something): *Doctors in the area do their best to fend off the disease. Sue's neighbours were very inquisitive, but she fended their interference off as well she could. The press had so many questions that the politician found it difficult to fend them off.*

keep up to continue or maintain (something): *Martha could not keep up the pretence any longer. It must be very expensive to keep that lifestyle up. We set such a high standard last year that it is difficult to keep it up.*

send off to tell (someone) to leave (a football pitch, etc) as a punishment. *The referee sent off three players in the first half of the match. It was difficult to see why the referee had sent so many players off.*

Do it Yourself

1 Replace the underlined word with a phrasal verb: *The council underline{established} strict guidelines for the design of new houses.*

2 Replace the underlined words with a phrasal verb: *You will be asked to leave if you cannot underline{act according to} the rules.*

3 Complete the phrasal verb: *Joseph decided to leave university because he did not feel that his results _____ **up** to the level he needed to get a good degree.*

4 Complete the phrasal verb: *Janice is not very popular because she tends to **look** _____ **on** other girls who are not as pretty as she is.*

5 Fill in the missing phrasal verb: *Susan was annoyed that the boss had _____ her _____ for criticism when she thought that the whole staff team had been at fault.*

6 Complete the phrasal verb: *The security guard refused to _____ anyone **through** to see the film star.*

7 Replace the underlined words with a phrasal verb: *The members of the audience all underline{commented on} how well the actress had played her part.*

8 Replace the underlined word with a phrasal verb: *The celebrity tried to underline{avoid} the attention of the press.*

9 Replace the phrasal verb with one word: *Andrea had been working very hard on her essay, but she was finding it difficult to **keep up** that level of study.*

10 Fill in the missing phrasal verb: *The referee _____ Ian _____ for swearing.*

23 In Financial Difficulties

Phrasal Verbs in Use

It was only half-way through the university session, but already Frank's bank account was overdrawn. He hadn't realized how bad the situation was, but a letter from the bank manager had just made him **face up to** the problem. It **dawned on** him that he would have to do something to reduce his overdraft right away. Sadly, he wasn't very good at **coping with** financial matters. He should have had enough money to cover all his expenses for the whole session, but he had been very careless with it. He **had frittered** a great deal of it **away** on beer and fast food, and he went to the cinema a lot. Then, for the first few weeks of term he had had a girlfriend with expensive tastes, and the gifts which she expected **had eaten into** his allowance. If at all possible, he did not want to **resort to** getting more money from his father. Besides, he would have to **explain away** his present financial predicament and that would not be easy. It was a pity that he **had fallen out with** his elder brother or he could have asked him to **cough up** a loan, until he got a job in the summer vacation. In the end he went to see his sister, who was quite a bit older than him and in a well-paid job. He **coaxed** her **into** giving him a loan and felt very fortunate that she had agreed so willingly.

Know the Meaning

face up to to accept (a difficult situation) and try to deal with it: *It's best to face up to your illness and get treatment for it. Reluctantly Ned faced up to the fact that he was bankrupt. Bill has gone for good and we must face up to it.*

dawn on to become obvious or apparent (to one): *It dawned on Sally that she was alone in the house. Suddenly the truth of the matter dawned on me.*

cope with to deal with (someone or something) successfully: *Clare had great difficulty in coping with her workload. Jill encountered many problems but coped with them easily.*

fritter away to waste (time, money, etc) gradually and foolishly: *Paul frittered all his money away on gambling. Kate frittered away her time watching television instead of studying. Dave's grandmother left him a lot of money, but he frittered it away.*

eat into gradually to use a great deal of (something): *Going on such an expensive holiday really ate into their savings. Ray had a substantial inheritance from his parents, but tax ate into it to a great extent.*

resort to to decide on or choose (some form of action) because all others have failed or are unsuitable, unavailable, etc: *The young men had to resort to sleeping on the streets when they had no money for rent. Murder is a serious crime and the young man did not have to resort to it.*

explain away to attempt to excuse or account for (something) so that the situation does not seem so bad as it first appeared: *Diane had been at an all-night party, but tried to explain away her tiredness in the morning by saying that she had been unable to sleep the night before. Joan's friends did not believe in the supernatural, but they were unable to explain her strange experience away. Freda had to tell the truth about her unofficial absence because she was unable to explain it away.*

fall out with to quarrel with (someone): *Children are always falling out with their friends. Pam won't speak to Pete — she fell out with him last week because he forgot her birthday.*

cough up (informal) to give or pay (sum of money): *Joe is hoping that his father will cough up the money for a new car. Rick owes me money but he refuses to cough up.*

coax into persuade (someone) by talking to him/her in a gentle, often flattering manner: *We eventually coaxed the child into taking some food. Bella didn't want to take part in the college play, but her friends coaxed her into it.*

Do it Yourself

1 Replace the underlined word with a phrasal verb: *Bill and Suzanne have finally <u>accepted</u> the fact that their marriage is over.*

2 Replace the underlined words with a phrasal verb: *It suddenly <u>became apparent to</u> Tina that Steve had been seeing someone else behind her back.*

3 Complete the phrasal verb: *I don't know how Jenny is going to **cope** _____ working full-time and looking after the children on her own.*

4 Complete the phrasal verb: *Charlotte **frittered** _____ all her money and could not afford to pay her rent.*

5 Fill in the missing phrasal verb: *Paying for the repairs to her car after the accident really _____ Kate's savings.*

6 Fill in the missing phrasal verb: *The young man was so hungry that he _____ stealing a sandwich from the shop.*

7 Replace the underlined words with a phrasal verb: *Keith had to admit he was having an affair because he could not <u>account for</u> the lipstick mark on his shirt.*

8 Replace the underlined words with a phrasal verb: *Jonathan is going to move out of his flat because he keeps <u>quarrelling with</u> his flat-mate.*

9 Replace the underlined word with a phrasal verb: *The manager is refusing to <u>pay</u> for the overtime that I worked last week.*

10 Complete the phrasal verb: *Sheila **coaxed** Ruth _____ going on holiday with her.*

24 The Winners

Phrasal Verbs in Use

Alex and Julie were preparing to play in the final of the tennis club mixed doubles. For several years in a row they had won it easily, but last year their opponents in the final had beaten them soundly and **had walked off with** the cup. Neither Alex nor Julie had played well and they felt that they **had shown** themselves **up**. They knew also that some people in the club **had levelled** a great deal of criticism **at** them because of their poor standard of play in the most important match of the year. This year they were determined to do well and to **win back** the trophy, although they **were pitted against** two very strong players who were considerably younger than they were. Because of this determination, they had trained hard and practised regularly. Much to the annoyance of Julie's husband and Alex's girlfriend, they had done very little but work and play tennis. They had even taken time to **rough out** a game plan. All this preparation, they hoped, should bring them victory. Despite the criticism which they had received, they still had loyal supporters, several of their friends being seated round the court all ready to **cheer** them **on**. When they went on court, they **were trusting to** luck as well as **banking on** their tennis skills. Indeed, luck was on their side. Both sets of players were evenly matched and it was a hard-fought match. However, Alex and Julie **carried off** the trophy.

Know the Meaning

walk off with to win (a prize, trophy, etc), especially easily: *Matt was the youngest competitor in the tournament, but he walked off with first prize. The tennis championship trophy was shared last year, but this year Nell played so well that she walked off with it.*

show up to make (oneself or someone) feel embarrassed or humiliated by one's bad behaviour, mistakes, etc: *The child started screaming in the supermarket and really showed her mother up. Maggie should never have entered the dance tournament — she danced very badly and showed herself up.*

level at to direct or aim at (something such as criticism, accusations, etc): *It was unfair to level accusations at Jim — he wasn't even present when the attack occurred. Bella was distressed that most of the criticism was levelled at her.*

win back to win or get back (something which one has had before and lost): *Our hockey team had trained hard and won back the trophy which we lost last year. The government is campaigning hard to win disillusioned voters back before the next election.*

pit against to put (someone or something) in competition with (someone else or something else): *In the tournament we were pitted against last year's champions. They pitted their superior skills against ours and won the quiz easily.*

rough out to draw or describe (something such as a plan or idea) roughly, and without much detail: *The architect has roughed out the plans for our new house. At the meeting a few people roughed out some ideas for raising money for repairs to the village hall.*

cheer on to support and encourage (someone such as a sports competitor) by cheering: *We need as many people as possible to cheer on our team in the final. The large crowd was cheering the young athlete on. The local football team has very few fans to cheer them on.*

trust to to place one's hopes on (someone or something), to rely on (someone or something): *We shall have to trust to Polly's good judgement and hope that she makes the right decision. There is nothing else the team can do but trust to their superior strength.*

bank on to rely on (someone or something), to expect (someone or something) to help one: *I'm banking on the train being on time. The relay team are banking on Judy — she's their most experienced runner.*

carry off to win (a prize, trophy, etc) *It was no surprise when Sophie carried off the prize for best all-round student. Emma carried all the English prizes off. There was a special trophy for creative writing and we knew that Ron would carry it off.*

Do it Yourself

1 Replace the underlined words with a phrasal verb: *The team had been playing very well all season, and they felt they had a good chance of <u>easily winning</u> the cup.*

2 Complete the phrasal verb: *Christine warned John that he was not to **show** her _____ at the office party by flirting with other women.*

3 Replace the underlined words with a phrasal verb: *Darren <u>directed</u> his criticism <u>at</u> the doctor for not diagnosing the illness sooner.*

4 Fill in the missing phrasal verb: *Jeff is doing his best to _____ his girlfriend's affection.*

5 Replace the underlined words with a phrasal verb: *Our team may not have a chance of getting through the next round — we are <u>in competition with</u> last year's champions.*

6 Replace the underlined words with a phrasal verb: *Steve has made an appointment with the bank manager so that he can <u>describe roughly</u> the plans for his new business.*

7 Complete the phrasal verb: *Lynne went to watch the race so that she could **cheer** _____ her friend.*

8 Replace the underlined words with a phrasal verb: *I'm too busy to organize the holiday and so I am going to <u>rely on</u> Pam to do it.*

9 Replace the underlined words with a phrasal verb: *William is <u>placing his hopes on</u> getting good enough marks to get into university.*

10 Replace the underlined word with a phrasal verb: *Tim was annoyed that Fred <u>won</u> the prize for the best player of the match.*

25 A Would-be Actor

Phrasal Verbs in Use

Tom was telling his parents how pleased he was by a newspaper review of a play in which he appeared. The play had been a local amateur production, but the newspaper critic **had hailed** Tom **as** a very promising young actor. Tom had always loved acting and here was proof, he thought, that he could **carve out** a career for himself on the stage. It was his opinion that the review might **open up** several opportunities. His parents **disagreed with** him, and were concerned that their son **was leading up to** telling them that he wanted to leave university right away and be an actor. In fact, they were right about this. When Tom did mention it, they both tried to **argue** him **out of** it. 'You're doing very well at university and acting is a very insecure career,' said Tom's father. 'You would have to **allow for** long periods without work and you need to have a means of making a living. I assume you don't want to **wind up** on unemployment benefit.' Tom replied, 'People always **trot out** the same old arguments against acting. I'm going to **opt out of** university and become an actor. That's my decision and I'm standing by it!' Tom's parents were not all that worried by this outburst, partly because they had read the review in the other local newspaper. It described both the play and Tom's role as very poor and amateurish. Tom said no more about a stage career.

Know the Meaning

hail as to be acknowledged and praised publicly as (someone or something): *The critics hailed Janet's latest book as a masterpiece. The young Irish writer was hailed as another James Joyce.*

carve out to make or create (something), often with difficulty or great effort: *It is extremely difficult to carve out a career in the theatre. The firm has gradually carved out a significant share of the fashion industry. Flora had a very successful career as an opera singer, but it took her years to carve it out.*

open up to cause (an opportunity, etc) to be available: *The course, which Donald is taking, could open up several career possibilities. The expanding computer market has opened up several marketing opportunities for the firm.*

disagree with not to agree with (someone or something), to have a different opinion from (someone or something): *Sally's parents disagreed with her about her choice of career. The two newspaper reports disagreed with each other.*

lead up to gradually to guide a conversation towards (a particular subject): *For days Jim has been talking about how little money he has, and I just knew that he was leading up to asking me for a loan.*

argue out of to persuade (someone) not to do something by pointing out the disadvantages, etc: *We tried in vain to argue Paddy out of buying the car. Tracy's parents tried to argue her out of leaving home.*

allow for to take into consideration (something which may happen in the future): *When you're arranging your appointment, you'll have to allow for the train being late. The winter was very cold, but luckily I had allowed for that, and had taken a lot of warm clothing with me.*

wind up to be in a place or situation, sometimes unpleasant, at the end of, and often as a result of, a series of events, to end up: *We were going to try a different holiday destination this year, but we wound up in the same old place again. If Pete does not take better care of himself, he will wind up in hospital.*

trot out to put forward (the same excuse, argument, etc) repeatedly and without thinking about it: *The politician has nothing new to say — he just trots out the same old policies. We've heard Bert's ideas on economics many times, but that does not stop him trotting them out.*

opt out of to decide no longer to be involved with (something): *Willie opted out of further education and got a job in the family business when he left school. Jessie was near the end of a nursing course when she suddenly opted out of it.*

Do it Yourself

1 Complete the phrasal verb: *The soldier was _____ as a hero when he returned to his home town.*

2 Replace the underlined word with a phrasal verb: *Lucy is determined to make a career as lawyer.*

3 Replace the underlined word with a phrasal verb: *If Gerry gets a good degree, it will create a wide range of opportunities for him.*

4 Replace the underlined words with a phrasal verb: *Tina did not agree with the way the company treated its customers.*

5 Complete the phrasal verb: *Bob was looking at rings in the jewellers, and Helen suspected that he was _____ up to proposing to her.*

6 Complete the phrasal verb: *Dom tried to argue Jane _____ of calling off the engagement.*

7 Replace the underlined words with a phrasal verb: *Chris was late for the meeting because he had not taken into consideration getting stuck in a traffic jam.*

8 Complete the phrasal verb: *If Russell and Pauline do not stop arguing all the time, I think they will wind _____ getting divorced.*

9 Complete the phrasal verb: *The children get bored because the teacher just trots _____ the same lesson every day.*

10 Replace the underlined words with a phrasal verb: *Since Caroline had missed so many classes through being ill, it would be best to decide not to continue with her college course and start again at the beginning of the year.*

26 *Buying a Car*

Phrasal Verbs in Use

Walter **was flicking through** some car magazines. 'I'm going to buy a car and I'm trying to find a model which I like,' he explained to his friend, Jim. 'Apparently prices vary a lot and so I intend to **shop around** until I find one that is reasonably priced. I don't have time to **hunt out** a real bargain, but I don't want to be overcharged.' Jim commented. 'There've been a lot of articles in the press recently which **have hit out at** dishonest car dealers. You have to be careful to choose a reliable one.' Walter and Jim went to a dealer, who had been recommended by Walter's father, and Walter immediately began to **enthuse over** one of the models on show. 'I had a buyer for that until this morning, but the deal **fell through**,' said the car dealer. He then went on to say, 'I'm prepared to **mark** it **down** for a quick sale because I have a lot of new cars coming in. Why don't you **try** it **out**?' Walter said that he would like to take the car on a test drive and the car's performance impressed him. His father knew quite a bit about cars and he loved to **tinker with** engines. Walter asked him to have a look at the car and he said that it was a good car for the money. 'I can **tune up** the engine for you — but, apart from that, it's fine.'

Know the Meaning

flick through to turn over the pages of (a magazine, book, document, etc) quickly in order to glance at them quickly: *We flicked through the film magazine to find out what the critics were recommending. I flicked through it, but the book did not have the information which I wanted.*

shop around to compare prices, quality, etc of something in various shops before purchasing (something): *If you shop around for a child's bike you'll find one much cheaper than that. We got a real bargain when we bought our new computer, but we had spent a lot of time shopping around for it.*

hunt out to find (something) after a hard search: *I hunted out these old wellingtons from the back of the cupboard. The old family photographs were in an old trunk in the attic and it took me some time to hunt them out.*

hit out at to criticize or attack (someone or something): *Many of the residents hit out at the new parking scheme in the town centre. People know that the local MP is not responsible for the government's economic policy, but many of them hit out at her about it, nevertheless.*

enthuse over to show great enthusiasm for (someone or something), to show that one is very pleased with (someone or something): *Our neighbours were enthusing over the new restaurant. I didn't really like the range of clothes in that shop, but Tanya enthused over them.*

fall through to fail, not to happen, not to be completed successfully: *The sale of the house fell through at the last minute. We made plans to work overseas, but they fell through because we could not get visas.*

mark down to reduce the price of (something): *The shopkeeper has marked down a lot of goods to make way for new stock. The car has been marked down for a quick sale. The dress had a slight flaw and so the sales assistant marked it down.*

try out to test (something) to find out if it is suitable, effective, etc: *Joanne is trying out a new recipe for chicken. The school is trying new truancy regulations out this term. Tim didn't like the motorbike when he tried it out.*

tinker with to work at (something such as an engine), sometimes in an unskilled way, to try to make minor repairs or improvements to it: *Colin is an accountant, but he loves tinkering with motorbikes as a hobby. Henry offered to fix my car, but I'm not letting him tinker with it — he ruined the engine of his father's car.*

tune up to adjust (a car engine, etc) so that it runs more efficiently or faster: *This car is going so much better since the mechanic tuned the engine up. You should get Mike to tune up your boat engine — it sounds a bit rough. Bill's sports car has been going a lot faster since he tuned it up.*

Do it Yourself

1 Complete the phrasal verb: *Trevor has been **flicking** _____ holiday brochures for days, but he has not booked anything.*

2 Complete the phrasal verb: *Sarah **shopped** _____ and got a really good deal on her new stereo.*

3 Complete the phrasal verb: *Dawn has asked me to give her back the book that she lent me and so I am going to have to _____ it **out**.*

4 Replace the underlined word with a phrasal verb: *The parents criticized the head teacher for not making sure that the climbing frame in the playground was secure.*

5 Replace the underlined words with a phrasal verb: *I would like to see the film that all the critics have been showing great enthusiasm for.*

6 Replace the underlined words with a phrasal verb: *Our plan to go on holiday did not happen because I fell and broke my leg the day before we were due to leave.*

7 Replace the underlined words with a phrasal verb: *Sue has rushed down to the clothes shop because she heard that they had reduced the price of the designer clothes.*

8 Complete the phrasal verb: *Jennifer is going to **try** _____ renting a cottage in the country for a few months before she decides if she will buy a house there.*

9 Complete the phrasal verb: *The television was working fine until Andrew started to **tinker** _____ it.*

10 Fill in the missing phrasal verb: *The car doesn't seem to be running very well — I think that it probably needs to be _____.*

27 A Health Scare

Phrasal Verbs in Use

Kim's father was in hospital. He had gone for a health check-up and they **had kept** him **in** because the doctors wanted to do some more tests on his heart. Since he smoked, had a stressful job and was overweight he **fell into** a category of people who had an increased risk of heart disease. Kim's mother was worried and had phoned her immediately. In fact, she was not surprised that her husband **had ended up** in hospital. She had been trying to get him to go to the doctor for months, but he had always **wriggled out of** going, despite the fact that he was having fairly regular chest pains. Finally, he **was frightened into** making an appointment when one of his colleagues died of a heart attack at work. The test results showed that Kim's father had no serious heart disease, but that he would have to **guard against** anything that might put any excessive strain on his heart. The doctor told him to **wake up to** the fact that he was going to have to change his lifestyle completely. He **warned** him **off** food with a high fat content, **sketched out** a sample diet sheet and told him to get more exercise and work fewer hours. Kim and her mother were very relieved that he was not seriously ill and went to collect the patient from hospital. Kim's father was relieved, too, but grumbling about the lifestyle that the doctors **had imposed on** him.

Know the Meaning

keep in to prevent (someone) from leaving somewhere: *The convict appealed against his sentence, but he lost and was kept in prison. The child is not well and her mother is keeping her in bed.*

fall into to belong to (a group, category, etc), to be classified as being part of (a particular group, etc): *Peter is very bright and, indeed, falls into the gifted children category. There are generous people and there are mean people — Tony falls into the latter class.*

end up to be in a place or situation, often unpleasant, eventually at the end of a series of events: *Joe kept breaking the law and ended up in prison.*

wriggle out of to avoid doing something that one should, to dodge (something): *It was Anne's turn to do the washing-up, but she succeeded in wriggling out of it. You promised to deliver those leaflets — don't try to wriggle out of it now.*

frighten into to make (someone) do something by making him/her afraid: *The bully frightened the other schoolboy into giving him money. The man who attacked Molly frightened her into not telling the police.*

guard against to try to make sure that something does not happen by being careful: *Hospitals should be kept clean to guard against infection. Jane should guard against being too trusting.*

wake up to to become aware of (a situation, often a difficult or dangerous one): *George suddenly woke up to the fact that his firm was in financial difficulties. The troops soon woke up to the danger they were in.*

warn off to tell or advise (someone) not to do something because he/she might be punished or face other unpleasant consequences: *We warned the children off taking sweets from strangers. Jo has been warned off drinking too much. Acting is a very uncertain profession, and Lucy's parents tried to warn her off against it.*

sketch out to describe (something) roughly and without details: *Mother sketched out her plans for the party. Emma wanted an exercise programme, and her coach sketched one out for her.*

impose on to make (someone) accept (something): *The president imposed a curfew on the citizens after the uprising. There is a limit on the amount of money we can take to school — it was imposed on us by the head teacher.*

Do it Yourself

1 Complete the phrasal verb: *The teacher threatened to **keep** the children _____ at lunchtime if they did not behave.*

2 Replace the underlined word with a phrasal verb: *Susan was a bright pupil and naturally belonged to the group that was expected to go to university.*

3 Fill in the missing phrasal verb: *The teacher warned the pupil that if he did not behave, he would _____ in the principal's office.*

4 Replace the underlined words with a phrasal verb: *Robert promised to take me on holiday, but now he is trying to avoid doing it.*

5 Complete the phrasal verb: *The salesman **frightened** Jane _____ buying a burglar alarm by saying that there had been a lot of break-ins in the area.*

6 Complete the phrasal verb: *When I go on holiday, I always try to _____ **against** pickpockets.*

7 Replace the underlined words with a phrasal verb: *Michelle became aware of the fact that her husband was unfaithful when she saw him kissing another woman.*

8 Complete the phrasal verb: *George **warned** Fred _____ eating in the canteen because it was horrible.*

9 Replace the underlined words with a phrasal verb: *Tracey made an appointment with the bank manager to describe roughly her plans for a new business venture.*

10 Complete the phrasal verb: *The editor has **imposed** a very tight deadline _____ all of his staff.*

28 Planning a Night Out

Phrasal Verbs in Use

Pam had decided that it would be a good idea to spend a night clubbing before the college term began. With this in mind she started to **ring round** some of her friends. She thought that clubbing was more fun with a group of people, and she intended to **track down** as many friends as possible. However, she wasn't having much luck and she **was running up** a large phone bill. Several of them were still out of town on holiday. Jane had said that her parents did not **approve of** her going clubbing, and Pam had heard that they were the sort to **interfere with** their daughter's social life. Trixie said that she was busy just then, but that she would **call back** and Vi **hung up**, saying that she was miserable because she and her boyfriend had parted. Pam thought that she was going to have to cancel the clubbing expedition, but Trixie called and said that she would go and that she would **round up** one or two others. Since they would be late coming home from the club, it was decided that Pam would **put** Trixie **up** for the night. Trixie's mother was an anxious person and would **wait up for** her, no matter how late it was. Pam shared a flat with two other students and so parents were not a problem.

Know the Meaning

ring round to telephone (several people) in order to ask about or discuss something: *I'll ring round all my friends and ask them to help in the search for the dog. Here's a list of people who are interested — I've already rung round a few of them.*

track down to find (someone or something) after a long or difficult search: *Mel has just tracked down her father who left home when she was a baby. It took the police several years to track the murderer down. There are very few first editions of the book, but we eventually tracked one down.*

run up to begin to be liable for, or to accumulate (debt, expenses, a bill, etc): *Tony has run up a huge credit card bill. You should not expect your parents to pay off these bills when it was you who ran them up.*

approve of to be pleased with or think well of (someone or something): *Jenny's parents do not approve of the student way of life. I had my hair cut and my family approved of the new style. Joan has made new friends, but her parents do not approve of them.*

interfere with to prevent or slow down the progress of (something): *Lack of staff interfered with the production of the new product. The bus schedule was running smoothly until bad weather interfered with it.*

call back to telephone (someone) who has telephoned you, to return (someone's) telephone call: *I'll just call Mary back — she left a message on my answering machine. I'll find out the information for you and call you back.*

hang up to end a telephone connection, often by putting the receiver back on the handset: *Trudy was very angry with Dave and she hung up before he could apologize. Meg said abruptly to the salesman that she did not want to buy anything and hung up.*

round up to gather together (a group of people or animals): *Let's try to round up a group of volunteers to paint the village hall. We watched the dogs round the sheep up. Many prisoners have escaped and the prison authorities are trying to round them up.*

put up to provide (someone) accommodation, usually temporarily and in one's home: *They put the homeless family up in a hotel. We can put up only one person. We can put you up for the night if you miss the last train.*

wait up for not to go to bed because one is waiting until (someone) has returned to the house: *You don't have to wait up for Sue — she's an adult now. Jean wants to be back home before midnight because her parents insist on waiting up for her.*

Do it Yourself

1 Replace the underlined word with a phrasal verb: *The manager had to telephone all the staff about the missing keys.*

2 Complete the phrasal verb: *Tom wanted a rare copy of an old record, and I eventually _____ it **down** in a charity shop.*

3 Replace the underlined word with a phrasal verb: *It was a very cold winter and granny accumulated a huge heating bill.*

4 Replace the underlined words with a phrasal verb: *Jean's parents do not think well of her boyfriend.*

5 Complete the phrasal verb: *Roger and Julie were looking forward to getting married, but his parents kept **interfering** _____ their plans for the wedding.*

6 Fill in the missing phrasal verb: *Can I _____ you _____ in half an hour? — I'm just washing my hair.*

7 Complete the phrasal verb: *Ruth explained to the customer that she could not help him, but he _____ **up** before she finished talking.*

8 Replace the underlined words with a phrasal verb: *The jumble sale would be very busy and so Lisa tried to gather together as many helpers as possible.*

9 Complete the phrasal verb: *Keith offered to _____ me **up** for a couple of nights while my flat was being decorated.*

10 Complete the phrasal verb: *I asked John not to **wait** _____ **for** me, but he was still awake when I got back after the party.*

29 Room-cleaning

Phrasal Verbs in Use

Patsy used the spare bedroom in her parents' house as a study and, by the end of the college term, it was looking very untidy. She decided that she would give it a good clean before she went on holiday. Then she went to collect dusters and other cleaning materials before starting to work. When she entered the room, there seemed to be papers and books everywhere. Patsy really did not know why she **had hoarded up** so much stuff. A great deal of it was completely worthless. She had too few bookshelves for the books, which she needed for college, and for her own collection of leisure books. Because of this she had asked her father to **fit** one of the cupboards **up with** shelves as soon as he could. Before he could do that, however, she had to **empty out** the cupboard. This proved to be a very boring task and consisted mainly of **filling up** several large rubbish bags. Having done this, she **turned out** the other cupboard, which contained bookshelves. Since many of the books were very dusty, she **dusted** them all **down** and **put** them **back** on the shelves, before turning her attention to the papers, which **were cluttering up** both the desk and floor. Patsy, unlike her mother, was not one of those people who **derive** satisfaction **from** cleaning. Indeed, she disliked the task very much. Therefore, she was very glad when she finally **filed away** the last set of papers.

Know the Meaning

hoard up to keep or store large quantities of (something): *Why did you hoard up so many tins of food — they're all past their sell-by date? We had to throw out a lot of old magazines when my aunt died — she had been hoarding them up.*

fit up with to equip or supply (someone or something) with (something): *Dad is fitting up the garden shed with a row of shelves. The cottage has a burglar alarm — my brother fitted it up with one last year.*

empty out to remove the contents from (something): *The milk was sour and we emptied out the bottle. We're getting the decorators in, but first we have to empty the front room out.*

fill up to make (someone or something) completely full: *Fill the tank up with unleaded petrol please. We filled up the container with fresh water. The teenagers are always hungry — it seems impossible to fill them up.*

turn out to empty (something, such as a room or cupboard): *We turned out the cupboard under the stairs and found lots of old bottles. It will be easier if we turn the bedrooms out one at a time. The kitchen cupboards are neat and tidy — we turned them out today.*

dust down to clean (something) by removing dust from it with a cloth, etc: *We had to remove all the books and dust the shelves down. Pat dusted down the wardrobe shelves before putting her new sweaters on them. The chairs in the old cottage were filthy, and we had to dust them down before we sat on them.*

put back to put (something) back where it was before it was moved, to replace (something): *I wish that you would put books back on the shelves and not leave them lying on the floor. Tom was able to put back the money which he had borrowed from the till. Stella took all her dresses out of the wardrobe and put them back again.*

clutter up to fill or cover (something) so that it is made untidy: *There were dirty dishes cluttering up the kitchen worktops. The students clutter their rooms up with beer cans and fast food containers. The room was far from tidy — there were old magazines and newspapers cluttering it up.*

derive from to get (something) from (something), to have (something) as a source of (something): *Sheila derives a great deal of enjoyment from her garden. Anne loves books — she derives so much enjoyment from them.*

file away to store (something) in a file for possible future use: *We filed the application forms away in the bottom drawer of the filing cabinet. The secretary filed away the day's correspondence. Don't throw away the reply to your complaint — file it away in case you need to refer to it again.*

Do it Yourself

1 Replace the underlined words with a phrasal verb: *The children were keeping lots of sweets for a midnight feast.*

2 Replace the underlined words with a phrasal verb: *Frank said that it made a huge difference to his heating bill since he had his house supplied with central heating.*

3 Complete the phrasal verb: *Vera had to _____ **out** the rabbit hutch so that she could clean it properly.*

4 Fill in the missing phrasal verb: *I asked Dave to _____ the bath with piping hot water.*

5 Replace the underlined words with a phrasal verb: *No-one would admit to stealing the money, and so the teacher asked all of the children to empty out their pockets.*

6 Complete the phrasal verb: *The vase looked as good as new once it had been **dusted** _____.*

7 Replace the phrasal verb with one word: *The security guard told the thief that if he **put back** the items that he had stolen he would not call the police.*

8 Complete the phrasal verb: *James is a very messy cook — he manages to _____ **up** every surface, even when he is making a simple meal.*

9 Replace the underlined words with a phrasal verb: *Tricia gets a great deal of pleasure from telling other people that they are wrong.*

10 Complete the phrasal verb: *Now that the meeting is over, I can **file** _____ the report.*

30 A Broken Leg

📋 Phrasal Verbs in Use

'What's wrong with you?' asked Maria as she saw Les limping down the road. He replied, 'I broke my leg some time ago and this is the first day that I've been able to **do without** crutches. I've wanted to **dispense with** them for ages because I found them very uncomfortable.' Les then told Maria the story of his accident. He had been unloading furniture from a van when he stepped back and **fell over** a chair. His friend, Kevin, laughed at first when he saw that he **had tripped over** something, but then realized that Les was in pain. It didn't **occur to** either of them that Les might have broken his leg until he tried to **stand up**. He was in such agony that Kevin phoned for an ambulance and the paramedics **lifted** Les **up** on to a stretcher and **carted** him **off** to hospital. When he got there, his leg was put in plaster and he had to learn to walk on crutches. 'I've been able to attend college and study all right,' said Les, 'but the accident's really **messed up** my part-time job. I work as a sports coach at the local gym and, of course, I haven't been able to do that. The trouble is that I really need the money and now I'm having to **live off** my parents.' 'I'm sure they don't mind,' said Maria comfortingly. 'They'll just want your leg to get back to normal as soon as possible.'

Know the Meaning

do without to manage without having (something): *Matt will not be happy if he has to do without a car. Our phone is broken and it is difficult to do without it.*

dispense with to stop using (something) or to do without (something): *Business is poor and so the firm has had to dispense with some of its staff.*

fall over to fall to the ground by accident, often because someone or something is in the way: *The child took some kind of fit and fell over. Mother fell over a toy which had been left in the hall. Don't leave your shoes there — someone will fall over them.*

trip over to knock one's foot against something and stumble and perhaps fall to the ground: *Watch that you don't trip over — those paving stones are loose. I tripped over a shopping bag in the shop doorway. There was a brick lying in the path and the old man tripped over it.*

occur to suddenly to think of something or to realize something: *It occurred to Fred that the car's engine was making an odd noise. Did it not occur to you that Jack might be lying?*

stand up to rise to one's feet after sitting down or lying down: *The children were asked to stand up and say good-morning to the new teacher. My leg does not hurt when I am sitting down — but it is painful when I stand up.*

lift up to hold (someone or something) in your hands or in your hands and arms and move him/her/it upwards, to raise (someone or something) to a higher position: *The gardener lifted up the tools and put them in the shed. Sally lifted the bottles up and put them in the bin. The baby was crying and Jane lifted her up.*

cart off to take (someone) somewhere, especially without asking his/her permission and sometimes rather abruptly or rudely: *Mrs Carson is always saying that her family want to cart her off to an old people's home. The child was screaming and his father carted him off to his room.*

mess up (informal) to spoil or ruin (something): *Having to resit his exams has messed up Jock's holiday plans. Certainly Freda has done wrong, but she should not let that one misdeed mess the rest of her life up. We had prepared an interesting schedule for the fete, but bad weather messed it up.*

live off to get all the money which you need for living from (someone or something): *Joe doesn't want a job — he's happy to live off his wife. Peter owns several flats and lives off the rent from them. Beth gets an allowance from her parents while she's studying, but she feels bad about having to live off them.*

Do it Yourself

1 Replace the underlined words with a phrasal verb: *Kevin is going to have to <u>manage without</u> an assistant in the shop because he cannot afford to pay any more wages.*

2 Replace the underlined words with a phrasal verb: *Louise <u>stopped using</u> her lawyer because he was useless and expensive.*

3 Complete the phrasal verb: *Susan had to go to hospital after she _____ **over** and banged her head.*

4 Complete the phrasal verb: *I twisted my ankle when I **tripped** _____ the curb.*

5 Complete the phrasal verb: *It did not _____ **to** Jane that she could just ask for a pay rise.*

6 Replace the underlined words with a phrasal verb: *The soldiers were ordered to <u>rise to their feet</u> when the officer entered the room.*

7 Fill in the missing phrasal verb: *The librarian _____ the pile of books and took them over to the shelves.*

8 Complete the phrasal verb: *The police **carted** the protesters _____ to the station for questioning.*

9 Replace the phrasal verb with one word: *Ruth **messed up** the plan to have a surprise party for Tom by telling him all about it.*

10 Complete the phrasal verb: *Peter does not think that the job will pay enough money for him to _____ **off**.*

31 Making a Job Move

Phrasal Verbs in Use

Barry **was looking out for** a new job. He hadn't been very happy with his present one for some time and **had been mulling over** a change. However, he wasn't actually miserable where he was and he had found it difficult to **muster up** enough energy to start actively seeking likely jobs. He **had come across** one or two, but these were no better than his present job. It was his girlfriend, Gina, who **was egging** him **on** to make a change. Barry earned so little that most of his salary **was swallowed up** by rent and food and Gina liked to go to the cinema and clubs. In fact, Gina **had** never **fathomed out** why Barry had taken a job with his present firm in the first place, as he had excellent qualifications and was worthy of something much better. It was she who **came up with** the idea of preparing a CV and sending it to various firms. Rather reluctantly Barry **geared** himself **up** to make some notes about his educational qualifications and work history. Gina then helped him to **flesh out** these notes into a formal CV, which Gina then sent to various prospective employers. It took quite a while for any replies to arrive and then there was a series of interviews, about which Barry got quite nervous. Within a very short time, however, Barry had a well-paid, interesting job. Gina's persuasion and hard work had not been in vain.

Know the Meaning

look out for to try to find, obtain, etc (something): *I've been looking out for that book for some time. Jan was so pleased to find a house in that street — she had been looking out for one for some time.*

mull over to think about (something) carefully and for a long time: *We mulled over the idea of moving house, but eventually decided to build an extension to this one. The committee members all mulled the problem over, but failed to suggest a solution. The firm's offer of work was a generous one, but, after mulling it over, Henry rejected it.*

muster up to gather (courage, energy, etc): *I cannot muster up any enthusiasm for the project. The general expected all his soldiers to muster up the courage to fight the strong enemy army.*

come across to find or meet by chance: *Julia came across an old school friend at the conference. I came across an interesting article on global warming in the local newspaper. It was a lovely pub and the young couple were glad to have come across it.*

egg on to encourage or urge (someone) to do something, often something foolish or wrong: *The students knew that they were wrong to egg on Tom to climb on the roof. The boy said that he would not have stolen the car if his friends had not egged him on.*

swallow up to use all of a supply of (money, resources, etc): *Phoning home from the payphone has swallowed up all my small change. Eating in expensive restaurants will soon swallow your allowance up. The student has a small grant but university textbooks swallow that up easily.*

fathom out to understand (someone or something), after thinking about it carefully for some time: *Even now the police cannot fathom out a motive for the murder. There is no point in trying to fathom Jane out — she is very secretive. Peggy left home suddenly — we cannot fathom it out.*

come up with to think of (an idea, plan, proposal etc) and suggest it: *The council have come up with a plan to solve the traffic problem. This is a good idea — who came up with it?*

gear up to prepare (someone) to do something, to get (someone or something) ready and able to do something: *The students decided that it was time that they started gearing themselves up for the exams. The firm is not geared up to cope with the large increase in orders. The football team is very inexperienced and unfit — it will be difficult to gear it up for the tournament.*

flesh out to add details to (something) to make it fuller or more comprehensive: *We hope to flesh out the proposal before the next meeting. That is interesting, but you need to flesh the idea out a bit. Your essay is too short — you will have to flesh it out with some more information.*

Do it Yourself

1 Replace the underlined words with a phrasal verb: *Lorraine bought the dress straight away — it was just what she had been <u>trying to find</u>.*

2 Replace the underlined words with a phrasal verb: *Fiona said that she would have to <u>think carefully about</u> the proposal that she move to another city to get a better job.*

3 Complete the phrasal verb: *Wendy somehow managed to **muster** _____ the courage to ask her boss for a promotion.*

4 Fill in the missing phrasal verb: *I _____ the advert in the local newspaper yesterday.*

5 Replace the underlined word with a phrasal verb: *The girl said that she had stolen the sweets from the shop because she had been <u>encouraged</u> by her brother.*

6 Replace the underlined words with a phrasal verb: *Paul complained that heating his flat was <u>using all of</u> his wages.*

7 Replace the underlined word with a phrasal verb: *I cannot <u>understand</u> why James left university — he always got excellent marks.*

8 Replace the underlined words with a phrasal verb: *The manager was very pleased with Robert for <u>thinking of</u> the idea of going on a team-building course.*

9 Complete the phrasal verb: *Dave is trying to **gear** himself _____ to sell his house.*

10 Complete the phrasal verb: *The editor told the journalist that she would need to **flesh** her article _____ a bit.*

32 The Exam Aftermath

Phrasal Verbs in Use

The first-year students at Worthington College had just finished a history exam and were discussing it as they went to the canteen for coffee. Bruce, who **tended towards** optimism, thought that it had been quite an easy exam. Douglas, who had done very little studying for the exam, had thought that it **verged on** being impossible, while Fraser, who had done even less preparation, **had** already **written off** the exam. Diane felt that she had been very fortunate, in that she had happened to **brush up on** two of the exam topics on the morning of the exam, but Liz had not been so lucky. She had chosen to **swot up on** what she believed to be likely exam topics, and only one of these had been in the exam paper. Harry and Rosalind **were vying with** each other in declaring how badly they thought they had done in the exam, but Robin thought that he might **have** just **scraped through**. He didn't know very many historical facts, but he was planning to be a professional writer and knew how to **pad out** a few facts into a successful essay. Sally was not with them, but everyone knew that she would not be worried. Not only was she good at history, but she also always studied hard. Undoubtedly she would **sail through** the exam. Len looked at his gloomy fellow-students and said, 'There's nothing we can do about it now. Let's stop **brooding over** the exam and have some fun!'

Know the Meaning

tend towards to show more of (a certain quality, etc) than others: *Jan is very generous, but Tom tends towards meanness. I wouldn't actually accuse Derek of sexism, but he is tending towards it.*

verge on to be very close or similar to, to border on: *Liz's laughter was verging on hysteria. They say that what Matt did was not an illegal act, but it was certainly verging on one.*

write off to regard (someone or something) as being of no further use or value, or unimportant, unsuccessful, etc: *Don't write off the job which you've been offered without finding out more details. It would be foolish to write catering off as a career without knowing more about it.*

brush up on to revise one's knowledge of (something): *Meg should brush up on the Highway Code before she takes her driving test. There was a question about Napoleon in the exam — thank goodness that I brushed up on him.*

swot up on to study or read up as much as one can about (a subject), often for a test or exam: *I can't go out tonight because I'm swotting up on grammar for tomorrow's test.*

vie with to compete with (someone or something), to try to do something better than (someone or something else): *Ella and Fay vied with each other for the English prize. It's difficult to predict who will win the golf trophy — several good players are vying for it.*

scrape through to only just avoid failing or being unsuccessful at (something), to pass (an exam, etc) with a very low mark: *Mark will have to study harder — he just scraped through last year's exams. Jenny thought that she had failed her driving test, but found that she had just scraped through it.*

pad out to add (information, etc) to (a piece of writing, etc) just to make it longer without making it any more relevant, informative, useful, etc: *The makers of this machine have padded the instructions out with a great deal of unnecessary detail. If you pad out your essay with a lot of irrelevant material, you will get a low mark for it. This guidebook about the city is very poor — the author has padded it out with a lot of silly anecdotes.*

sail through to pass or succeed at (something) very easily, to deal with (a situation) easily and successfully: *Dave sailed through his driving test at his first attempt. Polly just sails through life — she never seems to have any problems.*

brood over to think about (something unpleasant, difficult, etc) anxiously for a long time: *Sally keeps brooding over her divorce. It's a pity that you didn't get the job, but there's no point in brooding over it.*

Do it Yourself

1 Complete the phrasal verb: *Ivy does not like her new teacher — she _____ **towards** strictness.*

2 Replace the underlined words with a phrasal verb: *Fred was trying to keep a straight face when the policeman was talking to him, but he was <u>very close to</u> laughing the whole time.*

3 Complete the phrasal verb: *Trudy has **written** _____ her relationship with Peter because he refuses to talk about getting married.*

4 Replace the underlined words with a phrasal verb: *Tom is going to spend the day <u>revising his knowledge of</u> general knowledge in preparation for the quiz.*

5 Complete the phrasal verb: *Tony will have to **swot** _____ on algebra if he wants to do well in the test.*

6 Replace the underlined words with a phrasal verb: *Trevor and William have been <u>competing with</u> each other for the attention of the new girl at work.*

7 Complete the phrasal verb: *Liam did not run a very good race and was relieved that he managed to _____ **through** to the next round.*

8 Complete the phrasal verb: *My essay was a bit short, but I managed to **pad** it _____ with some quotes.*

9 Complete the phrasal verb: *Julie was very nervous about her job interview, but she **sailed** _____ it.*

10 Replace the underlined words with a phrasal verb: *Philip keeps <u>thinking anxiously about</u> the accident he had last week, but it was not his fault.*

33 A Winter Holiday

Phrasal Verbs in Use

Janet and several of her friends **huddled round** the fire of her parent's country cottage, where they were spending the weekend. It was a very cold day and they were all feeling slightly sleepy after lunch. After a short nap Jim was beginning to feel quite energetic and was trying to **prevail on** the others to go for a walk. At first Jill was in favour of the idea, but had now decided to **back out of** the walk, saying that she was too tired. Bill said that he **was**n't **feeling up to** walking and **plumped for** a game of Scrabble instead if anyone else was interested. Jessie, who was not a very energetic person, readily **fell in with** this proposal and went to get the Scrabble board and a dictionary. Jill said that she would like a game also, but Mark said that he would much prefer to read. Kate got up to **attend to** the fire, which was in need of more logs and coal, saying to Jim, 'You won't get anywhere by trying to **push** us **into** going with you. Why don't you go by yourself?' Jim replied, 'A good walk would **wake** you all **up**. Sitting around is making you sluggish.' The others ignored this and went on with what they were doing until Jim said, 'Goodbye then. I may be some time. I'm going to **call in at** the pub on the way back.' Suddenly several people changed their minds about going out.

Know the Meaning

huddle round to gather closely together, near to (something): *The children were very cold and huddled round the radiator. I can't even see the bonfire — there are too many people huddled round it.*

prevail on to persuade (someone) to do something although he/she may be reluctant: *We eventually prevailed on Toby to lend us his car. Ruby is very mean — I'm sure that you will not prevail on her to make a contribution to the charity.*

back out of to decide not to do something which one has already promised, arranged, etc to do, to withdraw from (an arrangement, promise, etc): *The two firms were planning to merge, but one of them backed out of the deal. The building contract had been drawn up, waiting to be signed, when the owner of the house backed out of it.*

feel up to to feel able and inclined to (do something): *Pat didn't feel up to cycling to work today — she has a sore leg. Amy is having a party but I've been ill and I don't feel up to going to it.*

plump for to choose (someone or something): *Pam and Beth were discussing holiday destinations and Pam plumped for Italy. You shouldn't criticize the party venue — you were the one who plumped for it.*

fall in with to accept and agree to (something): *Everyone happily fell in with Roger's suggestion. It is a very interesting idea, but some members of the committee may well not fall in with it.*

attend to to make sure that (someone or something) has what he/she/it needs, to help or deal with (someone or something): *Could you attend to that customer? — she wants a new hat. The bonfire needs more wood, but I can't attend to that at the moment.*

push into to force (someone) into (doing something): *The drama teacher pushed Celia into playing Ophelia in the college production of Hamlet although she was quite unsuitable. Val's father pushed her into studying medicine.*

wake up to make (someone) more alert: *A walk by the sea might wake the children up. Having a cold shower certainly woke up Jenny. Harry said that he was going for a swim to wake himself up.*

call in at to visit (somewhere) briefly: *James called in at a pub to have a quick pint. There's a new wine bar in the high street and we called in at it to see what it was like.*

Do it Yourself

1 Replace the underlined words with a phrasal verb: *The children gathered round the teacher while she told them the ghost story.*

2 Complete the phrasal verb: *The local residents **prevailed** _____ the council to change their mind about closing the school.*

3 Replace the underlined words with a phrasal verb: *Helen is furious at Ruth for changing her mind about going on holiday with her.*

4 Complete the phrasal verb: *I was sick last night and did not **feel** _____ going to work this morning.*

5 Replace the phrasal verb with one word: *After studying the menu for a long time, Bob eventually **plumped for** the chocolate mousse.*

6 Complete the phrasal verb: *We should get someone else to move in to share the cost of the rent, and I am hoping that she will **fall in** _____ the plan.*

7 Complete the phrasal verb: *I have a lot of outstanding bills to pay and I am going to _____ **to** them when I get paid at the end of the month.*

8 Complete the phrasal verb: *I'm not surprised that Yvonne has dropped out of university — her father **pushed** her _____ going.*

9 Complete the phrasal verb: *Peter needs a cup of strong black coffee in the morning to _____ him **up** before he starts work.*

10 Replace the underlined words with a phrasal verb: *Caroline briefly visited the office, where she used to work, to see her old colleagues.*

34 Sudden Illness

📝 Phrasal Verbs in Use

When Lucy and Sharon came back from lunch, there was an ambulance parked outside the office door. It **moved off** as they approached and, when they went into the office, everyone **was clustered round** the reception desk. 'Lucy!' said the receptionist, Anna. 'Thank goodness you're here! Linda has gone to hospital in the ambulance and she **is asking for** you.' Lucy was very worried, since Linda was her sister. When she asked what had happened, she was told that Linda had suddenly **blacked out** as she rose from her desk. She had not being feeling well and had thought that she **was coming down with** flu. When Lucy said that she would go to the hospital at once, several of the others offered to go, too, since they were all anxious about their colleague. However, Lucy said, 'I don't think that the hospital staff will want a whole crowd of people **descending on** them. I'll go and then I'll phone you.' When Lucy arrived at the hospital, several people in white coats **were buzzing round** Linda's bed. A doctor **took** Lucy **aside**, saying, 'We thought at first that your sister might have a brain tumour and that we would have to **operate on** it. We've done some tests and, thankfully, there is no tumour. Your sister has very high blood pressure and we have given her medication for it. All this **has taken** a lot **out of** her and she needs to rest.'

Know the Meaning

move off to start to leave: *The cyclist got on her bike and moved off. The protest march was over and the protesters were starting to move off.*

cluster round to gather around (someone or something) in a group which is very close together: *The students clustered around the notice-board to find out their exam results. When the film star arrived, a crowd of photographers clustered round her.*

ask for to say that one would like to see or talk to (someone): *The old lady was very ill and kept asking for her daughter. A man rang up and asked for you.*

black out to lose consciousness: *Celia blacked out for a few minutes after the stone hit her head. It was a heavy blow, but not enough to make him black out.*

come down with to catch or to suffer from (an illness): *Tim has a lot of spots on his body — I think he's coming down with chickenpox. Molly's sister has mumps and she thinks that she's coming down with it.*

descend on to arrive suddenly, often in large numbers and often unexpectedly or without being wanted: *Hordes of reporters descended on the politician's house when they heard the scandal about him. In the winter the town is a peaceful place, but in the summer, crowds of tourists descend on it.*

buzz round/around to move around (somewhere) busily and quickly: *There had obviously been an accident because there were police buzzing around all over the motorway. I wouldn't visit the castle today — there are parties of schoolchildren buzzing around it.*

take aside to separate (someone) from other people because one wants to have a private conversation with him/her: *The lecturer took Paula aside and told her the news of her father's accident. The pupil was obviously upset and the teacher took him aside to find out what was wrong.*

operate on to perform surgery (on someone or something): *The surgeon is going to operate on the patient this afternoon. The athlete's leg is badly injured and the surgeon is going to operate on it right away.*

take out of to make (someone) feel tired or weak: *Working such long hours has taken a great deal out of Tom. Anne needs a holiday — studying for exams has taken a lot out of her.*

Do it Yourself

1 Replace the underlined words with a phrasal verb: *Aileen switched on the indicator to show that she was about to <u>start to leave</u>.*

2 Replace the underlined words with a phrasal verb: *The police asked the crowd not to <u>gather round</u> the cyclist, who had an accident.*

3 Complete the phrasal verb: *I saw Paul at the party last night and he was **asking** _____ you.*

4 Replace the underlined words with a phrasal verb: *The boxer had to be taken to hospital after he <u>lost consciousness</u> at the end of the fight.*

5 Complete the phrasal verb: *Roger could not stop sneezing and he hoped he was not _____ **down with** a cold.*

6 Complete the phrasal verb: *Crowds of fans _____ **on** the hotel where the band were staying.*

7 Complete the phrasal verb: *Sheila's mother is _____ **around**, trying to finalize the arrangements for the wedding on Saturday.*

8 Fill in the missing phrasal verb. *The manager _____ Fiona _____ and warned her not to be late again.*

9 Replace the underlined words with a phrasal verb: *The doctor said that the only way that I will be able to use my arm again is to <u>perform surgery on</u> it.*

10 Complete the phrasal verb: *Lucy enjoyed climbing the mountain, but it **took** a lot _____ **of** her.*

35 Market Research

Phrasal Verbs in Use

Rod wondered what he **had let** himself **in for**. There he was on a Saturday morning, standing in the high street trying to **strike up** conversations with complete strangers. He was being employed by a market research company to ask shoppers a series of questions and **jot** their answers **down** on questionnaires. It was not an easy job. Many shoppers **had loaded** themselves **up** with various bags and packages, and did not want to stop and answer questions about their lifestyles. One woman **had** actually **flown into** a temper when he had tried to stop her, and had almost hit him with her umbrella. Rod had discovered that very few people were willing to be interviewed and rushed past him, **casting aside** any thought of politeness when they saw him. He was worried about his lack of progress because he **had clocked up** three hours at the job and had only completed two questionnaires. In order to get some tips on how to get people to talk to him, he had watched other market researchers at work. He had seen one hide in shop doorways and suddenly **leap out at** passers-by. Amazingly, some of these then **engaged in** conversation quite happily with him. This technique had not worked for Rod. Nor had any others. Just now a man **had broken off** a conversation with a friend to tell Rod to get lost. Rod decided that he would never be any good at the job and went home.

Know the Meaning

let in for to involve (oneself or someone) in something difficult, dangerous, unpleasant, expensive, etc: *When Josh's daughter got married he didn't know what he was letting himself in for — the wedding cost thousands of pounds. Rachel didn't know what she was letting her husband in for when she said that he would chair the meeting. My mother didn't know what she was letting me in for when she asked me to look after her neighbour's children — they were very badly behaved.*

strike up to begin (a conversation, friendship, etc): *They struck up an acquaintanceship on the plane. I struck up a conversation with the person next to me at the theatre.*

jot down to write (something) down often in a brief, informal form: *Just let me jot down your address. I jotted the appointment down in my diary. Phil couldn't find Marcia's phone number although he had jotted it down.*

load up to put a lot of things on (someone or something) and take them somewhere: *They loaded the boot of the car up with Christmas presents. Could you load the van up with the shopping? The donkey was very old, but its owner loaded it up with goods to take to market.*

fly into suddenly to go into (a state of anger): *Marge flew into a rage when Pete arrived late. Sally's father flew into a temper when she lost her job.*

cast aside to get rid (of someone or something): *Julie has now cast aside her religion. He had a daughter, but he cast her aside when he remarried.*

clock up to reach (a number of miles, hours, etc): *The car clocked up two thousand miles on the return trip. The tradesman charged us for more hours than he actually clocked up.*

engage in to take part in (something): *Joe wasn't allowed by his parents to engage in the travel business. Bill is engaged in banking. The man in the train tried to engage me in conversation.*

leap out at to move towards (someone) suddenly, often from a hidden position: *The attacker leapt out at the old man from a dark doorway. We were passing the gate when a large dog suddenly leapt out at us.*

break off to stop speaking suddenly, often for a very short time: *Sue was in the middle of a telephone conversation, but broke off to say goodbye to her daughter, who was just leaving.*

Do it Yourself

1 Complete the phrasal verb: *I feel sorry for Derek, but should have known what he was **letting** himself in _____ when he married Joan — she has a terrible temper.*

2 Replace the underlined word with a phrasal verb: *The train journey passed quickly after I <u>began</u> a conversation with the woman sitting beside me.*

3 Complete the phrasal verb: *Keith _____ **down** the date of the concert.*

4 Fill in the missing phrasal verb: *The family _____ the car with all the things that they needed.*

5 Replace the underlined words with a phrasal verb: *Julie was worried that Kevin would <u>suddenly go into</u> a rage when he realized that she had crashed the car.*

6 Replace the underlined words with a phrasal verb: *The children soon <u>got rid of</u> their favourite toys when their mother brought home a computer for them to play with.*

7 Complete the phrasal verb: *George decided to stop for a rest after he had **clocked** _____ eight hours of driving on the motorway.*

8 Replace the underlined words with a phrasal verb: *Joanna is a very shy girl and does not like to <u>take part in</u> social gatherings.*

9 Complete the phrasal verb: *Tracey got a terrible fright when the youth **leapt** _____ **at** her from behind.*

10 Replace the underlined words with a phrasal verb: *Monica was telling her friend about the surprise she had planned for her husband's birthday, but had to <u>suddenly stop speaking</u> when he walked in.*

36 Amateur Dramatics

Phrasal Verbs in Use

The local amateur dramatic society were holding their first meeting of the season after a long summer break. They had selected Harold as their director last season and he **had ferreted out** some scripts that he thought the members might like to perform. The various members **had thumbed through** these and had given their opinions. After a lot of discussion and some argument, a play had been chosen. Then Pam, who was in charge of costumes, **had handed round** coffee and biscuits. Now the director had begun to **parcel out** the parts and this always caused some controversy. The members, who had been in the society longest, always thought that they should get the best parts and sometimes overestimated their talent. Harold had no intentions of doing this. He told the members that it was absolutely necessary that they **improve on** last year's performance, and that he was not going to select anyone who was going to **ham up** their part. He went on to say that the society had acquired a reputation for being very amateurish after their last few performances, and that it was vital to **shake** this **off**. Because of this reputation, they had had found it difficult to **scrape together** a reasonably sized audience for their last production and this was causing financial problems. His comments **stirred up** some anger and resentment among the older members as he was quite new to the society, but several of the members **stuck up for** him.

Know the Meaning

ferret out (*informal*) to find (something) by searching for it thoroughly: *Trust Jan to ferret out the family's guilty secrets. Fred was the first reporter to ferret the scandal out. The information was useful and it hadn't taken long to ferret it out.*

thumb through to turn over the pages (of a book, etc) and glance at them briefly: *I thumbed through the catalogue to see what the clothes were like. This book looks as though many people have thumbed through it.*

hand round to pass (something) from one member of a group to another: *The waitress handed round a tray of sandwiches. I'll get my son to hand the drinks round at the party. That's the agenda for the meeting — could you hand it round?*

parcel out to divide (something) out among the members of a group: *The land was parcelled out among the four sons of the family. There were ten members of the committee and we parcelled out the various duties among us.*

improve on to make (a standard, result, etc) better: *The standard of football has not improved on last year's performance. Our profits were very high last year — I don't see how we can improve on them.*

ham up to exaggerate words and gestures, especially when one is acting in a play, etc: *The marketing manager was furious when Ben hammed up his presentation. The local dramatic society put on a production of Macbeth and really hammed it up.*

shake off to get rid of (something, such as a habit, reputation, etc): *I'm trying shake off the effects of a bad cold. Tom still smokes and says that he simply cannot shake the habit off. As a youth Mick got a reputation as the local bad boy, and he has never shaken it off.*

scrape together to get together or obtain with great difficulty (the amount or number which one needs): *Roy eventually scraped together a deposit on a flat. Can we scrape enough people together to hire a minivan? The monthly rent is high, but we usually manage to scrape it together.*

stir up to cause (trouble, strong feelings of some kind, etc) often deliberately: *The very name of the president stirred up hatred in many of the citizens. George is a very argumentative person and likes to stir up trouble. We thought that we had achieved peace, but some terrorists stirred things up again.*

stick up for to defend or support (someone): *Of course John stuck up for his elder brother. Emma was upset that no-one had stuck up for her in the argument.*

Do it Yourself

1 Replace the underlined word with a phrasal verb: *I am going to ask Jane to take me shopping with her — she always manages to <u>find</u> the best bargains.*

2 Complete the phrasal verb: *Peter has been **thumbing** _____ the property guide, but he has not seen any house which he likes.*

3 Complete the phrasal verb: *The teacher asked Jenny to **hand** _____ the books for the afternoon's lesson.*

4 Complete the phrasal verb: *There was a lot of work to do before they could set up camp and so the friends **parcelled** _____ the various jobs.*

5 Fill in the missing phrasal verb: *I agree that the team played well last year, but I still think that they can _____ their tactics.*

6 Replace the underlined word with a phrasal verb: *The referee told the football player to stop <u>exaggerating</u> his injury and to get on with playing the game.*

7 Replace the underlined words with a phrasal verb: *I cannot <u>get rid of</u> the feeling that someone has been going through my belongings.*

8 Replace the underlined words with a phrasal verb: *Charles finally managed to <u>get together</u> enough money to pay for the bill.*

9 Complete the phrasal verb: *The manager fired Elaine because she was always **stirring** _____ trouble in the office.*

10 Replace the underlined word with a phrasal verb: *Wilma <u>defended</u> Jean when the manager accused her of being useless at her job.*

37 Auditions

Phrasal Verbs in Use

There was great excitement at Langham College of Drama. A well-known theatrical company had contacted the college and said that they **were scouting around** for new talent. They had gone on to say that they would like to audition some of the college students for parts in their next productions, and had arrived to **weigh up** the merits of the students. Since the company **ranked among** the most successful in the country, it was a wonderful opportunity for the students and many of them **were brimming over with** enthusiasm. They were also nervous, knowing that the possibility of employment with the theatre company **hinged on** how well they performed on that one day. Emily said that a touch of nervousness **brought out** the best in her and improved her performance. Not many of the others agreed with that philosophy. They wished that they felt more confident about the whole thing. Matt was feeling particularly lacking in confidence. He had been trying to learn a long speech from Shakespeare, but **had got bogged down** in it. Now he was feeling very depressed. At the start of the auditions dozens of students **had trooped into** the section of the college assembly hall, which the organizers **had partitioned off** for the occasion. However, it was now mid-afternoon and those holding the auditions **were** gradually **whittling away at** the number of would-be actors. It would not be long before the students discovered which of them had been successful, and which would have to wait for another audition.

Know the Meaning

scout around to look in several places for (something which one wants): *When we arrived in the town we scouted around for somewhere cheap to eat. They eventually found their ideal house but they had to scout around for it.*

weigh up to consider (something) carefully, especially so as to come to a decision or make a choice: *We weighed the situation up and decided that we could not possibly win. Sheila weighed up the advantages and disadvantages of moving to the country, and decided to remain in the city. After weighing everything up, Charles decided to resign.*

rank among to have a place (in a particular group): *Fred's father ranks among the richest men in Britain. The inhabitants rank among the poorest people in the world.*

brim over with to be full of (something): *Her eyes were brimming over with tears. Muriel was brimming over with joy on her wedding day.*

hinge on to depend on (something): *The success of the venture hinges on large export sales. Ned needs a good degree — his future hinges on it.*

bring out to cause (something) to become obvious: *Cruelty to animals brings out the worst in Jack. Working with children has brought out Jean's gentler side.*

get bogged down in to make little progress with (something), perhaps because of paying too much attention to detail or minor problems: *James applied for a visa to work there, but he got bogged down in all the regulations. Les is trying to fill in his income tax form, but he's getting completely bogged down in it.*

troop into to go into (somewhere) in a large group: *We all trooped into the assembly hall to hear the results of our exams. The dance hall was ready, and all the students trooped into it.*

partition off to separate part (of something) from the rest by means of a partition: *Marie partitioned off part of her living-room to use as study. The dining-room is really part of the kitchen, but they have partitioned it off.*

whittle away at gradually to make something smaller, weaker, etc: *Being unemployed for a time whittled away at Garry's savings. Various unsuccessful by-elections whittled away at the government's majority. A series of weak kings had whittled away at the power of the monarchy.*

Do it Yourself

1 Complete the phrasal verb: *After we got off the train we decided to* **scout** _____ *for a place to stay.*

2 Replace the underlined words with a phrasal verb: *Ruth asked if she could have time to <u>consider carefully</u> the pros and cons of accepting the offer of a new job in another city.*

3 Replace the underlined words with a phrasal verb: *Steve <u>has a place as one of</u> the fastest sprinters in the country.*

4 Replace the underlined words with a phrasal verb: *Tony's parents were <u>full of</u> pride as they watched him receive his award for bravery.*

5 Replace the underlined words with a phrasal verb: *The sale of the house <u>depends on</u> the couple, who want to buy it, being able to sell their own house.*

6 Fill in the missing phrasal verb: *Needles _____ the coward in me — they just make me want to run away from the clinic.*

7 Complete the phrasal verb: *Lorraine resigned from the residents' committee because she was tired of* **getting** _____ **down in** *petty arguments.*

8 Complete the phrasal verb: *The children* **trooped** _____ *the dining hall to get their lunch.*

9 Replace the underlined words with a phrasal verb: *I think that we will have to <u>separate off</u> part of the lounge to use as an extra bedroom.*

10 Complete the phrasal verb: *Getting turned down for so many jobs has really* **whittled** _____ **at** *Emma's confidence.*

38 Bullying

Phrasal Verbs in Use

Tim's parents were very worried. A few weeks ago he had had to change schools and he was very unhappy. When he was younger he had been very shy, but he **had grown out of** that and **had joined in** all the activities at his previous school. At first Tim's parents thought that his misery would **blow over**. They assumed he was missing his old friends. Yesterday, however, they had discovered from another parent at the school that a bigger boy in Tim's class **was picking on** him. Although Tim was a pleasant, friendly boy, the other boy, called Nigel, had taken against him for some reason. Worse than this, he had encouraged several other boys to **gang up on** Tim and to **push** him **around**. Nigel and these boys both called him names and attacked him physically. Tim hadn't known what to do. He was afraid to **tell on** the bullies because they had said that, if he did, they would treat him even more badly. He had tried to ignore their bullying and to **walk away from** it, but that hadn't worked. They just bullied him more. On the other hand, the boys were all bigger than he was and he was afraid to **hit** them **back**. When his parents found out about the situation, they realized that it **had gone** far **beyond** teasing and reported it to the head teacher. Nigel was suspended from school and the other boys given a stern warning against bullying.

Know the Meaning

grow out of to stop (having or doing something, often something unpleasant or undesirable) when one grows older or more mature: *Gradually the little girl grew out of her fear of the dark. Jill had a bad habit of biting her nails, but she grew out of it.*

join in to take part in (an activity in which other people are involved): *Mona was feeling unhappy and refused to join in the dancing. There was applause for the show, but not everyone joined in it. The local boys were playing a game of football and Meg's sons soon joined in.*

blow over to stop and be forgotten about: *Martin and Joan had a serious quarrel last year, but fortunately it seems to have blown over now. There was trouble in the town over the new development, but the council think that it will blow over.*

pick on to treat (someone) badly and unjustly, often doing so repeatedly: *The teacher started picking on Jean as soon as she joined the class. Jack is smaller than the other boys and they pick on him in the playground.*

gang up on (informal) to get together in a group and attack (someone else) or treat (someone else badly and unfairly): *The school bully and her friends ganged up on the new girl. They were all ganging up on me to try to make me change my mind.*

push around to treat (someone) roughly and rudely and tell (him/her) what to do: *Stella is very ambitious and pushes the other workers around to get what she wants. Tom's elder brothers pushed him around when they were children.*

tell on (informal) to report (someone) to someone in authority or in charge for having done something wrong: *The children next door saw Jerry break the window and told on him. Tina told the teacher on Pam when she tore her painting.*

walk away from not to try to deal with (a difficult or unpleasant situation), but to leave it or ignore it: *It was difficult for Jenny to walk away from the insults and jeers of her colleagues. The man in the pub challenged Pete to a fight, but he walked away from it.*

hit back to hit (someone) after he/she has hit one: *Molly was not strong enough to hit her brother back. The school bully doesn't expect people to hit him back.*

go beyond to be more serious, extreme, etc than (something): *Josh thought it was funny, but his behaviour certainly went beyond a joke. The row went beyond the usual friendly family argument.*

Do it Yourself

1 Complete the phrasal verb: *The doctor told Jane not to worry about her son sucking his thumb, and that he would soon* **grow _____ of** *it.*

2 Replace the underlined words with a phrasal verb: *Suzanne was delighted when the other children asked her to <u>take part in</u> their game of chase.*

3 Complete the phrasal verb: *I bet the treasurer is relieved that the scandal about the missing money seems to have* **blown _____.**

4 Complete the phrasal verb: *Trudy complained to her manager that Donald had been* **picking _____** *her.*

5 Replace the underlined words with a phrasal verb: *The teacher gave the children a scolding for <u>getting together and attacking</u> the boy.*

6 Complete the phrasal verb: *Peter is a very strong character and does not let anyone* **push** *him* **_____.**

7 Complete the phrasal verb: *Jessica decided that she would* **tell _____.** *Robert for cheating in the test.*

8 Replace the underlined word with a phrasal verb: *Thomas was trying to pick an argument with me all morning but I just <u>ignored</u> it.*

9 Complete the phrasal verb: *Darren's father told him that he should have* **hit** *the other boy* **_____** *when he punched him.*

10 Replace the underlined words with a phrasal verb: *Stealing money from the till <u>was more serious</u> the usual schoolboy pranks.*

39 A Breakdown

📝 Phrasal Verbs in Use

Gordon and some of his friends were leaving for a holiday in the mountains, now that they had finished college for the summer. Since the weather should be fine, they had decided to **camp out**. They **had clubbed together** to hire a van to take them and their equipment to their destination. Since none of them had any tents, and since they couldn't afford to buy any, they **had chipped in** more money and gone to a shop which **rented** them **out**. They had packed the van earlier and they all **piled into** it and drove off. They were making good progress with Gordon as driver, when there was a loud bang and the van **veered off** the road. Realizing that a tyre had burst, they got out of the van and phoned a repair garage on Jack's mobile phone. All they could do was to **hang around** the van and wait since they were miles from any town. In the van were some provisions, but these had to last until they reached the campsite, and they had to **ration out** the food. Despite this, they decided to have some coffee. Mary poured it out of the Thermos flask into some plastic cups and they **gulped** it **down** gratefully. Then the repair man appeared and replaced the tyre. They all got back into the van, this time with Ralph at the wheel. 'Don't drive too fast!' Gordon warned, 'even if we do have to **make up for** lost time.'

Know the Meaning

camp out to sleep outdoors in a tent: *We couldn't afford a hotel and so we hired a tent and camped out. The children wanted to camp out in the back garden.*

club together (*of a group of people*) to give money so that a group can share the cost of something: *Polly is ill — let's club together and buy her some flowers. If the family club together, we should be able to buy a really nice present for mum.*

chip in to pay some money towards the cost of something: *The brief-case is expensive, but if we all chip in we can afford to buy it as a leaving present for Rick. We were able to have a party because we all chipped in.*

rent out to allow the use (of something) in return for money: *The farmer rents out one of his fields to the pony club. Phil has decided not to rent his flat out again. Rose inherited a cottage from her grandmother and now rents it out.*

pile in/into (*of a group*) to get into (a vehicle, room, etc) all together in an informal or disorganized way: *The students all piled into the hall to hear the concert. The children piled onto the train on their trip to the seaside. The bus is waiting — pile in!*

veer off suddenly to change direction: *Joe suddenly saw the exit sign and veered off the motorway. The police were chasing the thieves along the path when they suddenly veered off across the fields.*

hang around to stay (somewhere) for quite a long time doing nothing, perhaps because one is waiting for someone or something: *There's a suspicious-looking character hanging around the school gates. My dental appointment has been delayed and now I'll have to hang around here for another hour.*

ration out to give only small amounts of (something) to the members of a group of people, because one does not have much of it: *Jane rationed out the children's weekly allowance so that they did not eat the sweets all at once.*

gulp down to eat or drink (something) very quickly: *Adam got up late and had only time to gulp down a piece of toast. Here's a mug of coffee — you've time to gulp it down before the meeting.*

make up for to compensate for (something), to supply (a reward, substitute, etc) for a disappointment, loss, damage, etc that has taken place: *You'll have to find a way to make up for damaging Sara's dress. The insurance money did not really make up for the loss of Julie's jewellery — a lot of it had sentimental value. Our children couldn't go on the trip to the seaside, but we made up for it by taking them to the zoo.*

Do it Yourself

1 Replace the underlined words with a phrasal verb: *We decided that it would be nice to go down and sleep outdoors in a tent at the beach.*

2 Complete the phrasal verb: *If we all **club** _____, we can probably afford to buy Diana a necklace.*

3 Replace the underlined words with a phrasal verb: *Rachel's friends all paid money in order to buy her a birthday present.*

4 Complete the phrasal verb: *Alex is going to **rent** _____ his flat while he is working abroad.*

5 Replace the underlined words with a phrasal verb: *The tourists all got into the open-topped bus that would take them on a sightseeing tour of the city.*

6 Replace the underlined words with a phrasal verb: *The dog was chasing the cat along the street when it suddenly changed direction and went up an alley.*

7 Complete the phrasal verb: *Hurry up, I don't want to miss my train and end up having to **hang** _____ at the station.*

8 Replace the underlined words with a phrasal verb: *We are running low on food — we are going to have to give out small quantities of what we have got left.*

9 Complete the phrasal verb: *You will get indigestion if you **gulp** _____ your food.*

10 Replace the underlined words with a phrasal verb: *William tried to compensate for forgetting Hannah's birthday by buying her an expensive pair of earrings.*

40 A Visit to the Zoo

Phrasal Verbs in Use

A group of children from the local primary school were going to the zoo. Some of the parents had offered to help, and the teachers **had** gratefully **taken** them **up on** their offer. When they reached the gates of the zoo, the teachers **had paired** the children **off**, telling them to **hold onto** tightly the hand of their partners. Before they left the school, the children **had gathered round** the head teacher, while she told them to be good and stay with the teachers all the time they were at the zoo. They had promised faithfully to do so, but when they **were going round** the zoo some of the boys seemed to forget their promises and **hared off** in the direction of the ice cream kiosk. One of the teachers soon caught them and returned them to the group without any ice cream. Then some people who were queuing to see the penguins claimed that some of the schoolchildren **had** just **barged through** without queuing. Finally, they were watching the zoo-keepers **hosing down** the elephants when one of the teachers counted the children. She discovered that one of them, a little girl called Sylvia, was missing. Fortunately they soon found her. She **had slipped away** to see the monkeys. By this time, all the adults had had quite enough excitement for one day. One of the teachers phoned the bus driver to come and collect them, and they **headed back** to the school.

Know the Meaning

take up on to accept (an offer, etc) from (someone): *You should take Malcolm up on his offer to pay for the damage. Paula suggested that she lend Bert some money, but he declined to take her up on it.*

pair off to arrange (a group of people) so that each joins together with another to make a pair or couple, sometimes with the intention of encouraging romance: *The dance teacher paired off the children according to their ability. At the party George paired his daughter off with the son of a rich farmer. The children gathered in the playground and the teacher paired them off for the walk to the bus.*

hold onto to grip (something or someone) tightly: *Little Alice held onto her mother's hand as they crossed the street. When Mark fell in the river he reached up and held onto a branch until he could be rescued. Bill threw Jim a rope and he held onto it, until he was pulled up from the bottom of the cliff.*

gather round to form a group round (someone or something): *The tourists gathered round the guide at the cathedral. We all gathered round the Christmas tree to sing carols. The boys began to fight and a crowd gathered round them.*

go round to walk through all of (something): *We'll go round the museum tomorrow. The art gallery is over there — would you like to go round it?*

hare off to run off quickly: *Jo hared off down the street, hoping to catch the bus at the next stop. The dog picked up the piece of meat and hared off with it.*

barge through to push one's way rudely through a group of people: *The youths barged through the crowd of spectators so that they could see the puppet show better. A large number of people were protesting outside the bank building, and the workers had to barge through them to get to work.*

hose down to clean (someone or something) by using water from a hose: *I hosed my boots down in the garden because they were filthy. Bill hosed the dogs down because they were very hot. The car is very dusty and I'm just going to hose it down.*

slip away to leave (somewhere) quietly, often without being noticed: *Sylvia slipped away early from the party as she was feeling ill. The last bus leaves before the end of the concert, and so I'll have to slip away before the end.*

head back to start on the return journey to (somewhere): *We've walked a long way and it's getting late — we'd better head back to the car. If we head back now we'll reach home before nightfall.*

Do it Yourself

1 Complete the phrasal verb: *Ruth decided that she would **take** her boss _____ on his offer of a promotion.*

2 Fill in the missing phrasal verb: *Ella was looking forward to the party because Suzie had said that she would try and _____ her _____ with her cousin who was very handsome.*

3 Replace the underlined words with a phrasal verb: *Rose tightly gripped the handrail as she descended the steep stairs.*

4 Replace the underlined words with a phrasal verb: *The friends formed a group round the bonfire as it began to get cooler after the sun went down.*

5 Replace the underlined words with a phrasal verb: *The thief grabbed Mavis's bag, and then ran off quickly down the street.*

6 Complete the phrasal verb: *Our friends _____ **round** the exhibition last week.*

7 Complete the phrasal verb: *The police had to **barge** _____ the crowd of onlookers in order to get to the scene of the accident.*

8 Complete the phrasal verb: *I **hosed** _____ the windows, but they are still dirty.*

9 Replace the underlined words with a phrasal verb: *Tom told Helen that he planned to quietly leave before anyone made a fuss and insisted that he stay at the party.*

10 Replace the underlined words with a phrasal verb: *I think that we should begin our return journey — it looks like the weather is going to turn nasty.*

41 A Surprise Goes Wrong

Phrasal Verbs in Use

Fay's friends were planning a surprise party for her twentieth birthday. They didn't think it would be difficult to keep her from finding out as she **was** so **wrapped up in** her new boyfriend, Harry, that she was not noticing anything very much at the moment. However, Fay was growing suspicious that something was happening. When she saw Matt and Anne deep in conversation, they immediately **clammed up** when she joined them. Then she met Bill who **was crossing out** names on a list. As soon as Fay asked him what it was, Bill **screwed up** the piece of paper and put it in his pocket, saying it was nothing. Fay was sure that they were all keeping something from her, but she didn't know what. In fact, she **harped on** about it so much to Harry that he got quite angry and asked her to talk about something else. Next, she tried to **worm** some information **out of** her best friend, Amy, but she said nothing. She even tried to **bluff** Sara **into** telling her about the secret by pretending that she knew all about it, but the bluff was unsuccessful. Finally, she decided to have a long chat with Bob, who was known to be rather indiscreet. In the midst of a conversation he **blurted out** news of the party, but asked Fay not to say anything. She **played along** with the surprise and **cried out** in pretended amazement when she arrived at the party.

Know the Meaning

wrap up to be so involved with (someone or something) and spend so much time on him/her/it that one has little time for anyone else or anything else: *Jim was so wrapped up in his work that he spent hardly any time with his children. Joe and Annette are so wrapped up in each other that they rarely see their friends.*

clam up *(informal)* to become silent and refuse to say anything: *When the interviewer asked the film star about her private life, she clammed up. The youth clammed up about what he had seen when the police asked him questions.*

cross out to draw a line through (something, especially words or items on a page): *I crossed out that word because I had spelt it wrongly. She crossed the address out and replaced it with her new address. We made a list of tasks to be done and crossed them out as we completed them.*

screw up to twist and roll up (a piece of paper, etc): *Josh screwed the note up and threw it in the wastepaper basket. Did you screw up the piece of paper which was lying on my desk? Helen's phone number is on that piece of paper — don't screw it up.*

harp on to keep on talking about (something), although this may annoy or irritate other people: *Fred keeps harping on about how much he dislikes his boss. We feel sorry that Agnes lost the competition, but wish that she wouldn't harp on about it.*

worm out of to obtain (information, a secret, etc) from (someone) slowly and gradually, usually after some persuasion: *Bill composed the questions for the quiz, but there's no point in trying to worm the answers out of him.*

bluff into to persuade (someone) into doing (something) by deceiving or tricking him/her: *Beth bluffed Ray into believing that she was wealthy. At first the man denied that he had committed the crime, but the police bluffed him into admitting it.*

blurt out to say (something) suddenly and without thinking of the effect or consequences: *They were afraid that their fellow thief would blurt the truth out to the police. The child blurted out that she knew who her attacker was although the man was in the room with her. Amy's parents know that she was out all night — her brother blurted it out.*

play along to pretend to accept or believe in (something): *We think that Alan's plan is useless, but we're playing along with it because we don't want to upset him. The boss has some strange ideas about sales techniques, and Mike plays along with these to flatter her.*

cry out to shout suddenly because one is hurt, surprised, etc: *Ben dropped a brick on his foot and cried out in agony. 'Help!' the drowning man cried out.*

Do it Yourself

1 Replace the underlined word with a phrasal verb: *Katie was so involved in studying that she forgot to eat her dinner.*

2 Replace the underlined words with a phrasal verb: *Martin refused to say anything when the manager started quizzing him about where he had been all morning.*

3 Complete the phrasal verb: *Roger crossed _____ the items on the shopping list as he put them in the trolley.*

4 Complete the phrasal verb: *Anna screwed _____ the letter telling her that she had failed her exams, and threw it on the fire.*

5 Replace the underlined word with a phrasal verb: *At first I was pleased that Frank had won the race, but he keeps talking about it and it is getting on my nerves.*

6 Complete the phrasal verb: *No-one knows the name of Ben's new girlfriend, but Jean is determined to _____ it out of him.*

7 Complete the phrasal verb: *Ian bluffed his boss _____ believing that he had been working hard.*

8 Replace the underlined words with a phrasal verb: *Yvonne could not stand to keep it a secret any longer, and she suddenly said the name of the father of her baby.*

9 Complete the phrasal verb: *Sometimes I get the feeling that Howard is just playing _____ with Lily's plan to get married next year.*

10 Replace the underlined words with a phrasal verb: *Sharon shouted suddenly for help after the man snatched her handbag.*

42 A Murder Investigation

Phrasal Verbs in Use

A murder had been committed in the village of Langdon. The corpse had been found by the river in such a battered state that a young policeman **had keeled over** at the sight of it. Since the police had not yet caught the murderer, the villagers were getting nervous and angry. Although the local police **had subjected** several people **to** lengthy interviews, and although they **had been snowed under** by information and suggestions from the public, they still had not identified the killer. They **had sifted through** a lot of the information which they had acquired. They **had** even **keyed in** a lot of it, in case computerized records could reveal that the murder was similar to another one which had been committed elsewhere in the country. The police were irritated by the fact that the several members of the press **tagged along** wherever they went, anxious for the police to **gen** them **up** immediately **on** any new developments. Because the local police were not very experienced in murder investigations, the authorities had asked a senior police officer from the city to **take over** the enquiry although the local force had not really wanted a stranger to **horn in on** their investigation. In the end, the new officer did no better than the locals even though more evidence was considered. After some time he succeeded in **narrowing down** the list of suspects, but the police never succeeded in gathering enough evidence to charge anyone.

Know the Meaning

keel over (*informal*) to fall over suddenly: *One of the soldiers on parade keeled over in the intense heat. The man in front of me keeled over and lost consciousness.*

subject to to cause (someone) to experience or undergo (something unpleasant or difficult): *The terrorists subjected their hostages to terrible torture. The police subjected the suspect to intense questioning.*

snow under to be overwhelmed with (something), to have much more (work, etc) than one can easily cope with: *We were snowed under with replies to our job advertisement. Our competitors have very few orders, but we are snowed under with them.*

sift through to examine (something) carefully and thoroughly, often because one is looking for something: *We sifted through all the replies to the job advertisement, but we did not find our ideal applicant. It will take Lorna a long time to sift through those historical documents for her research.*

key in to type (something) on a keyboard, so as to store it in a computer: *Have you begun to key in the annual sales report? It will take some time to key all this information in.*

tag along to accompany or go along with (someone) although one has not been invited and one may be unwanted: *Ellen is annoyed because Jack's young sister tags along whenever they go out on a date. If you're all going to the cinema, do you mind if I tag along?*

gen up on (*informal*) to give (someone) as much information as possible about something: *The marketing director needs to be genned up on this month's sales figures before the meeting. We must gen the workers up on their rights before they accept the offer.*

take over to take charge of (something), to become responsible for (something): *Ms Jones has taken over the running of the senior school. Mike's daughter will take over his role in the firm when he retires. Fred was in charge of the team, but Bert took it over when Fred retired.*

horn in on to become involved in (something), without being invited and often without being wanted: *Another department is trying to horn in on our proposal for a new product range. The residents in the area had been organizing a protest movement for months, but Mark horned in on it at the last minute and took all the credit when it was successful.*

narrow down to reduce (the number of choices or possibilities), to consider a small number of choices from a much larger selection: *There is a competition for the best dog in the show and the judges have narrowed the candidates down to six dogs. The firm received many applications for the post, but they have narrowed them down to four.*

Do it Yourself

1 Replace the underlined words with a phrasal verb: *The hockey player <u>suddenly fell over</u> after the ball hit her head.*

2 Complete the phrasal verb: *The animals had been **subjected** _____ years of neglect.*

3 Replace the underlined word with a phrasal verb: *The company was <u>overwhelmed</u> with complaints after it failed to honour its promise to give each customer a free gift.*

4 Replace the underlined words with a phrasal verb: *I am going to spend the weekend <u>carefully examining</u> the replies to my ad for a second-hand bike.*

5 Complete the phrasal verb: *Fiona spent hours **keying** _____ the statistics for the annual report, but forgot to save her work.*

6 Replace the underlined words with a phrasal verb: *We are going to that new restaurant tonight and you are welcome to <u>accompany us</u>.*

7 Complete the phrasal verb: *The manager **genned** his staff _____ **on** what had happened at the directors' meeting.*

8 Replace the underlined words with a phrasal verb: *Fred expects that he will <u>take charge</u> as manager when Paul retires.*

9 Complete the phrasal verb: *Fiona was making a good job of her presentation to the committee, but Sam **horned** _____ **on** it and ruined it.*

10 Complete the phrasal verb: *The judges have **narrowed** _____ the number of contestants to three for the final round.*

43 A Wedding Invitation

Phrasal Verbs in Use

Val was absolutely delighted to have received an invitation to the wedding of her friend, Kate. As she explained to her boyfriend, Alan, later, Kate's father was very wealthy and was bound to **fork out for** a lavish reception. There would, undoubtedly, be caterers there who would **ply** the guests **with** tasty food and champagne. Because Alan was not ready to **tie** himself **down** to married life, he really didn't like all this wedding talk. Indeed, Val **had seized on** the chance to say how wonderful it would be to be married and to have children. At this point, Alan hastily changed the subject, and mentioned how expenses could **mount up** for wedding guests, by the time they **had shelled out** a lot of money for a present and had paid for the journey to the wedding destination. He had hoped to **pare down** the expenses by suggesting that Val did not really need a new outfit, but she **was** completely **opposed to** the idea of wearing one of her existing outfits. She **had been yearning for** an excuse to buy something new and had got her wish with the arrival of the wedding invitation. Alan just hoped that she would not go over their budget limit when she **was settling on** something. His wish was not granted. Val spent a great deal on an eye-catching dress and hat, leaving Alan to say gloomily that the bride and groom would now be getting a much cheaper present.

Know the Meaning

fork out (*informal*) to pay money for: *Beth's grandmother is forking out for her college fees. Mary forked out a whole month's salary on that dress.*

ply with to keep giving (someone) supplies of (something): *They were generous hosts and plied their guests with excellent wine all evening.*

tie down to restrict (someone's) freedom: *Bill wants to marry Becky, but she feels that she is too young to tie herself down. Roger's mother is afraid that Lucy is trying to tie Roger down before he finishes his degree. Meg has postponed having children because she thinks that they would tie her down.*

seize on to accept or grasp (something) enthusiastically: *Tim was desperate for volunteers for his project and he seized on Polly's offer of help. When Bob was offered a job overseas, he seized on the opportunity. It was an idea that would bring the company profit and they seized on it.*

mount up to increase: *The tension was mounting up as the time of the tournament final approached. Gail's parents were worried at how the wedding costs were mounting up. The children saved a little each week and were surprised at how this mounted up.*

shell out (*informal*) to pay (money) for something: *Tony's parents shelled out a great deal of money on his education, but he dropped out of college. The government has been asked to shell even more money out on the project. Paula is organizing a huge party and expecting her parents to shell out for it.*

pare down to reduce the size or extent of (something): *Father said that we had to try to pare down the cost of the heating bills. The holy men pared their possessions down to the bare minimum. Trudy has a massive collection of clothes and she's trying to pare it down.*

oppose to to be against (something), to disapprove of or disagree with (something): *Many of the townspeople were opposed to the closing of the local school. The proposal seemed an interesting one, but most of the committee were opposed to it.*

yearn for to want (something) very much, to long for (something): *It was mid-winter and we were all yearning for some sunshine. Sue finally achieved financial success, having yearned for it all her life.*

settle on to decide on (something), to choose (something), after thinking about it or discussing it: *We settled on bright yellow curtains for the kitchen. We asked the baby's name, but the parents have not settled on one yet.*

Do it Yourself

1 Replace the underlined words with a phrasal verb: *Steve decided that he was going to buy his own flat because he was sick of paying out money for rent.*

2 Complete the phrasal verb: *Dave wanted Sheila to forgive him and **plied** her _____ gifts, but she would not speak to him.*

3 Complete the phrasal verb: *Trisha felt that an early marriage would _____ her **down**.*

4 Complete the phrasal verb: *When Emma suggested that Louise could move into her spare room, she **seized** _____ the idea.*

5 Replace the underlined word with a phrasal verb: *Nervous tension was increasing amongst the students as the week of the exams drew closer.*

6 Replace the underlined word with a phrasal verb: *Lydia resented paying money for a meal that had been almost inedible.*

7 Complete the phrasal verb: *Phil admitted that he needed to **pare** _____ his book collection because it was taking up the whole of his front room.*

8 Replace the underlined words with a phrasal verb: *Oliver wanted to live abroad for a year, but Trudy was against the idea.*

9 Complete the phrasal verb: *Pamela has been on a diet for a week, and she is **yearning** _____ some chocolate.*

10 Replace the underlined words with a phrasal verb: *Simon and Mandy have decided on May 6th as the date for their wedding.*

44 The Missing Tickets

📝 Phrasal Verbs in Use

'According to my horoscope in the local paper, I'm **going through** a very lucky phase,' said Mary, who was a firm believer in astrology, 'and so I've bought three lottery tickets.' Because she had to go out when the winning numbers were announced on the television, she asked her brother, Tom, to **mark down** the numbers for her, and then **check** them **against** the numbers on her tickets. When Mary went out, Tom **was lolling about** on the sofa, idly changing television channels. Since there was nothing on any of the channels, which he wanted to watch, he quietly **drifted off**. He **woke up** about an hour later to discover that he had missed the programme which **gave out** the lottery numbers. Mary was going to be furious. He was just trying to **come up with** schemes to discover the winning numbers before Mary got back, when they were flashed on the screen for the benefit of those who had missed the lottery show. How relieved he was. Then he discovered a worse problem. He couldn't find Mary's lottery tickets anywhere. Perhaps their little sister **had torn** them **up** by mistake. Tom was absolutely frantic. What if he lost a winning lottery ticket? Just then Mary came in, saying that she didn't **believe in** astrology after all because she had taken a copy of her numbers and had checked them before she left work. Tom, once more, felt relieved and said nothing about the missing tickets.

Know the Meaning

go through to experience (something, often something unpleasant): *Pam's husband is in hospital and she's going through a difficult time just now. Jill says that she knows what the pain of childbirth is like, and she doesn't want to go through it again.*

mark down to write down (something): *I marked down the topics which I want to discuss at the meeting. Could you mark the number down on this piece of paper? If you give the name of the book, I'll mark it down.*

check against to compare (something) with (something else), for example to find out if these are the same: *When we checked his name against the hotel register, we discovered that it was not there. The parking attendant checked the registration number of Bill's car against those on his list and refused to let him use the firm's car park. Here is a list of those who promised to come — could you check it against those who actually attended?*

loll about to lie down or sit down in a lazy way, not doing very much: *It was late at night, and we were lolling about listening to music and drinking wine. Jim's father said that he should be mowing the lawn, not lolling about on a deck-chair.*

drift off to fall asleep gradually: *I was reading in bed and I drifted off with the light on. It is dangerous for drivers to drift off when they're at the wheels of their cars.*

wake up to become conscious again after being asleep: *I woke up in the middle of the night, thinking that I had heard a noise downstairs. 'Wake up!' said Jane's mother, 'you'll be late for work!'*

give out to announce (something), to make (something) known: *The mayor gave out the names of the winners at the end of the fete. The police are giving no further details out just now. I don't know the name of the murderer although the newsreader gave it out.*

come up with to think of (something) and suggest it: *The boys are trying to come up with ways to make money quickly. That was a brilliant idea and it was Kevin who came up with it.*

tear up to pull (something) into many small pieces: *Angrily Maggie tore the letter up and threw the pieces in the bin. We tore up old sheets to make dusters. None of the rest of us saw the boss's memo — Bill tore it up in a fit of temper.*

believe in to have faith or confidence in (someone or something): *Rona never consults a doctor — she believes in herbal medicine. Roy needs to believe in himself if he's going to do well in business.*

Do it Yourself

1 Replace the underlined word with a phrasal verb: *We really need a bigger house, but I can't bear to experience the ordeal of selling this one.*

2 Replace the underlined words with a phrasal verb: *Tom wrote down the name of the hotel where he was going to be staying and gave it to his parents.*

3 Complete the phrasal verb: *The waiter _____ our names against his booking list, but could not find our reservation.*

4 Complete the phrasal verb: *Yvonne had a wonderful holiday, lolling _____ in the sun and reading her book.*

5 Complete the phrasal verb: *The baby was just about to drift _____ when somebody slammed a door and woke it up.*

6 Fill in the missing phrasal verb: *I did not _____ until the alarm went off.*

7 Replace the phrasal verb with one word: *The teacher gave out the names of the pupils who had been chosen for the school football team.*

8 Replace the underlined words with a phrasal verb: *Phillip has thought of a brilliant plan for Samantha's birthday.*

9 Fill in the missing phrasal verb: *The actor _____ the article that criticized his performance in the play.*

10 Replace the underlined words with a phrasal verb: *Freddy has faith in astrology, and won't go anywhere without reading his stars.*

45 Lost Love

Phrasal Verbs in Use

Anna had had a row with her fiancé, Phil, and **had handed** him **back** the engagement ring, which he had given her. Later, she regretted doing this and suggested to him that they have a long talk to try to **iron out** their problems. To her dismay, he refused, saying that they had had several discussions of that kind recently, and that these had done nothing to **straighten out** the many difficulties of their relationship. He went on to say that he felt that there was no point in trying to **work through** their problems any more as Anna always **stormed off** in the middle of any discussions about them. Anna was very upset when he then said that he thought that they should **split up**, and walked away from her. Being convinced that he would change his mind and call her, she **mooned around** by the phone all day, irritating all the members of her family. She **was** just **toying with** the idea of ringing him when she heard from a friend that he already had another girlfriend. Her friends tried to cheer her up, but she seemed determined to **wallow in** self-pity. The mere mention of Phil was enough to **trigger off** a bout of weeping. Several things were suggested to Anna to help take her mind off her broken relationship — clubbing, a trip to the cinema, a meal in a good restaurant — without success. Then one day her friends realized that Anna was smiling again. She had a new boyfriend!

Know the Meaning

hand back to give (something) to (someone) after you have borrowed it or taken it from them, to return (something) to (someone): *The teacher handed the English essays back to the class. Please hand back my history notes which you borrowed — I need them for the exam. The doorkeeper looked at Joe's pass and handed it back to him.*

iron out to solve or overcome (problems, difficulties, etc): *Josh and I had a major disagreement, but eventually we ironed the problem out.*

straighten out to organize (something) and put it in order, getting rid of any confusion or difficulties: *Both parties had different views on how to proceed and we had to use tact to straighten out the situation. Old Mr Wilson left his affairs in a mess when he died — it'll take a long time to straighten things out.*

work through to deal with (something) gradually and thoroughly, in the hope of finding solutions to any problems: *It will take some time to work through all the objections to the proposal. Their marriage is experiencing difficulties, but they are prepared to work through these.*

storm off to leave or rush off suddenly, because one is very angry: *Stella would not listen to Pete's apology and stormed off. We tried to explain what had happened, but Rod stormed off without listening.*

split up (*of two people*) to end a relationship or marriage: *Jake and Muriel had been married for over twenty-five years, but they split up when the children left home. Their friends were not surprised when Ali and Tanya split up — they were always quarrelling.*

moon around/about to wander around not doing very much as if one is dazed, often because one is in love, unhappy, etc: *Julie is mooning about waiting for Jack to ask her out on a date. Mick and Nora have had a quarrel and they're both mooning around, waiting for the other to apologize.*

toy with to consider (something) but not in a very serious way: *The Smiths are toying with the idea of buying a smaller house, but they haven't started looking for one yet.*

wallow in to choose to be in a state or situation, even though this is an unhappy one, as though you were enjoying it, to indulge in (something): *His friends were sorry when Tom lost his job, but he's been wallowing in self-pity ever since. Her husband caused Kate a lot of misery when he left — but she appears to be wallowing in it.*

trigger off to start (something), to cause (something): *The President's announcement triggered off a major rebellion in the country. The child's had an asthma attack, but we don't know what triggered it off.*

Do it Yourself

1 Complete the phrasal verb: *The airport official studied Jenny's passport before **handing** it _____ to her.*

2 Replace the phrasal verb with one word: *The manager is hoping that the technical difficulties with the new computer have finally been **ironed out**.*

3 Replace the underlined word with a phrasal verb: *It took several hours to <u>organize</u> the house after it had been broken into and vandalized.*

4 Replace the underlined words with a phrasal verb: *James is determined to <u>deal with</u> the problems that he has been having with his flat-mates.*

5 Fill in the missing phrasal verb: *Anne _____ without saying goodbye when she saw Tony kissing another woman at the party.*

6 Replace the underlined words with a phrasal verb: *Al and Vera <u>ended their relationship</u> after they realized that they did not love each other any more.*

7 Complete the phrasal verb: *Carol should spend more time studying, and less time **mooning** _____ thinking about boyfriends.*

8 Replace the underlined word with a phrasal verb: *Karen is <u>considering</u> the idea of going back to work after the children start school.*

9 Complete the phrasal verb: *Walter has been **wallowing** _____ self-pity since Jackie left him.*

10 Replace the phrasal verb with one word: *Oliver thinks that it was eating the shellfish that **triggered off** his food poisoning.*

46 Hard Work Rewarded

✏️ Phrasal Verbs in Use

Greg was feeling very concerned because Mr Marr, his college director of studies, had asked to see him. Greg was afraid that, at the meeting he would be told that the college authorities were going to **send** him **down**, because he had missed quite a few lectures this term. Also he had rarely submitted his essays on time. The problem was that he was having to **juggle** his university course **with** two part-time jobs in order to have enough money to stay at university. Last term his father had given him an allowance, but a car had knocked him off his bike, and he was now unable to work because of the injuries he had received. Greg just hoped that Mr Marr had not **put** him **down as** a lazy student, and that he would **dissociate** him **from** other students who **stayed away from** lectures because their lives **centred on** their social engagements. However, Greg's mother **had confided in** Mr Marr and he was able to tell Greg that he could **put in for** a special student grant that the college kept for cases of financial hardship. He said that although the final decision **rested with** the college principal, he had personally advised that Greg's application be accepted. There was nothing in Greg's background that **debarred** him **from** applying and Mr Marr was optimistic. He was right to be so because the college authorities awarded Greg the grant, and he was able to give up the part-time jobs.

Know the Meaning

send down officially to ask (a student) to leave university because of bad behaviour: *Robert was sent down from his university for stealing money from other students. Anne's parents were very upset when she was sent down for attacking another student.*

juggle with to try to cope with (a number of things at once): *Martha did not realize how difficult it was to juggle child-rearing with a career. Terry is trying to juggle his role as father with his role as son — he's trying to look after both his young children and his elderly parents. Phil will have to give up one of his jobs — he's tried and failed to juggle with both of them.*

put down as to regard (someone or something) as being of a particular type or kind although this is often not true: *Sheila had put Rod down as a respectable citizen, but she soon discovered that she had been quite wrong. Ron had put her down as a stupid person, but Sara was the brightest student in the class.*

dissociate from not to associate (people or things) with each other, to show that there is no association or connection between (people or things): *We want to dissociate our town from the town which borders it — our town is a much cleaner, peaceful place to live. Freda's parents wish to dissociate themselves from their neighbours who have the same name because their neighbours are always in trouble with the police.*

stay away from not to go to (somewhere), to avoid (going somewhere): *Their parents found out that the pupils had been staying away from school at least once a week. Rose's father warned Mike to stay away from his house and to stop seeing his daughter.*

centre on to concentrate on (something), to be most concerned with (something): *Joan's life centres on her work and her family. Bill doesn't regard golf as a hobby — his whole life is centred on it.*

confide in to tell (someone) about a private or secret matter or problem: *Molly confided in her new neighbour that her husband was in jail. Matt is such a gossip that no-one ever confides in him.*

put in for to apply for or ask to be considered for (a job, grant, etc): *Walter put in for the job of supervisor. There is a college bursary for overseas study and Sylvia has put in for it.*

rest with to be the responsibility of (someone or something): *The final decision rests with the planning committee. You must ask the head teacher about hiring the school hall — the decision rests with her.*

debar from to prevent (someone) from (doing something), often officially: *Getting such marks in his final school exams does not debar him from going to college, but he won't get into the college of his choice. After the fight, Ben was debarred from entering the pub again.*

Do it Yourself

1 Replace the underlined words with a phrasal verb: *It was no surprise that John got officially asked to leave university for cheating in his exams.*

2 Complete the phrasal verb: *Pat tried to **juggle** studying _____ working full-time.*

3 Replace the underlined words with a phrasal verb: *At school Hannah was often regarded as stupid because she had difficulty spelling.*

4 Complete the phrasal verb: *Andrew wants to **dissociate** himself _____ the crowd that he used to hang around with because they are always causing trouble.*

5 Replace the underlined words with a phrasal verb: *The children were warned to not go to the derelict factory because it was not a safe place to play.*

6 Complete the phrasal verb: *Next year I am going to **centre** my attention _____ studying for my exams.*

7 Replace the underlined word with a phrasal verb: *Fiona told her father that she was having second thoughts about getting married to Terry.*

8 Replace the underlined words with a phrasal verb: *Hugh decided that it was time that he asked to be considered for a promotion.*

9 Replace the underlined words with a phrasal verb: *The outcome of the court case is the responsibility of the jury.*

10 Complete the phrasal verb: *Drew was **debarred** _____ the tennis club after he swore at the umpire.*

47 A Proposal with a Difference

Phrasal Verbs in Use

Kevin's friends were surprised to see him without his girlfriend, Margo. Ever since he **had fallen for** her a few months ago, he seemed always to be with her. Now he had joined them in the pub and was not looking happy. He explained that Margo had suddenly proposed to him last night, saying that women had as much right as men to propose marriage. Kevin had thought he was in love with Margo, but this **had** certainly **damped down** his ardour. When he had said that he was not ready for marriage, Margo had said bitterly that he **had** just **been stringing** her **along**. He had tried to **butter** her **up** by saying how wonderful she was, and **had got out of** giving an answer just then. However, he was meeting her very shortly and he had decided that he was definitely going to **turn down** her proposal. His sister, Stella, was convinced that Margo was just trying to **trap** him **into** marriage, just because she wanted to get married, not because she loved him. She **had delved into** Margo's past and **stumbled on** the fact that she had been engaged to be married twice before although she was still only twenty years old. In both cases, the man had changed his mind, and decided not to **go through with** the engagement. Kevin left the pub, saying that he was off to tell Margo the bad news. He was back in less than an hour, looking relieved.

Know the Meaning

fall for to be very attracted to (someone) and fall in love with him/her: *The new lecturer is very handsome, and all the female students have fallen for him.*

damp down to reduce the extent or intensity of (something): *Bad weather damped down their desire for a walk in the country. The fans supported the team loyally, but a series of lost matches damped their enthusiasm down. The boys started off their early morning jogging sessions, but lack of sleep soon damped it down.*

string along to deceive (someone) by giving him/her false hopes about a situation, often a romantic relationship: *The boss was stringing Bert along by promising him promotion — he gave the senior job to someone else.*

butter up (informal) to flatter (someone), to try to please (someone), often because one wants him/her to do something for you: *Jim's just buttering Val up because he wants to borrow some money from her. Val wants to borrow Pete's English notes and so she's buttering him up.*

get out of to avoid (something/doing something): *Jo's trying to get out of working night shift. I agreed to go the party, but I'm trying to get out of it.*

turn down to refuse, to say no to (someone or something): *We were surprised that the firm turned Sally down for the publicity job. The club has already turned down several applications for membership. Paul asked Sara to marry him, but she turned him down.*

trap into to trick or mislead (someone) into doing something: *His mother said that Alice had trapped Will into marrying her by pretending to be pregnant. Jill said that the police had trapped her into confessing to a crime which she did not commit.*

delve into to try hard to discover information about (something) by searching thoroughly: *The journalist is delving into the politician's past career to try to uncover a scandal. You'll probably discover something scandalous in the film star's background if you delve into it for long enough.*

stumble on to discover (something) unexpectedly: *Annette stumbled on her biological father's name when she was looking at some family papers. The journalist didn't know about the mayor's drink-driving offence — he stumbled on it when looking at an old court report.*

go through with to continue with (something difficult or unpleasant) until it is achieved, completed, etc: *The world's press were shocked when the president of the country went through with the execution of those who had opposed him. Ron threatened to commit suicide once or twice, but we didn't think that he would go through with it.*

Do it Yourself

1 Replace the underlined words with a phrasal verb: *Jane's parents think that the man that she has <u>fallen in love with</u> is likely to cause her trouble.*

2 Replace the underlined word with a phrasal verb: *Penny's enthusiasm for her new job was <u>reduced</u> when she got a new boss.*

3 Complete the phrasal verb: *Ernie discovered that Gina had just been **stringing** him _____ by saying that she might go into business with him.*

4 Replace the underlined words with a phrasal verb: *Samantha is <u>trying to please</u> her boss before she asks if she can have three weeks off.*

5 Complete the phrasal verb: *Donna promised to go to the cinema with Jake tonight, but now she is trying to _____ **out** _____ it.*

6 Fill in the missing phrasal verb: *Ralph was _____ for a job with the police because he was too short.*

7 Replace the underlined words with a phrasal verb: *Paula had been <u>tricked into</u> accepting the blame for the missing money.*

8 Complete the phrasal verb: *I lost my job because my employers **delved** _____ my past and found out that I did not have the qualifications.*

9 Replace the underlined words with a phrasal verb: *Heather <u>unexpectedly discovered</u> the advert for the holiday.*

10 Replace the underlined words with a phrasal verb: *It was a difficult decision, but Yvette and Paul decided to <u>continue with</u> their divorce.*

48 Permission for a Party

📝 Phrasal Verbs in Use

The Denham twins, Wendy and Peter, were about to be nine years old and had said that they would like to have a birthday party. Last year they had asked for one also, but their parents had **palmed** them **off with** a family tea and a visit to the cinema, saying that they were too busy to organize a party. Their father had just said no again and Wendy was trying to **choke back** her tears. This time, however, the rest of the family **were ranged against** their father. Their mother and the twins' elder brother and sister, Ben and Amy, all said that a party was a good idea. Mr Denham was in a bad mood, and he replied that he had given his answer and there was not going to be a party. However, Mrs Denham succeeded in persuading him to let them **press ahead with** it. Assuring him that he need not be involved, she said that they would just **invite over** a few of the children's school friends and **stock up with** suitable food and soft drinks. Ben and Amy said that they would buy some balloons and streamers to **jazz up** the living room for the party and that they would also **lay on** some music for it. At this Wendy's face **lit up** and Peter **launched into** a speech of thanks. Ben and Amy went off to buy decorations, while Mrs Denham baked a cake and the twins wrote out invitations.

Know the Meaning

palm off with to deceive or persuade (someone) into accepting (something which is inferior to what he/she should have got): *The family should have got thousands of pounds in compensation for the accident to their son, but they were palmed off with a few hundreds. The couple went to Barbados on holiday but palmed their children off with a holiday in a local seaside resort. Terry promised Celia a diamond ring, but palmed her off with a cheap imitation one.*

choke back to try to prevent (something) appearing or being obvious: *Bella succeeded in choking the tears back as she waved goodbye. Lucy could hardly choke back her laughter.*

range against to be opposed to (another person, side, etc): *We met several groups of protesters who were ranged against the government with regard to its economic policies. The council will find that many of the townspeople are ranged against them because of their decision.*

press ahead with to continue (with something) in a determined way, despite difficulty, opposition, etc: *The protesters could not believe that the council were pressing ahead with the demolition of the old building. The project will be expensive, but we have decided to press ahead with it.*

invite over to ask (someone/people) to visit one in one's home: *Jan said that she only invited over one or two of her colleagues, but they all came. We've invited a few friends over for dinner. Jack was lonely and so Adam invited him over for a drink.*

stock up with/on to buy and store supplies of (something): *The shops are closed for the holiday and so we are stocking up on bread. There is going to be a shortage of coffee here and so we are stocking up on it.*

jazz up (informal) to make (something) brighter, more decorative, more exciting, etc: *Josie decided to jazz up her plain, dark suit with a brightly-coloured scarf. Bert jazzed his rented room up with a few colourful posters. The article is informative but dull — you should try to jazz it up a bit.*

lay on to provide or supply (something): *The organizers are laying on refreshments after the performance. There was food at the exhibition, but I don't know who laid it on.*

light up to look happy or cheerful suddenly: *The child's face lit up when he saw the Christmas tree. Len's face lit up when Jean invited him to her party.*

launch into to begin (to speak, sing, etc) with great enthusiasm, passion, etc: *The customer launched into a series of complaints, as soon as the manager appeared. Tom forgot the words of the patriotic song after the first verse although he had launched into it with great confidence.*

Do it Yourself

1 Complete the phrasal verb: *Debbie had been expecting her father to buy her a new car, but he **palmed** her ____ **with** an old banger.*

2 Replace the underlined words with a phrasal verb: *Pauline was only just able to <u>prevent showing</u> her anger as her manager informed her that she was expected to work all weekend while he played golf.*

3 Replace the underlined words with a phrasal verb: *The residents were <u>opposed to</u> the plan to dig up the trees to build new houses.*

4 Complete the phrasal verb: *Ivy is going to **press** ____ **with** her plan to start her own business.*

5 Complete the phrasal verb: *Don't forget that Des and Mary have **invited** us ____ for dinner tonight.*

6 Replace the underlined words with a phrasal verb: *Irene is having her grandchildren to stay for the weekend and has <u>bought in supplies of</u> their favourite food.*

7 Fill in the missing phrasal verb: *Dave decided to ____ the table by putting out some candles and flowers.*

8 Complete the phrasal verb: *Kevin's father offered to **lay** ____ the transport to take people home after the party.*

9 Replace the underlined words with a phrasal verb: *Sharon's face <u>suddenly looked happy</u> when Sean asked her to marry him.*

10 Replace the underlined words with a phrasal verb: *Robert <u>passionately began telling</u> a string of excuses when the manager asked him why he was late for work.*

49 A Family Trip

Phrasal Verbs in Use

The Brown family were getting ready to go away for a few days to visit some friends. Mr Brown was trying to **squeeze** the luggage **into** the boot, saying that it was just as well the car had a roof rack and **marvelling at** the amount of luggage two adults and two children needed for a long weekend. Several times Mrs Brown **had dug into** a series of bags to make sure that she had all that was required on the journey. She **had** also **dished out** games and toys to the children to play with on the journey, only to discover that they were arguing over who should have which game. Now, at last, the children **had been strapped into** their seats and their next-door neighbour **was waving** the family **off**. The parents were going to share the driving, planning to **switch over** at the halfway mark. Mr Brown was driving first, but he did not get far before he joined a traffic queue. There had been an accident and cars and lorries **were tailing back** for miles. The children, Charlie and Sophie, got bored very quickly and wanted to know if they were nearly there when they were still in the traffic jam. Their parents tried to **jolly** them **along**, but then Sophie said that she thought that she was going to **throw up**. Fortunately, she did not and the traffic jam soon cleared. They were on their way at last.

Know the Meaning

squeeze into to put (someone or something) into a place although there is not really enough space: *Meg cannot possibly squeeze any more clothes into that wardrobe. They closed the theatre doors, saying that they could not squeeze in any more people. I had forgotten to pack my book, but I squeezed it into my rucksack.*

marvel at to be very surprised at, sometimes in an admiring way: *We marvelled at Mel's ability to get her own way. Jock's friends marvelled at the way in which he coped with bringing the children up on his own. When you see Tricia's skill with a paintbrush, you can only marvel at it.*

dig into to put your hand (into a pocket, bag, etc) to search for something: *Sue dug into her pocket to find change to give the beggar. George held Mary's rucksack while she dug into it to find the map.*

dish out (informal) to give (an amount of something) to each person, to distribute (something): *Could you dish out these leaflets to anyone who wants one? Peggy offered to dish the application forms out to the students.*

strap into to fasten (someone) securely into a seat, using a belt or strap: *Everyone must be strapped into their seats before the plane takes off. Will you strap the baby into his car seat? I found the baby's highchair and I'll strap her into it.*

wave off to wave to (someone) as he/she leaves somewhere: *The children waved their father off to work. Your granny's leaving now — are you going to wave her off?*

switch over to change (from one person or thing) to another: *The factory used to use those machines, but we have these now — we switched over last year. There are two drivers on the coach — they switch over every four hours.*

tail back (of traffic, vehicles, etc) to form a long, very slow-moving or stationary queue, usually because of roadworks, an accident or a broken-down vehicle: *They are building a new roundabout, which means that traffic tails back during the rush hour. A lorry has overturned on the motorway and the traffic is tailing back for miles.*

jolly along to keep (someone) in a good mood, often so that he/she will behave well or do as you wish: *We tried to jolly the children along by telling stories and playing games, but they were very tired of the train journey. My sister doesn't really want to act as babysitter, but I'm trying to jolly her along until I can find someone else.*

throw up (informal) to be sick, to vomit: *Bill drank too much wine and threw up all over Diana's new carpet. The food was so horrible that it made me want to throw up.*

Do it Yourself

1 Complete the phrasal verb: *The bus was full but the driver let me **squeeze** _____ it because it was pouring with rain and I was soaking wet.*

2 Replace the underlined words with a phrasal verb: *Everyone <u>was surprised at</u> Julia's performance in the play.*

3 Replace the underlined words with a phrasal verb: *The inspector waited patiently while Ruth <u>searched in</u> her bag to find her ticket.*

4 Replace the underlined word with a phrasal verb: *The teacher asked Veronica to <u>distribute</u> the books for the lesson to the children.*

5 Complete the phrasal verb: *The taxi driver would not set off until he knew that everyone was **strapped** _____ their seats.*

6 Complete the phrasal verb: *Sarah felt like crying as she **waved** her brother _____ when he left home to go to university.*

7 Replace the underlined words with a phrasal verb: *Tracey was watching a film on television, but it was boring and she <u>changed channels</u> to watch a comedy show instead.*

8 Fill in the missing phrasal verb: *The traffic always _____ on this stretch of road at the weekends.*

9 Complete the phrasal verb: *Ian tried to **jolly** everyone _____, but they were bored and wanted to go home.*

10 Replace the phrasal verb with one word: *Travelling by bus always makes me **throw up**.*

50 A Successful Take-over Bid

Phrasal Verbs in Use

In the 1980s George Bryant had founded a PR company. It had been extremely successful and for a long time George and the other shareholders **had raked in** a lot of profit. Now George was getting old, and there were a great many competitors around. Several of his employees thought that the firm **was crying out for** a more modern business approach. They were secretly hoping that one of the bigger companies would **take** the firm **over**, but George's wife, Ella, was opposed to this, and they knew that he **deferred to** her in all business matters. Apart from anything else, it was Ella's father who **had put up** the capital for the firm in the first place. However, there was now a problem because of George's reluctance to modernize. Some of George's competitors had started to **cream off** the most talented of their staff, and several of the competitors had said that they would like to buy the firm. A few of them, at least, had said that a take-over would not necessarily **divest** George **of** a role in the firm. Despite Ella's objections, George was at heart a businessman and decided to **play** the interested firms **off against** each other. He felt that he would like some more leisure time and time to spend with his wife and family. In his opinion it would be foolish to **pass up** such an opportunity, as it probably would not **come up** again. Therefore, he transferred ownership of the firm.

Know the Meaning

rake in (*informal*) to make or earn a lot of (money) easily: *The company has been raking in excessive profits for years. The family have a lot of money — during the war they owned a munitions factory, which raked it in.*

cry out for to need (something) very much: *I'm glad there has been a change of management — the company was crying out for it.*

take over to gain control of (a company) by buying a majority of its shares: *Old Mr Massie does not want his family firm to be taken over, but his son wants to sell it. It was a multinational company that took over the local computer firm.*

defer to to accept (someone's) decision or opinion, often someone in authority, whatever one's own opinion is: *The court deferred the case to a higher court. I cannot deal with this matter — I have deferred it to our managing director.*

put up to provide (money) to pay for something: *The townspeople put up the money to build a war memorial. An anonymous benefactor put up half the cost of the new church. We collected quite a lot of money ourselves for the scheme, and the local council put up the rest.*

cream off to take away (from a group) the most talented members: *The top universities cream off the brightest students from the schools. The most successful final-year students have already been creamed off by industrial firms. We had a number of very talented marketing people in our training scheme, but a rival company creamed them off.*

divest of to take (something) away from (someone or something): *George was divested of his role as club treasurer when some money went missing. The new owners will certainly divest Michael of his position as marketing director.*

play off against to cause (people) to compete with (each other) or to argue with (each other) so that one gains some kind of advantage for oneself: *Tom played the two prospective buyers off against each other and got a very good price for his house. The children approached their parents separately about the possibility of getting a dog and tried to play one off against the other.*

pass up not to take advantage of (something, such as an opportunity): *Paula felt that she could not pass up the chance to see her favourite pop group. I cannot believe that Roe passed such an opportunity up. Paddy was offered the opportunity to work overseas, but he decided to pass it up.*

come up to happen, to occur: *some important work has come up and I cannot meet you tonight. The chance to buy this property will not come up again for a long time.*

Do it Yourself

1 Replace the underlined words with a phrasal verb: *Ron has been <u>making a lot of money by earning huge wages</u>.*

2 Replace the underlined words with a phrasal verb: *The old church is in a bad state of repair — it <u>needs</u> a new roof <u>very much</u>.*

3 Replace the underlined words with a phrasal verb: *It is sad that the large supermarkets have <u>gained control of</u> the small, local shops.*

4 Complete the phrasal verb: *The teacher **deferred** the decision regarding Hamish's future at the school _____ the head teacher.*

5 Replace the underlined words with a phrasal verb: *Fiona's parents <u>provided the money for</u> the deposit of her house.*

6 Complete the phrasal verb: *It is difficult for small businesses to compete with the large ones who **cream** _____ the best workers.*

7 Complete the phrasal verb: *Elaine was _____ **of** her position as a local councillor after she was charged for corruption.*

8 Complete the phrasal verb: *Claire has two boyfriends and she is always **playing** them _____ each other.*

9 Replace the underlined words with a phrasal verb: *Charlotte had to <u>not take advantage of</u> the offer of a free holiday because she could not get any time off work to go.*

10 Replace the phrasal verb with one word: *I won't be able to come with you to the theatre tonight because an emergency has **come up** at work.*

51 Assembling Furniture

Phrasal Verbs in Use

Mary and Danny had just bought a flat. Previously, they had been in furnished rented accommodation and so they needed furniture for the flat. Danny was suggesting that they should buy the items of furniture in flat packs and **put** them **together** themselves. They could not afford, he said, to **lay out** more money than they needed to. Then Mary pointed out that if things went wrong they would have to **add in** the cost of employing someone to put things right. Danny **laughed** this **off**. He would not need anyone, he said, to **bail** him **out** because he had studied carpentry at school and he just needed to **mug up on** the basics. Danny was particularly pleased that he had been able to **beat down** the price of various items of furniture because their packaging was damaged. The furniture was even more of a bargain than he had expected. The problems began when he **took off** the packaging. He couldn't decide what to do with all the pieces although he didn't like to admit this to Mary. Carefully he **read through** all the instructions and arranged all the pieces. When he started to assemble a wardrobe, however, the finished article looked all wrong. There were several screws left over. Nevertheless, he began on a bedside cabinet, but this looked even worse. Eventually he realized that he **had muddled up** the instructions, and thought that they should contact a professional carpenter. Mary readily agreed.

Know the Meaning

put together to assemble (something), to join together (the parts of something) in order to produce it: *The doll's house was sold in a flat pack and Lucy's father and mother had to put the parts together. Colin bought a model aeroplane kit for his son, but could not put it together.*

lay out to spend (money, often a lot of money) on something: *Mr and Mrs Campbell laid out a fortune on their children's education. Mr Jones is refusing to lay any more money out on his son's old car.*

add in to include as part of (something): *The cost of the flight may be cheap, but, if you add in accommodation and food, the holiday will be quite expensive. By the time they added delivery charges in, the firm's furniture was very expensive.*

laugh off to regard or pretend to regard (something difficult, serious, etc) as amusing or unimportant: *Jim tried to laugh off his gambling losses, but they had left him without any money. They can't laugh the matter off — it could have a serious effect on all of us.*

bail out to help (someone) out of a difficult situation: *Her parents have bailed Sue out again by paying off her debts. Jack needs somewhere to stay for a few days, and we bailed him out by offering him our spare room.*

mug up on (informal) to study (something) very hard, usually for a short period of time and often in preparation for an exam: *I'm mugging up on economics — the exam's tomorrow. Sam's sure that there will be a question on World War 2 in the history exam — he's mugging up on it now.*

beat down to reduce (the price of something) by bargaining or haggling: *The stall-holder asked us for $300 for the rug, but we beat the price down to $250. In some countries traders expect buyers to try to beat down prices. That price is too high — try to beat it down.*

take off to remove (something) from (something) from where it was: *Meg took the wrapping off the meat. There were two pieces of wrapping paper round the present and we took off the outer one. There's a brown paper cover on the book — could you take it off, please?*

read through to read the whole of (something): *The lecturer said that she had read through all the essays. The director read the report through and frowned. I gave Jo the letter and he read it through right away.*

muddle up to cause (things) to be mixed up or in the wrong order, to confuse (things): *Fran muddled up the directions which we were given to get here. Les is so vague that he always muddles things up. Sally took both Jane's and Meg's clothes to the laundrette and now she's muddled them up.*

Do it Yourself

1 Complete the phrasal verb: *Martin could not **put** the shelves _____ because he did not have a screwdriver.*

2 Replace the underlined word with a phrasal verb: *May and Bob were going to get divorced, but they decided not to bother when they realized that they would both have to spend a fortune on legal fees.*

3 Replace the underlined word with a phrasal verb: *Amy reminded Douglas to include a tip for the waitress when he paid the bill.*

4 Complete the phrasal verb: *Dennis has been trying to **laugh** _____ the fact that he did not get the job that he applied for.*

5 Complete the phrasal verb: *Tracey's childminder let her down at the last minute, but Nicola was able to **bail** her _____ by agreeing to watch the children while she was at work.*

6 Replace the underlined word with a phrasal verb: *I am going to spend the evening studying the Highway Code before my driving test.*

7 Complete the phrasal verb: *The salesman wanted $5,000 for the car, but I **beat** it _____ to $4,000.*

8 Fill in the missing phrasal verb: *The librarian _____ the book _____ the shelf and gave it to the customer.*

9 Replace the underlined words with a phrasal verb: *The lawyer read all of the case notes before meeting his client.*

10 Complete the phrasal verb: *We had to find an alternative hotel because the travel agent had **muddled** _____ our booking.*

52 The College Prize

Phrasal Verbs in Use

Gail was quite determined to win the college prize for best final year student. Her parents were very poor and had made many sacrifices to **put** her **through** college. Therefore she had to reward all their hard work. With the prize in mind, she had worked very hard throughout the course and **had waded through** all the work without complaint. Her whole college career **had been geared towards** being the most successful student. As she approached the end of the college year, however, she had begun to feel that she could perhaps **ease up** a little and still win the prize. Indeed, the stress and strain of all her hard work were beginning to **tell on** her, and who could blame her if the standard of her work began to **taper off** a bit? There was a new student called Karen in the class, and Gail had at first **warmed to** her. Soon she realized that Karen was very bright and very hard-working, and Gail's attitude to Karen began to **savour of** jealousy. She felt that Karen **was gaining on** her as far as the end-of-year prize was concerned. She began to study harder than ever. After all this time, Gail had not thought that she would ever have to **take on** a rival for her coveted prize. Now she had no choice but to view Karen as a competitor. In the end, however, Gail's fears were unnecessary and she won the prize easily.

Know the Meaning

put through to pay the expenses of (someone) who is studying, training etc: *Her parents put Sara through drama college although they wanted her to go to university. Jock is working part-time in a factory to put himself through college.*

wade through to read (a great deal of written material) with much time and effort: *I've got to wade through all these books for my research project. These documents contain new regulations and we've all got to wade through them.*

gear towards to be designed for or to be directed at (someone or (something): *The course is geared towards the brighter students. The housing development is geared towards the needs of young families. Joan wants a well-paid job and her studies are geared towards it.*

ease up not to work quite as hard as previously, not to put as much effort into (something): *Mick has been training very hard for the new football season, but has been told by his coach to ease up a bit. Joanna is suffering from stress because of working too hard and the doctor told her to ease up.*

tell on to have a bad effect on (someone or something)): *The long journey was beginning to tell on the old lady, and she looked exhausted. Sue wasn't sleeping properly and this began to tell on her work. Frank has been doing a great deal of overtime and it is beginning to tell on him — he looks ill.*

taper off gradually to become smaller in size, amount or quantity: *The number of tourists begins to taper off in late autumn. The side effects of the drug will start to taper off after a few days.*

warm to to begin to like (someone or something), to become fond of (someone or something): *I didn't like Joe at first, but I warmed to him when he helped to fix my bike. The committee rejected the idea at first, but they are now warming to it.*

savour of to suggest or seem like (something, usually something unpleasant): *Carl's actions savour of revenge. Marge's attitude towards her neighbours savours of envy.*

gain on gradually get closer to (someone) whom one is chasing or trying to pass: *The firm has a sales competition and this month Ted is gaining on Molly, who usually wins it. We thought that Jill would win the race easily, but Celia began to gain on her just before the finish.*

take on to begin to compete against (someone or something): *Next week our team takes on the team which won the league last year. The firm, although small, is prepared to take the market leaders on. I would not take Toby on at chess — he's a brilliant player.*

Do it Yourself

1 Complete the phrasal verb: *Gail's employers are going to _____ her **through** a computer course.*

2 Complete the phrasal verb: *The lawyer is going to **wade** _____ past case reports to see if she can find any instances of similar cases being dropped.*

3 Replace the underlined words with a phrasal verb: *The exercise class is designed for people who are already quite fit.*

4 Replace the underlined words with a phrasal verb: *The doctor told Des to not to put as much effort into his jogging because of his age.*

5 Replace the underlined words with a phrasal verb: *The stress of bringing up two children on her own is beginning to have a bad effect on Colette.*

6 Fill in the missing phrasal verb: *The manager said that she had expected sales to _____ after the Christmas rush.*

7 Complete the phrasal verb: *Ruth **warmed** _____ her new teacher from the first day they met.*

8 Complete the phrasal verb: *I don't like my new boss — his manner **savours** _____ bullying.*

9 Replace the underlined words with a phrasal verb: *The sprinter was gradually getting closer to the leader when he fell and twisted his ankle.*

10 Fill in the missing phrasal verb: *I would not like to _____ John _____ in an argument — he has a fierce temper.*

53 A Skating Trip Goes Wrong

Phrasal Verbs in Use

Mike had arrived home to tell his family that the local pond **had frozen over** and that some of his friends were going skating. He was going to join them. It was rare for the pond to **ice over** completely, but this was a particularly hard winter. Mike's mother immediately began to worry that the ice might crack and people drown. Mike **set aside** her fears, and asked his sister, Emma, to **listen out for** the doorbell as his friends were going to collect him on their way to the pond. She had been invited to join them but **had opted out** of the skating party because it was too cold. Their younger brother, James, tried to **muscle in on** the trip, but his mother said no. Mike had gone to find his skates, but returned to say that someone must **have made off with** them because they were not in his room. His mother replied that since he hardly ever used them, she **had stowed** them **away** in the cupboard under the stairs. Impatiently Mike began **rooting about** in the cupboard, trying to find the skates. He pulled various articles out into the hall and finally found the skates. However, he had not put everything back properly and some ski poles **were jutting out** of the cupboard. In his hurry, Mike fell over these and twisted his ankle. Instead of going skating he had to lie on the sofa and rest his ankle.

Know the Meaning

freeze over to become covered with a layer of ice: *The village pond has frozen over and the ice is thick enough to skate on.*

ice over to become covered with a layer of ice: *The pond has iced over, but the layer of ice is quite thin. It's very cold and the water in the dog's bowl in the yard has iced over.*

set aside to ignore (something), to pay no attention to (something): *There's no point in complaining about the food — the restaurant management just sets any complaints aside. Try to set aside your worries — I'm sure the children will be quite safe. Many people raised objections to the scheme, but the council set these aside.*

listen out for to be alert so that one will hear (something expected) when it happens: *I must listen out for the postman ringing the doorbell — I need to sign for a parcel. This monitor lets us listen out for the baby crying. I didn't hear the car drive up although I was listening out for it*

opt out of to decide not to join or be involved in (something): *Stella has opted out of going to Tim's party because she is feeling tired. Julia has organized a trip to the theatre, but Harry has opted out of it.*

muscle in on to force one's way into (something) when one has not been invited and is not wanted: *Ron tried to muscle in on our annual picnic, but he is not a member of the club. This is a private family party and your friends are not going to muscle in on it.*

make off with to take (something) that does not belong to one, to steal (something) and take it away: *The pickpocket made off with Ken's wallet and watch. The meat's not on the kitchen table — I think the dog made off with it.*

stow away to put or store (something) somewhere until it is required: *Kate stowed away the toys in the cupboard until the children returned from holiday. The baggage handlers have stowed the luggage away in the hold. We won't need these heavy sweaters until next winter — I'll stow them away in the attic.*

root about/around (informal) to search among (things), moving them around, because one is looking for something, to rummage around: *Pat was rooting around the stuff in the attic when she found a valuable china vase. The dog is rooting about in the rubbish, looking for his bone.*

jut out of to stick out from (something), to extend beyond (something): *A few trees jutted out of the rock face. Gordon walked past the garden shed and tripped over a rake that was jutting out of it.*

Do it Yourself

1 Replace the underlined words with a phrasal verb: *Just because the water has become covered with a layer of ice does not mean that it is safe to walk on.*

2 Replace the underlined words with a phrasal verb: *The windscreen of the car had become covered with a layer of ice during the night.*

3 Replace the phrasal verb with one word: *The manager set aside his staff's concerns about having to work at weekends.*

4 Complete the phrasal verb: *Please lower the volume of your music — I'm listening _____ for the phone ringing.*

5 Replace the underlined words with a phrasal verb: *Hal decided not to be involved with the holiday at the last minute.*

6 Replace the underlined words with a phrasal verb: *Marion phoned the police when the youths tried to force their way into her party.*

7 Complete the phrasal verb: *Melanie was helpless as she watched the thief _____ off with her bag.*

8 Complete the phrasal verb: *Sarah stowed the presents _____ under the bed so that the children would not find them.*

9 Replace the underlined words with a phrasal verb: *Charlie was rummaging around in the garden shed looking for his old tennis racket.*

10 Replace the underlined words with a phrasal verb: *The car was sticking out from the driveway and got hit by a bus.*

54 A City Attack

Phrasal Verbs in Use

Carl was taking his girlfriend, Sophie, to the city for the day. He **had dipped into** his savings so that they could have a meal out as well as doing some shopping. When his mother tried to **drum into** him how dangerous some of the areas of the city could be, he had not paid much attention. Besides, he had had some training in the martial arts and felt sure that he would be able to **protect** both himself and Sophie **from** any muggers. He and Sophie were wandering about the old part of the city, feeling sad that so many beautiful old buildings **had fallen into** such a state of disrepair, when someone **grabbed at** him from behind. Somehow Carl had always assumed that he would be able to **face** an attacker **down**, but he was held in a strong grip from behind. When he tried to struggle he felt something sharp **cut into** his thick jacket. Then he heard Sophie screaming just as he collapsed on the pavement. When some paramedics **brought** him **round**, he could remember very little about the stabbing. However, Sophie, who was determined that the attacker would not **get away with** his crime, was able to give a description of him to the police. Furthermore, the police thought they knew someone who **answered to** that description, and asked her to go down to the police station. There they showed her some photographs of known criminals and she was able to identify Carl's attacker.

Know the Meaning

dip into to spend some of (the money that one has been saving): *The couple dipped into their retirement savings to buy a new car. Your savings won't grow if you keep dipping into them.*

drum into to repeat (something) regularly to (someone) in the hope that he/she will remember it and pay attention to it: *They drummed into their children that they must not accept sweets from strangers. Frank's mother had a great regard for honesty and drummed this into him when he was a child. We had the need for cleanliness drummed into us as children.*

protect from to try to (prevent someone or something) from harming or affecting (someone or something): *The hut protected the travellers from the wind and rain. The dog tried to protect his master from the attacker. There was danger out there and we were powerless to protect ourselves from it.*

fall into to begin to be in (a particular state or condition): *a lot of the old traditions have fallen into disuse. They were beautiful houses once, but they have fallen into a state of neglect.*

grab at to attempt to get hold of (someone or something): *Bob thought he was drowning and grabbed at the edge of the boat. The child grabbed at the last cake before anyone else could take it. Jock looked like a generous man and the beggar grabbed at his sleeve.*

face down to look at someone boldly and confidently in the hope of overcoming or defeating him/her: *The government minister hoped to face down the Opposition MPs. The soldier turned round and faced down his pursuer. The mugger didn't expect the old man to face him down.*

cut into to make a cut or tear in (something) with a knife, scissors, etc: *The dressmaker was almost afraid to cut into the beautiful, expensive cloth. The meat was placed on the table and father cut into it to serve us all.*

bring round to make (someone) conscious again: *When he collapsed, the paramedics tried to bring Matt round by calling his name. The patient was in a coma and his relatives tried to bring her round by speaking to her.*

get away with to avoid being punished for (something): *Becky should not get away with being so rude to people. Jack definitely committed the crime, but he got away with it.*

answer to to have the features or characteristics mentioned in (a description, etc): *The man in the next room answers to the description circulated by the police. If this description's accurate, then the police have got the wrong woman — the accused does not answer to it all.*

Do it Yourself

1 Replace the underlined words with a phrasal verb: *Ian had to spend some of his rent money to pay the electricity bill.*

2 Complete the phrasal verb: *The manager **drummed** _____ his staff the importance of treating customers well.*

3 Complete the phrasal verb: *Rick and Fay are trying to **protect** their children _____ the effects of the divorce.*

4 Replace the underlined words with a phrasal verb: *The hotel used to be beautiful, but it has begun to be in disrepair.*

5 Replace the underlined words with a phrasal verb: *The drunk man attempted to get hold of his drink before he was thrown out of the pub.*

6 Complete the phrasal verb: *Julie decided to turn round and **face** _____ the man that was following her.*

7 Replace the underlined words with a phrasal verb: *The little girl made a cut into her birthday cake with delight.*

8 Complete the phrasal verb: *The first-aid team were able to **bring** the player _____ before the ambulance arrived.*

9 Replace the underlined words with a phrasal verb: *Phil was relieved that he had escaped without being punished for lying to his girlfriend.*

10 Complete the phrasal verb: *The stray cat **answered** _____ the description of the cat that Jack had lost.*

55 *Locked Out*

Phrasal Verbs in Use

Joan had been to the opening of a new art gallery and had just returned to her aunt's house, which she was looking after for a few weeks. Her friend, Paul, who was an art critic, **had taken** her **along to** the exhibition as his guest. Since Paul was able to **rattle off** a great deal of information about the paintings and the artists, it had been a very interesting evening. The organizers had publicized the event well and **had pulled in** a considerable number of people. Paul **had seen** her **to** the front door before getting the taxi to take him to his own flat, but now she couldn't find the key. Joan remembered that she **had put** it **away** in her handbag, but then she had changed bags before going to the exhibition. She was faced with the fact that she **had locked** herself **out**. It **was getting on for** midnight and she couldn't **puzzle out** how to get into the house. Just as she was about to start panicking, a woman appeared who said that she was her aunt's next-door neighbour, Mrs Grimes. She had been disturbed by the noise of Joan trying to get in and **had looked out** the spare key that Joan's aunt had given her for emergencies. Joan was very grateful and was soon indoors trying to get warm. After her night-time adventure she **warmed up** some soup and went to bed.

Know the Meaning

take along to to get (someone) to accompany you to (something or somewhere): *George went to the football match and took along two of his friends to it. I can take a guest to the reception and so I'm taking my daughter along to it. Meg is visiting me and so I'm taking her along to my dance class.*

rattle off (*informal*) to say (something) very rapidly and without effort: *Peggy asked Jim if he knew of any plumbers in the area, and he rattled off a list of names. The tour guide rattled off a list of all the famous buildings in the city. The pupil knows the dates of all the battles — she rattled them off in a few minutes.*

pull in to attract (people) to (an event, etc), often in large numbers: *If you don't advertise the concert, you won't pull in enough people to make a profit. The advertising posters certainly pulled the crowds in. There were crowds of people at the meeting and it was definitely the advertising campaign that had pulled them in.*

see to to go (somewhere) with (someone) to make sure that he/she gets there safely, to escort (someone) to (somewhere): *Elsie's escort saw her to the door of her flat. Bill didn't go in the taxi with his mother, but he saw her to it.*

put away to place (something) tidily (somewhere): *Bert forgot to put away the lawnmower in the garden shed. Mother put the tins of food away in the kitchen cupboards. Could you put the boots away in the cupboard until you need them again?*

lock out to prevent (someone) from entering (somewhere) because the doors are locked and he/she does not have a key. *Her flat-mates accidentally locked Jan out because they didn't realize that she was still out when they went to bed. His parents locked out Tim and his friends because they didn't know that he didn't have a key. Freda locked herself out when the door slammed shut and she didn't have her keys.*

get on for (*of time*) to be nearly (a certain time): *It's getting on for lunch time. It must have been getting on for 6 o'clock.*

puzzle out to think hard (about a problem) in order to find a solution: *We finally puzzled out why Vera was behaving in that weird way. Finding our way there will not be easy, but we're sure that Rick will puzzle it out.*

look out to search for and find (something that has been stored away): *I'll look out Jock's address for you — it's in my old address book. Jess promised to look a few things out for the jumble sale.*

warm up to heat up (cold food, etc) on a cooker, etc: *Molly warmed up the stew and served it with bread. Could you warm the soup up, please?*

Do it Yourself

1 Complete the phrasal verb: *Wilma is worried about going to the hospital and so she is going to **take along** her brother _____ the appointment.*

2 Replace the underlined words with a phrasal verb: *I asked Tom what sort of music he liked and he <u>rapidly said</u> a long list of bands that he listened to.*

3 Complete the phrasal verb: *Offering free wine certainly helped to **pull** the crowds _____.*

4 Complete the phrasal verb: *The nurse **saw** the patient _____ the ambulance.*

5 Complete the phrasal verb: *The teacher told the children to _____ **away** their books and get ready for gym class.*

6 Complete the phrasal verb: *Janet was furious with Jim for being late — so she **locked** him _____ of their flat.*

7 Complete the phrasal verb: *It is **getting** _____ **for** 2 am and I think that we should go home.*

8 Replace the underlined words with a phrasal verb: *The secretary finally managed to <u>think hard and find a solution to</u> what had happened to the missing cash.*

9 Replace the underlined words with a phrasal verb: *Helen promised to <u>search for and find</u> the recipe for me.*

10 Complete the phrasal verb: *Tim could not sleep and so he **warmed** _____ some milk and made himself a cup of cocoa.*

56 Party Clean-up

Phrasal Verbs in Use

Katy came downstairs one Sunday morning to find that her brother, Josh, **was** taking some painkillers and **washing** them **down** with a lot of water. She was not surprised. At the party the night before, Josh had drunk rather a lot of beer and now had a hangover. Katy looked with horror at the kitchen and living room. What a mess! Some of their friends had stayed the night, but they had all left. She wanted to **go after** them and get them to help, but there was no time. Their parents were returning that evening and their father would **hold forth** about the state of the house if they did not clean it. First she got Josh to **gather up** some of the empty beer cans and take them to the rubbish bin at the foot of the garden. She thought that she would never **get** the stains **off** the carpet. However, she managed to **scrape off** some of the sticky stuff and **scrubbed off** the rest. Unfortunately, someone **had pushed over** a vase and cracked it. When Josh said that he would try to **patch** it **up**, Katy said that there was no time and that they could get it repaired later. Hopefully, their parents wouldn't notice the crack until then. Meanwhile, Josh **was slapping** some paint **on** part of the kitchen wall which had been damaged. Just as they finished cleaning, their parents arrived back, pleased to see the house looking so clean and tidy.

Know the Meaning

wash down to drink something after eating (food, etc) or while eating (food, etc): *The diners washed down the food with some excellent wines. They washed the sandwiches down with beer. Wilma took a sleeping tablet and washed it down with a glass of water.*

go after to follow or pursue (someone): *The police went after the burglars, but did not catch them. Jill left the room in tears and Mike went after her to apologize.*

hold forth to talk (about something) for a long time, often in a boring or a pompous way: *As usual George was holding forth about how clever his children are. Peggy started to hold forth once again about her views on the educational system and we all left the room.*

gather up to bring (things) together in a group, to collect (things) together: *Fred gathered up the old newspapers and burnt them. We gathered the leaves up and put them in sacks. There was a great deal of litter in the park, but someone must have gathered it up.*

get off to remove (something) from (something): *Sara couldn't get the ink stain off the tablecloth. The children have got paint on the curtains and I can't get it off.*

scrape off to remove (something) from (something) by rubbing it with something sharp, such as a knife: *We scraped the dried mud off the carpet. The cooker in the flat was filthy and the tenants had to scrape a lot of grease off it. There was dog dirt on the floor and we asked its owner to scrape it off.*

scrub off to remove (something) from (something) by rubbing hard with a cloth or brush: *Joe scrubbed the wine marks off the carpet. Molly eventually managed to scrub the dirt off the kitchen floor. There is dried blood on the floor — someone will have to scrub it off.*

push over to push (someone or something) so that he/she/it falls to the ground: *Jack pushed the chair over when he was dancing. The boy did not even stop when he pushed over the old lady. The vase is broken — the dog pushed it over with his tail.*

patch up to mend (something) roughly and perhaps temporarily: *The roofer patched the roof up to keep the rain out, but it needs to be completely re-covered. Jeff wonders if you can patch up this old garden shed for him. Bits of the kitchen wallpaper are torn — I'm going to try to patch it up.*

slap on to apply (something) to (something) quickly and carelessly: *I'll just slap on some makeup and I'll be ready to leave. Sue slapped some butter on a piece of toast and ate it as she went out the door. Here's a can of paint — I'll just slap some on that dirty bit of wall.*

Do it Yourself

1 Complete the phrasal verb: *Victoria **washed** _____ the nuts with a glass of juice.*

2 Replace the phrasal verb with one word: *Yvonne **went after** the customer who was suspected of stealing from the shop.*

3 Replace the underlined words with a phrasal verb: *Sid looked at his watch as Fred talked for a long time about his holiday in Spain.*

4 Replace the underlined words with a phrasal verb: *Tracey collected together the dirty clothes and put them in the washing machine.*

5 Complete the phrasal verb: *Nicola could not **get** the grass stain _____ her jeans.*

6 Complete the phrasal verb: *Before we could begin to decorate, we had to **scrape** _____ the old wallpaper.*

7 Complete the phrasal verb: *It took a long time to **scrub** _____ the grease from the cooker.*

8 Complete the phrasal verb: *At the end of the argument, Bob lost his temper and **pushed** Howard _____.*

9 Replace the underlined words with a phrasal verb: *Wendy said that she would try to temporarily and roughly repair the old dress, but that Jane would need to buy a new one soon.*

10 Replace the underlined words with a phrasal verb: *You had better quickly apply some sunscreen before we go to the beach.*

57 No Sea View

Phrasal Verbs in Use

Celia and three of her friends, Caroline, Rod and Peter, had just arrived at their holiday destination. Although Peter would have preferred a country cottage in Scotland, the others **had insisted on** somewhere sunny and warm. They had chosen a self-catering apartment in Spain, which, according to the brochure, had a view of the sea. Peter had nothing against such a holiday and happily **fell in with** their plans. However, the apartment which they had been given did not have a view of the sea, but a view of a concrete wall. Moreover, the apartment was very dirty. They went to **put** their complaints **to** the manager, but he could not **make out** what they were saying although both Caroline and Rod spoke some Spanish. By the time they found the travel company's courier, Celia was in such a bad temper that she immediately started to **lash out at** her. Rod pointed out that if they just calmly **laid** the facts **before** her, she would be more likely to **hear** them **out** and try to help. When he listed their complaints to the rep, Rod tried to **push for** a change of apartment, but she said that, being mid-summer, everywhere was full. She was, however, able to make the manager **get** someone **in** to clean the apartment thoroughly. They were lovely apartments, she said, but she was going to tell her firm that the present manager **was** not **keeping** them **up** properly. Thus, Celia and her friends got a clean apartment, if no sea view.

Know the Meaning

insist on to say firmly that (something) is what one must have and refuse to have anything else: *Bob is insisting on sending his children to private schools. Beth insisted that they went to a restaurant with a no-smoking area. Joe didn't really want a large, white wedding but Sophie insisted on it.*

fall in with to accept and agree to (something): *Maurice refused to fall in with the rest of the family's holiday plans. If you make the travel arrangements we will all fall in with them.*

put to to present (something) to (someone), to bring (something) to (someone's attention) for his/her consideration: *Let us put the matter of truancy to the headmaster. The union put out the workers' demands to management. This department does not deal with complaints — you will have to put them to the Customer Service Department.*

make out to understand (something that may be difficult to understand): *I can't make out why Rod likes Edith so much — she can be very nasty. The woman was saying something to me in a foreign accent and I couldn't make it out.*

lash out at to speak to (someone) in a very angry way: *Amy has a very hot temper and lashes out at people who really haven't done anything wrong. Phil tried to apologize to Jane for being late, but she lashed out at him and walked away.*

lay before to bring (something) to (someone's) attention so that he/she can consider it: *We are to lay our proposal before the committee tomorrow. We drew up the building plan and laid it before the council.*

hear out to listen to what someone has to say without interrupting him/her: *The teacher never hears the pupils out, but assumes she knows what they are going to say. Paula had a good reason for being late, but the boss refused to hear her out and gave her an official warning.*

push for to try very hard to achieve (something), for example by persuading others of its importance: *The parents are pushing for a new school and have contacted the local councillors and MP.*

get in to get (someone) to come and do (something) for you: *Bella would prefer to get a professional decorator in to redecorate the house, but Ron wants to do the work himself. DIY is all very well but you should get in an expert for the electrical work.*

keep up keep (a building, etc) in good condition, to maintain (a building, etc) properly: *It takes quite a lot of money to keep these old buildings up. The church authorities don't have the resources to keep up all the churches and many of them are in disrepair. I had to sell the cottage — I just couldn't keep it up, as the quotation for the repairs was very expensive.*

Do it Yourself

1 Complete the phrasal verb: *George's parents **insisted** _____ him going to university but he would have preferred to get a job.*

2 Replace the underlined words with a phrasal verb: *Sue happily agreed with and accepted her friend's plan to get a flat together.*

3 Complete the phrasal verb: *Greg **put** his complaint about the new development _____ his local councillor.*

4 Replace the phrasal verb with one word: *It was a bad connection, and I could not **make out** what Don was trying to say.*

5 Complete the phrasal verb: *Gavin **lashed** _____ **at** Grant for damaging his computer.*

6 Complete the phrasal verb: *Robbie **laid** his proposal _____ the directors.*

7 Complete the phrasal verb: *I suspect that he is guilty of stealing the money but I think that we should **hear** him _____ before we decide what to do.*

8 Replace the underlined words with a phrasal verb: *Mary is trying hard to achieve a pay rise and, if she does not get it, she will look for another job.*

9 Complete the phrasal verb: *My washing machine was leaking and I had to **get** a plumber _____ to fix it.*

10 Replace the underlined word with a phrasal verb: *It takes a lot of money to maintain these old buildings.*

58 Work Comes to a Halt

Phrasal Verbs in Use

All was not well at Rowlands' factory. They **had** just **put in** a new production system the previous week, and it had suddenly stopped working for no obvious reason. Everyone **had gone by** the manufacturer's instructions and nothing seemed to be broken. Some of the workers had not liked the new machinery. They would have preferred to **revert to** their old system. This was not possible, as all the old equipment **had been traded in** for the present lot. The reason management had decided to buy the new system was so that they would be in a better position to **stave off** the competition, which was getting more and more fierce. Now they were afraid that the competitors would hear about the break-down of their machinery and try to **do** them **down** by telling people that Rowlands had production problems. If that **got around** it would seriously affect their orders. It was not as if they had bought a cheap system. Their production manager had thought it unwise to try to **keep** costs **down**, when such vital machinery was involved. Instead, he had advised them to **invest in** state-of-the-art equipment which was much more modern than that of any of their competitors. Unfortunately, this had now proved to be a disappointment and everyone remembered that the old machinery **had** never **broken down**. Soon all was well. A representative of the manufacturers of the new system arrived and made a small adjustment. The machines were soon working again.

Know the Meaning

put in to put (something) in place, to install (something): *Our neighbours have put in a new central heating system. Beth's had a fitted kitchen put in. We've put an open fireplace in. That's a lovely window — when did you put it in?*

go by to use (something) as a guide or help in doing something: *We're not sure if we'll get there — all we have to go by is some barely legible directions. The pupils were told that if they went by the rule, they would not get into trouble.*

revert to to return to a previous state or condition, often one that is thought less desirable in some way, to begin to use (something) again which one had used before, but stopped using: *Our central heating system's broken down and so we've had to revert to electric fires. For a while Jill seemed happy, but now she's reverted to her gloomy old self.*

trade in to give (something, such as a car) to a dealer etc in part exchange for a new model so that one gets this at a reduced price: *Bert traded in his old motorbike for a much more powerful one. I wonder if I can trade my computer in for a more modern version. Jill doesn't have her sports car any more — she traded it in for a family saloon.*

stave off to keep away or prevent (something unpleasant, etc): *I'm trying to stave this cold off. A bank loan won't stave off the collapse of the firm. The enemy launched an attack and our army failed to stave it off.*

do down to criticize (someone) and try to make him/her seem unimportant or unsuccessful: *Sara is so critical that she even does her own family down. I can't believe Bruce would do down his best friend like that. Brian is a very clever person, but he has low self-esteem and is always doing himself down.*

get around (of information, news, etc) to become known by a large number of people: *Linda doesn't want news of her engagement to get around until she can tell her parents. Rose was cautioned by the police and she was scared that news of this would get around in her home town.*

keep down to keep (something) at a low level: *We're trying to keep down the cost of house repairs. Try to keep the noise down — the baby is sleeping. The supermarket prices are still high although they claim to be keeping them down.*

invest in to spend money on (something) in the hope of getting some benefit, such as a profit: *Beth's financial adviser said that she should invest in property.*

break down (of a machine, etc) to stop working: *The car broke down and we had to get it towed to a garage. We were just about to watch television when the set broke down.*

Do it Yourself

1. Replace the underlined word with a phrasal verb: *The Browns had an alarm system <u>installed</u> after their next door neighbour's house was broken into.*

2. Complete the phrasal verb: *I **went** _____ the recipe, but the cake turned out to be inedible.*

3. Complete the phrasal verb: *Paul had given up drinking, but he **reverted** _____ it after his wife left him.*

4. Complete the phrasal verb: *I **traded** _____ my old car and bought a brand new one.*

5. Replace the underlined words with a phrasal verb: *Dave managed to <u>keep away</u> his hunger by eating a banana.*

6. Complete the phrasal verb: *Frank left his last job because he had a manager who was always **doing** him _____.*

7. Replace the underlined words with a phrasal verb: *News about the assault soon <u>became known by a large number of people in</u> the small community.*

8. Complete the phrasal verb: *Mavis has asked her daughter to try and **keep** _____ the cost of the wedding reception.*

9. Replace the underlined words with a phrasal verb: *My mother always advised me to <u>spend money on</u> a good pair of walking shoes.*

10. Replace the underlined words with a phrasal verb: *I had to hand wash all my clothes when the washing machine <u>stopped working</u>.*

A Dictionary of Phrasal Verbs

A

abide by

to act according to (a rule, law, etc): *The players were asked to abide by the referee's decision. Those are the school rules and pupils must abide by them.*

act as

to carry out the work or duties of (someone or something): *The assistant manager acts as head of department when the manager is away. This sofa acts as a bed as well as something to sit on.*

act on

to act according to (what someone has advised, suggested, etc): *Paddy refused to act on my advice. I made various suggestions, but the committee did not act on any of them.*

add in

to include as part of (something): *The cost of the flight may be cheap, but if you add in accommodation and food the holiday will be quite expensive. By the time they added delivery charges in, the firm's furniture was very expensive.*

agree with

to say the same as (someone or something), to have the same opinion as (someone): *I agree with you that something must be done. The information which Jack gave to the police agreed with that given by Bill.*

allow for

to take into consideration (something which may happen in the future): *When you're arranging your appointment, you'll have to allow for the train being late. The winter there was very cold, but luckily I had allowed for that and had taken a lot of warm clothing with me.*

angle for

to try to get (something, such as a compliment, invitation, etc) without actually asking for it: *When Jody asked us to her party, Amy stood close by, obviously angling for an invitation. Paul didn't pay Tricia any compliments although she was obviously angling for one.*

answer to

to have the features or characteristics mentioned in (a description, etc): *The man in the next room answers to the description circulated by the police. If this description's accurate, then the police have got the wrong woman — the accused does not answer to it all.*

approve of

to be pleased with or think well of (someone or something): *Jenny's parents do not approve of the student way of life. I had my hair cut and my family approved of the new style. Joan has made new friends, but her parents do not approve of them.*

argue out of

to persuade (someone) not to do something, by pointing out the disadvantages, etc: *We tried in vain to argue Paddy out of buying the car. Tracy's parents tried to argue her out of leaving home.*

arrive at

to reach (a place): *We arrived at the hotel rather late. The cottage is still a considerable distance away and we won't arrive at it until morning.*

ask for

to say (to someone) that you would like to have (something), to request (something) from (someone): *Fred has gone to the bank to ask for a loan. If you want some water ask the waitress for it.*

ask for

to say that one would like to see or talk to (someone): *The old lady was very ill and kept asking for her daughter. A man rang up and asked for you.*

ask in

to invite (someone) to go into a house: *Jill's mother told her to ask the visitors in. I knocked at the door but Mr Brown did not ask me in.*

attend to

to make sure that (someone or something) has what he/she/it needs, to help or deal with (someone or something): *Could you attend to that customer? — she wants a new hat. The bonfire needs more wood, but I can't attend to that at the moment.*

B

back away

to move slowly backwards away from (someone or something): *We all backed away from the man with the knife in his hand. Terry looked at the angry dog and quietly backed away from it.*

back out of

to decide not to do something which one has already promised, arranged, etc to do, to withdraw from (an arrangement, promise, etc): *The two firms were planning to merge, but one of them backed out of the deal. The building contract had been drawn up, waiting to be signed, when the owner of the house backed out of it.*

bail out

to help (someone) out of a difficult situation: *Her parents have bailed Sue out again by paying off her debts. Jack needs somewhere to stay for a few days, and we bailed him out by offering him our spare room.*

bank on

to rely on (someone or something), to expect (someone or something) to help one: *I'm banking on the train being on time. The relay team are banking on Judy — she's their most experienced runner. Dad may lend us his car, but don't bank on it. Phil is banking on getting a loan from his parents. I hope that Muriel gets a good mark in her exam because she's banking on it.*

barge through

to push one's way rudely through a group of people: *The youths barged through the crowd of spectators so that they could see the puppet show better. A large number of people were protesting outside the bank building, and the workers had to barge through them to get to work.*

bear up

to remain cheerful and confident: *Try to bear up — you'll be out of hospital soon. Sally is not bearing up very well under the strain of all this overtime.*

beat down

to reduce (the price of something) by bargaining or haggling: *The stall-holder asked us for $300 for the rug,*

but we beat the price down to $250. In some countries traders expect buyers to try to beat down prices. That price is too high — try to beat it down.

beat off

to prevent (someone) from defeating or overcoming you: *Geoff beat off several other competitors to win the golf championship. Julia beat her rivals off easily. The opposition was strong but we beat it off.*

beat up

to strike or kick (someone) very badly: *The youths beat up the stranger, but they did not steal his wallet. The same gang have beaten several people up. Whenever they see a pupil from another school they beat him up.*

believe in

to have faith or confidence in (someone or something): *Rona never consults a doctor — she believes in herbal medicine. Roy needs to believe in himself if he's going to do well in business.*

black out

to lose consciousness: *Celia blacked out for a few minutes after the stone hit her head. It was a heavy blow, but not enough to make him black out.*

blow over

to stop and be forgotten about: *Martin and Joan had a serious quarrel last year, but fortunately it seems to have blown over now. There was trouble in the town over the new development, but the council think that it will blow over.*

bluff into

to persuade (someone) into doing (something) by deceiving or tricking him/her: *Beth bluffed Ray into believing that she was wealthy. At first the man denied that he had committed the crime, but the police bluffed him into admitting it.*

blurt out

to say (something) suddenly and without thinking of the effect or consequences: *They were afraid that their fellow thief would blurt the truth out to the police. The child blurted out that she knew who her attacker was although the man was in the room with her.*

break down

to stop working: *The car broke down and we had to get it towed to a garage. We were just about to watch television when the set broke down.*

break into

to enter (a building, etc) illegally and often by using force: *Thieves broke into the jewellers in the high street. The building had an alarm system, but burglars broke into it, nevertheless.*

break off

to stop speaking suddenly, often for a very short time: *Sue was in the middle of a telephone conversation, but broke off to say goodbye to her daughter, who was just leaving.*

brim over with

to be full of (something): *Her eyes were brimming over with tears. Muriel was brimming over with joy on her wedding day.*

bring out

to cause (something) to become obvious: *Cruelty to animals brings out the worst in Jack. Working with children has brought out Jean's gentler side.*

bring round

to make (someone) conscious again: *When he collapsed, the paramedics tried to bring Matt round by calling his name. The patient was in a coma and his relatives tried to bring her round by speaking to her.*

brood over

to think about (something unpleasant, difficult, etc) anxiously for a long time: *Sally keeps brooding over her divorce. It's a pity that you didn't get the job, but there's no point in brooding over it.*

brush aside

to pay no attention to (something), to take no notice of (something). *The boss always brushed aside any suggestions made by the workers. The boss brushed our complaints aside very rudely. We tried to make a protest to the council, but they brushed it aside.*

brush up on

to revise one's knowledge of (something): *Meg should brush up on the Highway Code before she takes her driving test. There was a question about Napoleon in the exam — thank goodness that I brushed up on him.*

burst into

to enter (somewhere) suddenly and sometimes violently: *The couple were watching television when the burglar burst into the room.*

butter up

(informal) to flatter (someone), to try to please (someone), often because one wants him/her to do something for one: *Jim's just buttering Val up because he wants to borrow some money from her. Val wants to borrow Pete's English notes and so she's buttering him up.*

buzz round/around

to move around (somewhere) busily and quickly: *There had obviously been an accident because there were police buzzing around all over the motorway. I wouldn't visit the castle today — there are parties of schoolchildren buzzing around it.*

C

call back

to telephone (someone) who has telephoned you, to return (someone's) telephone call: *I'll just call Mary back — she left a message on my answering machine. I'll find out the information for you and call you back.*

call in at

to visit (somewhere) briefly: *James called in at a pub to have a quick pint. There's a new wine bar in the high street and we called in at it to see what it was like.*

call off

to cancel (an arrangement, event, etc): *We had to call off our plans to move house. Not enough people applied and so the university called the whole conference off. Matt and Katie had arranged their wedding but they called it off.*

call on

to ask or appeal to (someone) for something or to do something: *The minister called on all the villagers to* help the poor. The president called on neighbouring countries to assist him against the rebel army. Fiona and Colin are reliable people — you can call on them to help.

call out

to say (something) loudly, to shout: Anne called out from the back of the bus that she was cold. 'Watch! You're driving too fast!' called out Lou. Their neighbour called out a greeting as he passed.

camp out

to sleep outdoors in a tent: We couldn't afford a hotel and so we hired a tent and camped out. The children wanted to camp out in the back garden.

carry off

to get hold of (someone or something) and take (it/him/her) away by carrying: The robbers carried off the bag of jewels. The soldiers watched the enemy carry their friend off. We tried to save the bird, but the cat carried it off.

carry off

to win (a prize, trophy, etc) It was no surprise when Sophie carried off the prize for best all-round student. Emma carried all the English prizes off. There was a special trophy for creative writing and we knew that Ron would carry it off.

carry out

to act according to (instructions, etc), to put (something) into practice: The team carried out the captain's orders. The teachers are just carrying government policy out. That was the head teacher's suggestion and we are carrying it out.

cart off

to take (someone) somewhere, especially without asking his/her permission, and sometimes rather abruptly or rudely: Mrs Carson is always saying that her family want to cart her off to an old people's home. The child was screaming and his father carted him off to his room.

carve out

to make or create (something), often with difficulty or great effort: It is extremely difficult to carve out a career in the theatre. The firm has gradually carved out a significant share of the fashion industry. Flora had a very successful career as an opera singer, but it took her years to carve it out.

cast aside

to get rid (of someone or something): Jack cast his wife aside for a younger woman. Julie has now cast aside her religion. He had a daughter, but he cast her aside when he remarried.

catch up with

to come level with and sometimes overtake (someone or something): We were unlikely to catch up with our friends as they left long before us. The other group of walkers left first, but we caught up with them at lunchtime.

centre on

to concentrate on (something), to be most concerned with (something): Joan's life centres on her work and her family. Bill doesn't regard golf as a hobby — his whole life is centred on it.

chase after

to spend a lot of time and energy trying to get (someone or something): Jim's a newspaper reporter and is always chasing after exclusive stories. The other girls don't like Molly because she chases after all the male students. Sylvia finally got information about her biological father — after spending years chasing after it.

check against

to compare (something) with (something else), for example to find out if these are the same: When we checked his name against the hotel register, we discovered that it was not there. The parking attendant checked the registration number of Bill's car against those on his list and refused to let him use the firm's car park. Here is a list of those who promised to come — could you check it against those who actually attended?

cheer on

to support and encourage (someone such as a sports competitor) by cheering: We need as many people as possible to cheer on our team in the final. The large crowd was cheering the young athlete on. The local football team have very few fans to cheer them on.

chip in

to pay some money towards the cost of something: The briefcase is expensive, but if we all chip in we can afford to buy it as a leaving present for Rick. We were able to have a party because we all chipped in.

choke back

to try to prevent (something) appearing or being obvious: *Bella succeeded in choking the tears back as she waved goodbye. Lucy could hardly choke back her laughter.*

chop down

to make (usually a tree) fall to the ground by cutting through it with an axe etc: *The farmer is going to chop down some fir trees and sell them as Christmas trees. We chopped the older trees down last winter. I wondered where the old oak tree was and was told that the owner had chopped it down.*

clam up

(informal) to become silent and refuse to say anything: *When the interviewer asked the film star about her private life, she clammed up. The youth clammed up about what he had seen when the police asked him questions.*

clear out

to make something tidy by getting rid of what is not needed: *Alice cleared out the kitchen cupboards. We cleared the attic out in one day. The room is now very neat because we cleared it out yesterday.*

clock up

to reach (a number of miles, hours, etc): *The car clocked up two thousand miles on the return trip. The tradesman charged us for more hours than he actually clocked up.*

club together

(of a group of people) to give money so that a group can share the cost of something: *Polly is ill — let's club together and buy her some flowers. If the family club together, we should be able to buy a really nice present for mum.*

cluster round

to gather around (someone or something) in a group which is very close together: *The students clustered around the notice-board to find out their exam results. When the film star arrived, a crowd of photographers clustered round her.*

clutter up

to fill or cover (something) so that it is made untidy: *There were dirty dishes cluttering up the kitchen worktops. The students clutter their rooms up with beer cans and fast food containers. The room was far from tidy — there were old magazines and newspapers cluttering it up.*

coax into

persuade (someone) by talking to him/her in a gentle, often flattering manner: *We eventually coaxed the child into taking some food. Bella didn't want to take part in the college play, but her friends coaxed her into it.*

come across

to find or meet by chance: *Julia came across an old school friend at the conference. I came across an interesting article on global warming in the local newspaper. It was a lovely pub and the young couple were glad to have come across it.*

come down with

to catch or to suffer from (an illness): *Tim has a lot of spots on his body — I think he's coming down with chicken pox. Molly's sister has mumps and she thinks that she's coming down with it.*

come round

to become conscious again, to regain consciousness: *The pregnant woman fainted in the heat but soon came round.*

come up

to happen, to occur: *some important work has come up and I cannot meet you tonight. The chance to buy this property will not come up again for a long time.*

come up with

to think of (an idea, plan, proposal etc) and suggest it: *The council have come up with a plan to solve the traffic problem. This is a good idea — who came up with it? The boys are trying to come up with ways to make money quickly. That was a brilliant idea and it was Kevin who came up with it.*

confide in

to tell (someone) about a private or secret matter or problem: *Molly confided in her new neighbour that her husband was in jail. Matt is such a gossip that no-one ever confides in him.*

cook up

to put (something) together falsely or dishonestly: *The children cooked up some story about someone stealing their pocket money, but they spent it. Trust Fred to cook a story up about seeing an alien. Don't' believe Ron's excuse — he just cooked it up to avoid going to the meeting.*

cope with

to deal with (someone or something) successfully: *Clare had great difficulty in coping with her workload. Jill encountered many problems but coped with them easily.*

cough up

(informal) to give or pay (sum of money): *Joe is hoping that his father will cough up the money for a new car. Rick owes me money but he refuses to cough up.*

cover up

to place (something) over (someone or something) in order to hide or protect him/her/it: *The thieves covered the stolen bike up with a sheet of tarpaulin. The murderers had covered up the body with a pile of leaves. The baby is getting cold — we had better cover her up with a shawl.*

cream off

to take away (from a group) (the most talented, etc members): *The top universities cream off the brightest students from the schools. The most successful final-year students have already been creamed off by industrial firms. We had a number of very talented marketing people in our training scheme, but a rival company creamed them off.*

cross out

to draw a line through (something, especially words or items on a page): *I crossed out that word because I had spelt it wrongly. She crossed the address out and replaced it with her new address. We made a list of tasks to be done and crossed them out as we completed them.*

cry out

to shout suddenly because one is hurt, surprised, etc: *Ben dropped a brick on his foot and cried out in agony. 'Help!' the drowning man cried out.*

cry out for

to need (something) very much: *The situation cries out for immediate action. I'm glad there has been a change of management — the company was crying out for it.*

cut into

to make a cut or tear in (something) with a knife, scissors, etc: *The dressmaker was almost afraid to cut into the beautiful, expensive cloth. The meat was placed on the table and father cut into it to serve us all.*

cut off

to disconnect (a telephone service): *The engineer accidentally cut off our phone when repairing the line. Bad weather had cut our phones off. The cottage had a telephone connection, but the thieves cut it off.*

cut off

to remove by cutting by a knife, scissors, etc: *We cut off some of the dead blooms from the bush. The child cut all her hair off. Some of the branches of the tree were blocking the view and so we cut them off.*

D

damp down

to reduce the extent or intensity of (something): *Bad weather damped down their desire for a walk in the country. The fans supported the team loyally, but a series of lost matches damped their enthusiasm down. The boys started off their early morning jogging sessions, but lack of sleep soon damped it down.*

dawn on

to become obvious or apparent (to one): *It dawned on Sally that she was alone in the house. Suddenly the truth of the matter dawned on me.*

deal with

to take action with regard to (someone or something): *That department deals with customers' complaints. Harry has financial problems, but he is dealing with them.*

debar from

to prevent (someone) from (doing something), often officially: *Getting such marks in his final school exams does not debar him from going to college, but he won't get into the college of his choice. After the fight, Ben was debarred from entering the pub again.*

decide on

to choose (something), often after careful thought: *We looked at various holiday destinations but decided on Paris. My parents spent a long time looking at wallpaper and I'm surprised that they decided on that.*

defer to

to accept (someone's) decision or opinion, often someone in authority, whatever one's own opinion is: *The court deferred the case to a higher court. I cannot deal with this matter — I have deferred it to our managing director.*

delve into

to try hard to discover information about (something) by searching thoroughly: *The journalist is delving into the politician's past career to try to uncover a scandal. You'll probably discover something scandalous in the film star's background if you delve into it for long enough.*

derive from

to get (something) from (something,), to have (something) as a source of (something): *Sheila derives a great deal of enjoyment from her garden. Anne loves books — she derives so much enjoyment from them.*

descend on

to arrive suddenly, often in large numbers and often unexpectedly or without being wanted: *Hordes of reporters descended on the politician's house when they heard the scandal about him. In the winter the town is a peaceful place, but in the summer, crowds of tourists descend on it.*

deter from

to prevent or discourage (someone) from doing something, often by showing him/her how dangerous, difficult, unpleasant, etc it is: *Fear of being attacked in the street deters many women from going out at night. Clara knows that smoking may well damage her health, but that does not deter her from it.*

dig into

to put your hand (into a pocket, bag, etc) to search for something: *Sue dug into her pocket to find change to give the beggar. George held Mary's rucksack while she dug into it to find the map.*

dig up

to remove (something) by digging, to remove (something) from the ground: *We dug up the potatoes and cooked them for dinner. They dug the whole crop up. The rose bushes no longer bloomed and so we dug them up.*

dip into

to spend some of (the money that one has been saving): *The couple dipped into their retirement savings to buy a new car. Your savings won't grow if you keep dipping into them.*

disagree with

not to agree with (someone or something), to have a different opinion from (someone or something): *Sally's parents disagreed with her about her choice of career. The two newspaper reports disagreed with each other.*

dish out

(*informal*) to give (an amount of something) to each person, to distribute (something): *Could you dish out these leaflets to anyone who wants one? Peggy offered to dish the application forms out to the students.*

dispense with

to stop using (something) or to do without (something): *Business is poor and so the firm has had to dispense with some of its staff.*

dissociate from

not to associate (people or things) with each other, to show that there is no association or connection between (people or things): *We want to dissociate our town from the town which borders it — our town is a much cleaner, peaceful place to live. Freda's parents wish to dissociate themselves from their neighbours who have the same name because their neighbours are always in trouble with the police.*

divest of

to take (something) away from (someone or something): *George was divested of his role as club treasurer when some money went missing. The new owners will certainly divest Michael of his position as marketing director.*

divide up

to share (something) out among the members of a group: *The children divided the sweets up among them. The burglars divided up the stolen goods. We collected a lot of money, but it has to be divided up among several charities.*

do away with

to get rid of (something): *We did away with that old garden shed. The Smiths had an open fire in the study, but they did away with it and put in an electric heater.*

do down

to criticize (someone) and try to make him/her seem unimportant or unsuccessful: *Sara is so critical that she even does her own family down. I can't believe Bruce would do down his best friend like that. Brian is a very clever person, but he has low self-esteem and is always doing himself down.*

do without

to manage or survive without having (something): *Anne finds it difficult to do without sugar. Joe likes meat, but he can do without it.*

dote on

to love (someone) very much, sometimes to the extent of being foolish, to adore (someone): *Anne dotes on her granddaughter and is always giving her presents. I don't know what old Phil will do when his cat dies — he dotes on it.*

drift off

to fall asleep gradually: *I was reading in bed and I drifted off with the light on. It is dangerous for drivers to drift off when they're at the wheels of their cars.*

drink up

to finish (a drink) completely: *Drink up your tea — it's time to leave. The child was told to drink her milk up. The coffee was very hot, but I drank it up.*

drop off

(of a car-driver, etc) to let (a passenger) out of a vehicle: *The bus dropped the passengers off at the town hall. We gave Pat a lift and dropped her off at her home.*

drop out of

to stop being involved in or taking part in (something), to withdraw from (something): *Alan dropped out of university because he found the work too hard. The group dropped out of society and went to live in a commune on a remote island. It was a boring course and several students dropped out of it.*

drum into

to repeat (something) regularly to (someone) in the hope that he/she will remember it and pay attention to it: *They drummed into their children that they must not accept sweets from strangers. Frank's mother had a great regard for honesty and drummed this into him when he was a child. We had the need for cleanliness drummed into us as children.*

duck out of

(informal) to avoid (something or doing something): *It's raining and some of the pupils are trying to duck out of the hockey match. The next meeting is on Christmas Eve and I think most people will duck out of it.*

dust down

to clean (something) by removing dust from it with a cloth, etc: *We had to remove all the books and dust the shelves down. Pat dusted down the wardrobe shelves before putting her new sweaters on them. The chairs in the old cottage were filthy, and we had to dust them down before we sat on them.*

E

ease up

not to work quite as hard as previously, not to put as much effort into (something): *Mick has been training very hard for the new football season, but has been told by his coach to ease up a bit. Joanna is suffering from stress because of working too hard and the doctor told her to ease up.*

eat into

gradually to use a great deal of (something): *Going on such an expensive holiday really ate into their savings. Ray had a substantial inheritance from his parents, but tax ate into it to a great extent.*

egg on

to encourage or urge (someone) to do something, often something foolish or wrong: *The students knew that they were wrong to egg on Tom to climb on the roof. The boy said that he would not have stolen the car if his friends had not egged him on.*

eke out

to make (something) last as long as possible or supply as many people as possible: *The walkers had to eke out their water supply. We're going to have to eke out the fuel supply until the end of the week. Don't put too much butter on the sandwiches — there's not much and we have to eke it out.*

empty out

to remove the contents from (something): *The milk was sour and we emptied out the bottle. We're getting the decorators in, but first we have to empty the front room out.*

end up

to be in a place or situation, often unpleasant, eventually at the end of a series of events: *Joe kept breaking the law and ended up in prison.*

engage in

to take part in (something): *Joe wasn't allowed by his parents to engage in the travel business. Bill is engaged in banking. The man in the train tried to engage me in conversation.*

enter into

to become involved in (something), to take part in (something): *Fay entered into the spirit of the game. We had a discussion about possible holiday destinations, but Malcolm refused to enter into it.*

enthuse over

to show great enthusiasm for (someone or something), to show that one is very pleased with (someone or something): *Our neighbours were enthusing over the new restaurant. I didn't really like the range of clothes in that shop, but Tanya enthused over them.*

explain away

to attempt to excuse or account for (something) so that the situation does not seem so bad as it first appeared: *Diane had been at an all-night party, but tried to explain away her tiredness in the morning by saying that she had been unable to sleep the night before. Joan's friends did not believe in the supernatural, but they were unable to explain her strange experience away. Freda had to tell the truth about her unofficial absence because she was unable to explain it away.*

F

face down

to look at someone boldly and confidently in the hope of overcoming or defeating him/her: *The government minister hoped to face down the Opposition MPs. The soldier turned round and faced down his pursuer. The mugger didn't expect the old man to face him down.*

face up to

to accept (a difficult situation) and try to deal with it: *It's best to face up to your illness and get treatment for it. Reluctantly Ned faced up to the fact that he was* bankrupt. *Bill has gone for good and we must face up to it.*

fall back on

to use (something) or seek help from (someone) that you know that you can rely on when everything else has failed: *We have an open fire which we can fall back on if the central heating system fails. Sheila does some temporary work for us — we can always fall back on her.*

fall for

to be very attracted to (someone) and fall in love with him/her: *Les has fallen for his secretary and left his wife. The new lecturer is very handsome, and all the female students have fallen for him.*

fall in with

to accept and agree to (something): *Everyone happily fell in with Roger's suggestion. It is a very interesting idea, but some members of the committee may well not fall in with it. Maurice refused to fall in with the rest of the family's holiday plans. If you make the travel arrangements we will all fall in with them.*

fall into

to begin to be in (a particular state or condition): *a lot of the old traditions have fallen into disuse. They were beautiful houses once, but they have fallen into a state of neglect.*

fall into

to belong to (a group, category, etc), to be classified as being part of (a particular group, etc): *Peter is very bright and, indeed, falls into the gifted children category. There are generous people and there are mean people — Tony falls into the latter class.*

fall out with

to quarrel with (someone): *Children are always falling out with their friends. Pam won't speak to Pete — she fell out with him last week because he forgot her birthday.*

fall over

to fall to the ground by accident, often because someone or something is in the way: *The child took some kind of fit and fell over. Mother fell over a toy which had been left in the hall. Don't leave your shoes there — someone will fall over them.*

fall through

to fail, not to happen, not to be completed successfully: *The sale of the house fell through at the last minute. We made plans to work overseas, but they fell through because we could not get visas.*

fathom out

to understand (someone or something), after thinking about it carefully for some time: *Even now the police cannot fathom out a motive for the murder. There is no point in trying to fathom Jane out — she is very secretive. Peggy left home suddenly — we cannot fathom it out.*

feel up to

to feel able and inclined to (do something): *Pat didn't feel up to cycling to work today — she has a sore leg. Amy is having a party but I've been ill and I don't feel up to going to it.*

fend off

to try to prevent, keep away or avoid (someone or something): *Doctors in the area do their best to fend off the disease. Sue's neighbours were very inquisitive, but she fended their interference off as well she could. The press had so many questions that the politician found it difficult to fend them off.*

ferret out

(*informal*) to find (something) by searching for it thoroughly: *Trust Jan to ferret out the family's guilty secrets. Fred was the first reporter to ferret the scandal out. The information was useful and it hadn't taken long to ferret it out.*

file away

to store (something) in a file for possible future use: *We filed the application forms away in the bottom drawer of the filing cabinet. The secretary filed away the day's correspondence. Don't throw away the reply to your complaint — file it away in case you need to refer to it again.*

fill up

to make (someone or something) completely full: *Fill the tank up with unleaded petrol please. We filled up the container with fresh water. The teenagers are always hungry — it seems impossible to fill them up.*

find out

to learn or discover (something): *At last we found out where he was. Now they have found all the facts out. The information is up-to-date — we've just found it out.*

fish out

(*informal*) to take (something) out of somewhere, often with difficulty or after a search: *The teacher opened a desk drawer and fished out a piece of chalk. Moira searched in her handbag and fished a bar of chocolate out. I have a pen in my bag — I'll just fish it out.*

fit into

to feel comfortable (in a group, etc) as though one belonged: *Elaine felt that she did not fit into her husband's family. The group consisted of very academic people and Tony did not fit into it.*

fit up with

to equip or supply (someone or something) with (something): *Dad is fitting up the garden shed with a row of shelves. The cottage has a burglar alarm — my brother fitted it up with one last year.*

fix up

to arrange (something): *We have fixed up a meeting of the club for next week. Have you had time to fix the next game up? We're going on a cruise next year but we haven't fixed it up yet.*

flesh out

to add details to (something) to make it fuller or more comprehensive: *We hope to flesh out the proposal before the next meeting. That is interesting, but you need to flesh the idea out a bit. Your essay is too short — you will have to flesh it out with some more information.*

flick through

to turn over the pages of (a magazine, book, document, etc) quickly in order to glance at them quickly: *We flicked through the film magazine to find out what the critics were recommending. I flicked through it, but the book did not have the information which I wanted.*

fly into

suddenly to go into (a state of anger): *Marge flew into a rage when Pete arrived late. Sally's father flew into a temper when she lost her job.*

foist on

to make (someone) take or accept (someone or something) that he/she does not really want: *We don't have room to have people to stay, but our son has foisted his friends on us. Meg doesn't look after the children very often — she usually foists them on her parents.*

force into

to make (someone) do something against his/her will: *The kidnappers forced the child into entering the old bar. Val didn't want to sell the house but financial circumstances forced her into it.*

fork out

(informal) to pay money for: *Beth's grandmother is forking out for her college fees. Mary forked out a whole month's salary on that dress.*

freeze over

to become covered with a layer of ice: *The village pond has frozen over and the ice is thick enough to skate on.*

frighten into

to make (someone) do something by making him/her afraid: *The bully frightened the other schoolboy into giving him money. The man who attacked Molly frightened her into not telling the police.*

fritter away

to waste (time, money, etc) gradually and foolishly: *Paul frittered all his money away on gambling. Kate frittered away her time watching television instead of studying. Dave's grandmother left him a lot of money, but he frittered it away.*

G

gain on

gradually get closer to (someone) whom one is chasing or trying to pass: *The firm has a sales competition and this month Ted is gaining on Molly, who usually wins it. We thought that Jill would win the race easily, but Celia began to gain on her just before the finish.*

gang up on

(informal) to get together in a group and attack (someone else) or treat (someone else badly and unfairly): *The school bully and her friends ganged up on the new girl. They were all ganging up on me to try to make me change my mind.*

gather round

to form a group round (someone or something): *The tourists gathered round the guide at the cathedral. We all gathered round the Christmas tree to sing carols.* *The boys began to fight and a crowd gathered round them.*

gather up

to bring (things) together in a group, to collect (things) together: *Fred gathered up the old newspapers and burnt them. We gathered the leaves up and put them in sacks. There was a great deal of litter in the park, but someone must have gathered it up.*

gear towards

to be designed for or to be directed at (someone or (something): *The course is geared towards the brighter students. The housing development is geared towards the needs of young families. Joan wants a well-paid job and her studies are geared towards it.*

gear up

to prepare (someone) to do something, to get (someone or something) ready and able to do something: *The students decided that it was time that they started gearing themselves up for the exams. The firm is not geared up to cope with the large increase in orders. The football team is very inexperienced and unfit — it will be difficult to gear it up for the tournament.*

gen up on

(informal) to give (someone) as much information as possible about something: *The marketing director needs to be genned up on this month's sales figures before the meeting. We must gen the workers up on their rights before they accept the offer.*

get around

(of information, news, etc) to become known by a large number of people: *Linda doesn't want news of her engagement to get around until she can tell her parents. Rose was cautioned by the police and she was scared that news of this would get around in her home town.*

get away with

to avoid being punished for (something): *Becky should not get away with being so rude to people. Jack definitely committed the crime, but he got away with it.*

get behind with

to be late or slow in (doing something), not to make as much progress with (something) as might be expected: *Molly is studying in the library all day because she has got behind with her vacation reading list. The students are given so many essays to write that most of them get behind with them. I've been working late and have got behind with the housework. The students have several essays to write and some of them have got behind with them.*

get bogged down in

to make little progress with (something), perhaps because of paying too much attention to detail or minor problems: *James applied for a visa to work there, but he got bogged down in all the regulations. Les is trying to fill in his income tax form, but he's getting completely bogged down in it.*

get down to

to start working hard at (something): *The students had better get down to finding somewhere to live. I have three essays to write — I need to get down to them right away.*

get in

to get (someone) to come and do (something) for you: *Bella would prefer to get a professional decorator in to redecorate the house, but Ron wants to do the work himself. DIY is all very well but you should get in an expert for the electrical work.*

get off

to remove (something) from (something): *Sara couldn't get the ink stain off the tablecloth. The children have got paint on the curtains and I can't get it off.*

get on at

to criticize or scold (someone) continually: *The children would like a teacher who does not get on at them all the time. Terry's parents never praise him — they just get on at him.*

get on for

(of time) to be nearly (a certain time): *It's getting on for lunch time. It must have been getting on for 6 o'clock.*

get out of

to avoid (something): *Jo's trying to get out of working night shift. I agreed to go to the party, but I'm trying to get out of it. I'm trying to get out of tomorrow's meeting.*

Ella tried to get out of tidying her room. Joan has made a date with Tim, but she's trying to get out of it.

get through to

to make (someone) understand (something): *They just cannot get through to their daughter that hitchhiking can be dangerous. How can we get the importance of eating healthily through to them?*

get to

to reach, to arrive at (somewhere): *We want to get to the city before nightfall. The coast is still a long way off — I don't think you'll get to it tonight.*

get up

to get out of bed, to rise: *We have to get up very early to catch the first bus.*

give out

to announce (something), to make (something) known: *The mayor gave out the names of the winners at the end of the fete. The police are giving no further details out just now. I don't know the name of the murderer although the newsreader gave it out.*

give out

to distribute (something), to hand out (something): *Please give these leaflets out to all the students. We gave out free sweets to the children on the day of the fete. We had several books, but we gave them out.*

give up

to stop doing or taking (something) because one is no longer interested in it, because it is bad for one, etc: *Giles keeps getting chest infections and has been advised to give up smoking. Tess used to play tennis, but she had to give it up when she injured her arm. Mike gave smoking and drinking up at the same time. I don't take sugar in tea — I gave it up.*

go after

to follow or pursue (someone): *The police went after the burglars, but did not catch them. Jill left the room in tears and Mike went after her to apologize.*

go beyond

to be more serious, extreme, etc than (something): *Josh thought it was funny, but his behaviour certainly went beyond a joke. The row went beyond the usual friendly family argument.*

go by

to use (something) as a guide or help in doing something: *We're not sure if we'll get there — all we have to go by is some barely legible directions. The pupils were told that if they went by the rule, they would not get into trouble. That road map is out of date — we cannot possibly go by that.*

go over to

to change to a different system, organization, set of beliefs, etc: *Paula's parents are dissatisfied with state education and have gone over to the private system. There's a new youth club in the village and many of our members have gone over to it.*

go round

to walk through all of (something): *We'll go round the museum tomorrow. The art gallery is over there — would you like to go round it?*

go through

to examine (something) carefully, sometimes in order to search for (something): *Mary went through her friend's entire wardrobe looking for something to wear to the party. There is no error in the company books — the accountant has gone through them twice.*

go through

to experience (something, often something unpleasant): *Pam's husband is in hospital and she's going through a difficult time just now. Jill says that she knows what the pain of childbirth is like, and she doesn't want to go through it again.*

go through with

to continue with (something difficult or unpleasant) until it is achieved, completed, etc: *The world's press were shocked when the president of the country went through with the execution of those who had opposed him. Ron threatened to commit suicide once or twice, but we didn't think that he would go through with it.*

grab at

to attempt to get hold of (someone or something): *Bob thought he was drowning and grabbed at the edge of the boat. The child grabbed at the last cake before anyone else could take it. Jock looked like a generous man and the beggar grabbed at his sleeve.*

grow out of

to stop (having or doing something, often something unpleasant or undesirable) when one grows older or more mature: *Gradually the little girl grew out of her fear of the dark. Jill had a bad habit of biting her nails, but she grew out of it.*

guard against

to try to make sure that something does not happen by being careful: *Hospitals should be kept clean to guard against infection. Jane should guard against being too trusting.*

gulp down

to eat or drink (something) very quickly: *Adam got up late and had only time to gulp down a piece of toast. Here's a mug of coffee — you've time to gulp it down before the meeting.*

H

hail as

to be acknowledged and praised publicly as (someone or something): *The critics hailed Janet's latest book as a masterpiece. The young Irish writer was hailed as another James Joyce.*

ham up

to exaggerate words and gestures, especially when one is acting in a play, etc: *The marketing manager was furious when Ben hammed up his presentation. The local dramatic society put on a production of Macbeth and really hammed it up.*

hammer out

to produce (something) after much effort, discussion, etc: *The two firms eventually hammered out an agreement and they merged. Management and unions finally reached a compromise, but it took all night to hammer it out.*

hand back

to give (something) to (someone) after you have borrowed it or taken it from them, to return (something) to (someone): *The teacher handed the English essays back to the class. Please hand back my history notes which you borrowed — I need them for the exam. The doorkeeper looked at Joe's pass and handed it back to him. I asked Nora to hand back the books which she had borrowed from me. Nora absolutely refused to hand the books back, saying that I had given them to her as a present.*

hand in

to give (something) to (someone) or take (something) to (somewhere) so it can be dealt with: *Joe has gone to the office to hand in his job application. How can the teacher mark your essay if you do not hand it in?*

hand round

to pass (something) from one member of a group to another: *The waitress handed round a tray of sandwiches. I'll get my son to hand the drinks round at the party. That's the agenda for the meeting — could you hand it round?*

hang around

to stay (somewhere) for quite a long time doing nothing, perhaps because one is waiting for someone or something: *There's a suspicious-looking character hanging around the school gates. My dental appointment has been delayed and now I'll have to hang around here for another hour.*

hang up

to end a telephone connection, often by putting the receiver back on the handset: *Trudy was very angry with Dave and she hung up before he could apologize. Meg said abruptly to the salesman that she did not want to buy anything and hung up.*

hare off

to run off quickly: *Jo hared off down the street, hoping to catch the bus at the next stop. The dog picked up the piece of meat and hared off with it.*

harp on

to keep on talking about (something), although this may annoy or irritate other people: *Fred keeps harping on about how much he dislikes his boss. We feel sorry that Agnes lost the competition, but wish that she wouldn't harp on about it.*

head back

to start on the return journey to (somewhere): *We've walked a long way and it's getting late — we'd better head back to the car. If we head back now we'll reach home before nightfall.*

head for

to go or move towards (something) to go towards (something), to move in the direction of (something): *We're heading for London but we're staying overnight in York. With poor sales figures like these the firm is heading for disaster.*

hear of

to get information about (something), to learn about (something): *My doctor says he's never heard of the painkiller that's being advertised. That picture's by Jane's favourite artist — have you ever heard of him?*

hear out

to listen to what someone has to say without interrupting him/her: *The teacher never hears the pupils out, but assumes she knows what they are going to say. Paula had a good reason for being late, but the boss refused to hear her out and gave her an official warning.*

help out

to give (someone) some assistance, often temporarily or in an emergency: *I lent Edna the money because I felt that I should help out an old friend. Jane helps her neighbour out by looking after her children occasionally. The driver said that he had run out of petrol and asked us if we could help him out.*

herd into

to gather (people or animals) together into a group, often in an uncomfortable or not very polite way: *The police herded the protesters into a police van. A huge number of people wanted to hear the concert and the organizers tried to herd them all into far too small a hall.*

hinge on

to depend on (something): *The success of the venture hinges on large export sales. Ned needs a good degree — his future hinges on it.*

hint at

to suggest (something) in an indirect way: *My parents hinted at moving house. Anne did not actually say that she was leaving, but she hinted at it.*

hit back

to hit (someone) after he/she has hit one: *Molly was not strong enough to hit her brother back. The school bully doesn't expect people to hit him back.*

hit on

to think of (an idea, solution, etc): *The Kellys hit on the idea of letting a room out to make some money. I think I've hit on the answer to our problem.*

hit out at

to criticize or attack (someone or something): *Many of the residents hit out at the new parking scheme in the town centre. People know that the local MP is not responsible for the government's economic policy, but many of them hit out at her about it, nevertheless.*

hoard up

to keep or store large quantities of (something): *Why did you hoard up so many tins of food — they're all past their sell-by date? We had to throw out a lot of old magazines when my aunt died — she had been hoarding them up.*

hold forth

to talk (about something) for a long time, often in a boring or a pompous way: *As usual George was holding forth about how clever his children are. Peggy started to hold forth once again about her views on the educational system and we all left the room.*

hold onto

to grip (something or someone) tightly: *Little Alice held onto her mother's hand as they crossed the street. When Mark fell in the river he reached up and held onto a branch until he could be rescued. Bill threw Jim a rope and he held onto it until he was pulled up from the bottom of the cliff.*

horn in on

to become involved in (something), without being invited and often without being wanted: *Another department is trying to horn in on our proposal for a new product range. The residents in the area had been organizing a protest movement for months, but Mark horned in on it at the last minute and took all the credit when it was successful.*

hose down

to clean (someone or something) by using water from a hose: *I hosed my boots down in the garden because they were filthy. Bill hosed the dogs down because they were very hot. The car is very dusty and I'm just going to hose it down.*

huddle round

to gather closely together, near to (something): *The children were very cold and huddled round the radiator. I can't even see the bonfire — there are too many people huddled round it.*

hunt out

to find (something) after a hard search: *I hunted out these old wellingtons from the back of the cupboard. The old family photographs were in an old trunk in the attic and it took me some time to hunt them out.*

I

ice over

to become covered with a layer of ice: *The pond has iced over, but the layer of ice is quite thin. It's very cold and the water in the dog's bowl in the yard has iced over.*

idle away

to spend (a period of time) not doing very much: *It was lovely to idle away a few hours sitting in the garden. On holiday we idled whole days away just sitting on the beach. The college term was nearly over and Adam had idled it away.*

impose on

to make (someone) accept (something): *The president imposed a curfew on the citizens after the uprising. There is a limit on the amount of money we can take to school — it was imposed on us by the head teacher.*

impress on

to make (someone) realize how important something is: *The boss impressed on the staff the need for speed. His parents impressed on him the importance of studying hard. The head teacher impressed it on the pupils that school uniform must be worn.*

improve on

to make (a standard, result, etc) better: *The standard of football has not improved on last year's performance. Our profits were very high last year — I don't see how we can improve on them.*

indulge in

to do or be involved in (something) which one really enjoys: *The girls were planning to indulge in a shopping trip. The men indulged in a drinking bout and got severe hangovers. Smoking is a harmful habit, but Joe enjoys it and has indulged in it for years.*

insist on

to say firmly that (something) is what one must have and refuse to have anything else: *Bob is insisting on sending his children to private schools. Beth insisted on going to a restaurant with a no-smoking area. Joe didn't really want a large, white wedding but Sophie insisted on it.*

interfere with

to prevent or slow down the progress of (something): *Lack of staff interfered with the production of the new product. The bus schedule was running smoothly until bad weather interfered with it.*

invest in

to spend money on (something) in the hope of getting some benefit, such as a profit: *Beth's financial adviser said that she should invest in property.*

invite over

to ask (someone, people) to visit one in one's home: *Jan said that she only invited over one or two of her colleagues, but they all came. We've invited a few friends over for dinner. Jack was lonely and so Adam invited him over for a drink.*

iron out

to solve or overcome (problems, difficulties, etc): *The young couple are trying to iron out the things which cause difficulties in their relationship. Josh and I had a major disagreement, but eventually we ironed the problem out.*

J

jazz up

(informal) to make (something) brighter, more decorative, more exciting, etc: *Josie decided to jazz up her plain, dark suit with a brightly-coloured scarf. Bert jazzed his rented room up with a few colourful posters. The article is informative but dull — you should try to jazz it up a bit.*

join in

to take part in (an activity in which other people are involved): *Mona was feeling unhappy and refused to join in the dancing. There was applause for the show, but not everyone joined in it. The local boys were playing a game of football and Meg's sons soon joined in.*

jolly along

to keep (someone) in a good mood, often so that he/she will behave well or do as you wish: *We tried to jolly the children along by telling stories and playing games, but they were very tired of the train journey. My sister doesn't really want to act as babysitter, but I'm trying to jolly her along until I can find someone else.*

jot down

to write (something) down, often in a brief, informal form: *Just let me jot down your address. I jotted the appointment down in my diary. Phil couldn't find Marcia's phone number although he had jotted it down.*

juggle with

to try to cope with (a number of things at once): *Martha did not realize how difficult it was to juggle child-rearing with a career. Terry is trying to juggle his role as father with his role as son — he's trying to look after both his young children and his elderly parents. Phil will have to give up one of his jobs — he's tried and failed to juggle with both of them.*

jut out of

to stick out from (something), to extend beyond (something): *A few trees jutted out of the rock face. Gordon walked past the garden shed and tripped over a rake that was jutting out of it.*

K

keel over

(informal) to fall over suddenly: *One of the soldiers on parade keeled over in the intense heat. The man in front of me keeled over and lost consciousness.*

keep down

to keep (something) at a low level: *We're trying to keep down the cost of house repairs. Try to keep the noise down — the baby is sleeping. The supermarket prices are still high although they claim to be keeping them down.*

keep from

to stop oneself from (doing something), but with difficulty: *Jill was organizing a surprise party for Jo's return home, but she was so excited that she could scarcely keep from telling everyone about it. Tim is so conceited that he cannot keep from admiring himself in every mirror.*

keep in

not to let (someone) leave (somewhere): *Mary is keeping her child in bed until his cold's better. Jack is not home yet — the doctor is keeping him in hospital. The convict appealed against his sentence, but he lost and was kept in prison. The child is not well and her mother is keeping her in bed.*

keep off

to cause (someone or something) to stay away from: *Try to keep the child's attention off the sweets at the supermarket check-out. The fence is supposed to keep people off the grass. If the young people have a club, it helps to keep them off the streets.*

keep up

keep (a building, etc) in good condition, to maintain (a building, etc) properly: *It takes quite a lot of money to keep these old buildings up. The church authorities don't have the resources to keep up all the churches and many of them are in disrepair. I had to sell the cottage — I just couldn't keep it up as the quotation for the repairs was very expensive.*

keep up

to continue or maintain (something): *Martha could not keep up the pretence any longer. It must be very expensive to keep that lifestyle up. We set such a high standard last year that it is difficult to keep it up.*

key in

to type (something) on a keyboard so as to store it in a computer: *Have you begun to key in the annual sales report? It will take some time to key all this information in.*

knock out

to cause (someone) to become unconscious: *The fierce blow knocked out Mr Smart. The attacker hit the old man on the head and knocked him out. The burglar lifted a baseball bat and knocked the shopkeeper out with it.*

knock over

to make (something) fall, often accidentally: *The woman knocked over a valuable vase with her handbag. The child knocked the paint tin over. The bottle was full of wine and the dog knocked it over.*

L

lag behind

to move more slowly than (someone) and so be further behind than him/her: *Adam was the best runner in the race, but on that day he lagged behind the winners. Phil walked so fast that the other hill-walkers soon lagged behind him.*

land on

to come to rest on (something): *The child jumped and landed on a sand castle. There was a field near by and the helicopter landed on it.*

lash out at

to speak to (someone) in a very angry way: *Amy has a very hot temper and lashes out at people who really haven't done anything wrong. Phil tried to apologize to Jane for being late, but she lashed out at him and walked away.*

last out

to survive, to continue to exist or function in a difficult situation: *The travellers were cold and hungry and just hoped that they could last out until help arrived. Jim is supposed to have stopped smoking, but he won't last out until tonight without a cigarette.*

laugh off

to regard or pretend to regard (something difficult, serious, etc) as amusing or unimportant: *Jim tried to laugh off his gambling losses, but they had left him without any money. They can't laugh the matter off — it could have a serious effect on all of us.*

launch into

to begin (to speak, sing, etc) with great enthusiasm, passion, etc: *The customer launched into a series of complaints as soon as the manager appeared. Tom forgot the words of the patriotic song after the first verse although he had launched into it with great confidence.*

lay before

to bring (something) to (someone's) attention so that he/she can consider it: *We are to lay our proposal before the committee tomorrow. We drew up the building plan and laid it before the council.*

lay on

to provide or supply (something): *The organizers are laying on refreshments after the performance. There was food at the exhibition, but I don't know who laid it on.*

lay out

to spend (money, often a lot of money) on something: *Mr and Mrs Campbell laid out a fortune on their children's education. Mr Jones is refusing to lay any more money out on his son's old car.*

lead up to

gradually to guide a conversation towards (a particular subject): *For days Jim has been talking about how little money he has, and I just knew that he was leading up to asking me for a loan.*

leap out at

to move towards (someone) suddenly, often from a hidden position: *The attacker leapt out at the old man from a dark doorway. We were passing the gate when a large dog suddenly leapt out at us.*

leave aside

not to consider (something) at the present time: *Let us leave aside the question of payment until the work has been completed. The committee decided to leave the details aside and concentrate on the general principle. We can talk about expanding the firm later, but let us leave it aside just now.*

leave behind

not to take (someone or something) with you, sometimes deliberately, sometimes accidentally: *We had to leave some of our belongings behind as the removal van was too small. I can't find my umbrella — I must have left it behind at the office.*

leave off

to stop doing something: *We had to leave off sunbathing as it began to rain.*

let down

to fail (someone) in some way, not to help (someone) when he/she is relying on you to do so: *Moira felt that her husband had let the children down by being late for the party. Robert let down his entire family by not coming home for Christmas. Sheila won't let you down — if she promised to accompany you, she will.*

let in

to allow (someone) to enter somewhere, often by opening the door: *The doctor's receptionist let the patients in. If you let in all those people the hall will be far too crowded. Open this door and let me in at once!*

let in for

to involve (oneself or someone) in something difficult, dangerous, unpleasant, expensive, etc: *When Josh's daughter got married he didn't know what he was letting himself in for — the wedding cost thousands of pounds. Rachel didn't know what she was letting her husband in for when she said that he would chair the meeting. My mother didn't know what she was letting me in for when she asked me to look after her neighbour's children — they were very badly behaved.*

let through

to allow (someone or something) to pass or enter: *The street was closed off and the police refused to let any more people through. The striker gave the ball a powerful kick and the goalkeeper let it through.*

level at

to direct or aim (something such as criticism, accusations, etc) at: *It was unfair to level accusations at Jim — he wasn't even present when the attack occurred. Bella was distressed that most of the criticism was levelled at her.*

lift up

to hold (someone or something) in your hands or in your hands and arms and move him/her/it upwards, to raise (someone or something) to a higher position: *The gardener lifted up the tools and put them in the shed. Sally lifted the bottles up and put them in the bin. The baby was crying and Jane lifted her up.*

light up

to look happy or cheerful suddenly: *The child's face lit up when he saw the Christmas tree. Len's face lit up when Jean invited him to her party.*

line up

to place (people or things) in a row or queue: *The organizers lined the audience up outside the concert hall. Mary lined up the chairs in preparation for the meeting. The teacher moved the desks and lined them up against the wall.*

listen out for

to be alert so that one will hear (something expected) when it happens: *I must listen out for the postman ringing the doorbell — I need to sign for a parcel. This monitor lets us listen out for the baby crying. I didn't hear the car drive up although I was listening out for it.*

listen to

to pay attention to (someone) and to follow his/her advice: *Rena refused to listen to her parents and married Jack against their wishes. Mark warned Bill that Bob was a rogue, but Bill would not listen to him.*

live for

to regard (someone or something) as being the most important thing in your life: *Clare just lives for her children. The boys live for football and are always training and practising. The old couple have no children and live for each other.*

live off

to get all the money which you need for living from (someone or something): *Jo doesn't want a job — he's happy to live off his wife. Peter owns several flats and lives off the rent from them. Beth gets an allowance from her parents while she's studying, but she feels bad about having to live off them.*

live on

to eat (something) as one's only type of food: *Very young children live on milk. I like vegetables, but I would not like to live on them.*

load up

to put a lot of things on (someone or something) and take them somewhere: *They loaded the boot of the car up with Christmas presents. Could you load the van up with the shopping? The donkey was very old, but its owner loaded it up with goods to take to market.*

lock out

to prevent (someone) from entering (somewhere) because the doors are locked and he/she does not have a key: *Her flat-mates accidentally locked Jan out because they didn't realize that she was still out when they went to bed. His parents locked out Tim and his friends because they didn't know that he didn't have a key. Freda locked herself out when the door slammed shut and she didn't have her keys.*

loll about

to lie down or sit down in a lazy way, not doing very much: *It was late at night, and we were lolling about listening to music and drinking wine. Jim's father said that he should be mowing the lawn, not lolling about on a deck chair.*

look after

to take care of (someone), to attend to the needs of (someone): *Their grandmother looks after the children during the school holidays when their parents are at work. Jan's parents are both elderly and she has given up work to look after them.*

look down on

to regard and treat (someone or something) as being inferior or unimportant: *Fred is very rich and looks down on the other householders in the street. Amy's parents cannot afford expensive toys and the other children look down on her.*

look for

to try to find (something), to search for (something): *Jack has mislaid his notebook and is looking for it. The visitors are looking for an inexpensive hotel. Sally is looking for a new car. Mary has lost a glove and she is looking for it.*

look out

to search for and find (something that has been stored away): *I'll look out Jock's address for you — it's in my old address book. Jess promised to look a few things out for the jumble sale.*

look out for

to try to find, obtain, etc (something): *I've been looking out for that book for some time. Jan was so pleased to find a house in that street — she had been looking out for one for some time.*

look over

to examine or inspect (a piece of property) fairly quickly to see if it is satisfactory and suitable: *The estate agent gave us the keys and we looked over the cottage last night. We looked over several properties. I know the house — we looked over it last month.*

look to

to rely on (someone) to provide help: *Nigel looked to his parents to pay for his college fees. Mr and Mrs Walters have four children and they all look to them for financial assistance.*

look up

to look at (a reference book, set of instructions, etc) to try to find some information: *We looked up a* dictionary to find out what the word meant. I'll have to look up the instructions to find out how the machine works.

lump together

to consider (people or things) to be the same as each other and so treat them in the same way: *You can't lump together everyone who stays in that area — many of them are quite respectable. They lump all old people together and decide that they are of no further use to society. These children are at several different stages in their education — it would be wrong to lump them together.*

M

make do with

to have to use (something) instead of something else which is more suitable, desirable etc, to have to use a less acceptable, often inadequate substitute or alternative: *I really need cream for this recipe, but I'll just have to make do with milk. The family had to make do with much less money after their father lost his job.*

make for

to go towards (somewhere): *We're making for the nearest town. We didn't reach the city although we were making for it.*

make off with

to take (something) that does not belong to one, to steal (something) and take it away with one: *The pickpocket made off with Ken's wallet and watch. The meat's not on the kitchen table — I think the dog made off with it.*

make out

to claim or pretend that (something is true): *He made out that he was a millionaire, but, in fact, he had very little money.*

make out

to understand (something that may be difficult to understand: *I can't make out why Rod likes Edith so much — she can be very nasty. The woman was saying something to me in a foreign accent and I couldn't make it out.*

make up for

to compensate for (something), to supply (a reward, substitute, etc) for a disappointment, loss, damage,

etc that has taken place: *You'll have to find a way to make up for damaging Sara's dress. The insurance money did not really make up for the loss of Julie's jewellery — a lot of it had sentimental value. Our children couldn't go on the trip to the seaside, but we made up for it by taking them to the zoo.*

mark down

to reduce the price of (something): *The shopkeeper has marked down a lot of goods to make way for new stock. The car has been marked down for a quick sale. The dress had a slight flaw and so the sales assistant marked it down.*

mark down

to write down (something): *I marked down the topics which I want to discuss at the meeting. Could you mark the number down on this piece of paper? If you give the name of the book, I'll mark it down.*

marvel at

to be very surprised at, sometimes in an admiring way: *We marvelled at Mel's ability to get her own way. Jock's friends marvelled at the way in which he coped with bringing the children up on his own. When you see Tricia's skill with a paintbrush, you can only marvel at it.*

measure up to

to reach the standard of (someone or something), to be as good as (someone or something): *Carol's quite a good tennis player, but she does not measure up to the rest of the team. The team coach sets such a high standard that few players measure up to it.*

meet up with

to meet (someone), often by arrangement, but sometimes by chance: *The plan is to meet up with Ellie and Lucy at the airport. We were introduced to Sally and Mike at Frank's wedding, but we didn't expect to meet up with them again so soon.*

mess up

(informal) to spoil or ruin (something): *Having to resit his exams has messed up Jock's holiday plans. Certainly Freda has done wrong, but she should not let that one misdeed mess the rest of her life up. We had prepared an interesting schedule for the fete, but bad weather messed it up.*

moon around/about

to wander around not doing very much, as if one is dazed, often because one is in love, unhappy, etc: *Julie is mooning about waiting for Jack to ask her out on a date. Mick and Nora have had a quarrel and they're both mooning around, waiting for the other to apologize.*

mount up

to increase: *The tension was mounting up as the time of the tournament final approached. Gail's parents were worried at how the wedding costs were mounting up. The children saved a little each week and were surprised at how this mounted up.*

move off

to start to leave: *The cyclist got on her bike and moved off. The protest march was over and the protesters were starting to move off.*

move on

to tell (someone) to move from a particular place: *The police moved the beggars on. The driver had parked his car at a bus stop and the police moved him on.*

muddle through

to succeed in doing (something), although not very well, despite the fact that one does not know much about it: *Somehow I muddled through the interview test although it was very difficult. I knew very little about the last question in the exam, but I muddled through it.*

muddle up

to cause (things) to be mixed up or in the wrong order, to confuse (things): *Fran muddled up the directions which we were given to get here. Les is so vague that he always muddles things up. Sally took both Jane's and Meg's clothes to the laundrette and now she's muddled them up.*

mug up on

(informal) to study (something) very hard, usually for a short period of time and often in preparation for an exam: *I'm mugging up on economics — the exam's tomorrow. Sam's sure that there will be a question on World War II in the history exam — he's mugging up on it now.*

mull over

to think about (something) carefully and for a long time: *We mulled over the idea of moving house, but eventually decided to build an extension to this one. The committee members all mulled the problem over, but failed to suggest a solution. The firm's offer of work was a generous one, but, after mulling it over, Henry rejected it.*

muscle in on

to force one's way into (something) when one has not been invited and is not wanted: *Ron tried to muscle in on our annual picnic, but he is not a member of the club. This is a private family party and your friends are not going to muscle in on it.*

muster up

to gather (courage, energy, etc): *I cannot muster up any enthusiasm for the project. The general expected all his soldiers to muster up the courage to fight the strong enemy army.*

N

narrow down

to reduce (the number of choices or possibilities), to consider a small number of choices from a much larger selection: *There is a competition for the best dog in the show and the judges have narrowed the candidates down to six dogs. The firm received many applications for the post, but they have narrowed them down to four.*

nose out

(informal) to find (something) by searching: *The journalist soon nosed out the scandal involving the politician. It took us a long time but we nosed all the facts out eventually. If there are bargain goods to be had, Harry will nose them out.*

note down

to write (something) down, sometimes informally: *I'll just note down your address and post the information to you. If you note the details down, the manager will deal with your complaint. Bess noted down Charlie's address on a piece of paper, but she can't find it.*

O

occur to

suddenly to think of something or to realize something: *It occurred to Fred that the car's engine was making an odd noise. Did it not occur to you that Jack might be lying?*

open up

to cause (an opportunity, etc) to be available: *The course which Donald is taking could open up several career possibilities. The expanding computer market has opened up several marketing opportunities for the firm.*

open up

to unlock the door to a building so that people can get in: *Mark rarely opens up the office before 9.15 although he should open at 9 o'clock. Mario doesn't open his restaurant up until the evening. There was a queue outside the shop and so we opened it up early.*

operate on

to perform surgery (on someone or something): *The surgeon is going to operate on the patient this afternoon. The athlete's leg is badly injured and the surgeon is going to operate on it right away.*

opposed to

to be against (something), to disapprove of or disagree with (something): *Many of the townspeople were opposed to the closing of the local school. The proposal seemed an interesting one, but most of the committee were opposed to it.*

opt out of

to decide no longer to be involved with (something): *Will opted out of further education and got a job in the family business when he left school. Jessie was near the end of a nursing course when she suddenly opted out of it. Stella has opted out of going to Tim's party because she is feeling tired. Julia has organized a trip to the theatre, but Harry has opted out of it.*

P

pad out

to add (information, etc) to (a piece of writing, etc) just to make it longer without making it any more relevant, informative, useful, etc: *The makers of this machine have padded the instructions out with a great deal of unnecessary detail. If you pad out your essay with a lot of irrelevant material, you will get a low mark for it. This guidebook about the city is very poor — the author has padded it out with a lot of silly anecdotes.*

pair off

to arrange (a group of people) so that each joins another to make a pair or couple, sometimes with the intention of encouraging romance: *The dance teacher paired off the children according to their ability. At the party George paired his daughter off with the son of a rich farmer. The children gathered in the playground and the teacher paired them off for the walk to the bus.*

palm off with

to deceive or persuade (someone) into accepting (something which is inferior to what he/she should have got): *The family should have got thousands of pounds in compensation for the accident to their son, but they were palmed off with a few hundreds. The couple went to Barbados on holiday but palmed their children off with a holiday in a local seaside resort. Terry promised Celia a diamond ring, but palmed her off with a cheap imitation one.*

parcel out

to divide (something) out among the members of a group: *The land was parcelled out among the four sons of the family. There were ten members of the committee and we parcelled out the various duties among us.*

pare down

to reduce the size or extent of (something): *Father said that we had to try to pare down the cost of the heating bills. The holy men pared their possessions down to the bare minimum. Trudy has a massive collection of clothes and she's trying to pare it down.*

part with

to give or hand over (money or something of value) to someone else: *Reg is very rich because he rarely parts with any money. The book is of great sentimental value to Pam and she cannot bear to part with it.*

partition off

to separate part (of something) from the rest by means of a partition: *Marie partitioned off part of her living-room to use as study. The dining-room is really part of the kitchen, but they have partitioned it off.*

pass on

to give to or tell (someone) something which was given or told to you: *My mother passed on a few cooking tips to my sister. Beth was chosen to pass the bad news on to the others. That was good advice and I passed it on to my friends.*

pass over

to ignore or reject (someone): *The boss passed June over again and promoted her assistant. Jill applied for a job in another department, but she was passed over and was not even given an interview. Jack said that he wished to be considered for the post of deputy manager but the directors passed him over.*

pass up

not to take advantage of (something, such as an opportunity): *Paula felt that she could not pass up the chance to see her favourite pop group. I cannot believe that Roe passed such an opportunity up. Paddy was offered the opportunity to work overseas, but he decided to pass it up.*

patch up

to mend (something) roughly and perhaps temporarily: *The roofer patched the roof up to keep the rain out, but it needs to be completely re-covered. Jeff wonders if you can patch up this old garden shed for him. Bits of the kitchen wallpaper are torn — I'm going to try to patch it up.*

pay for

to give (money) for (something): *Joan's parents are paying for the holiday. Rachel would love that coat, but she would never be able to pay for it.*

pay off

to pay all the money that is owing with regard to a bill, loan, etc so that one is no longer in debt: *Robert's monthly instalments are so low that it will be years before he pays off his car loan. I took out a loan to buy a boat, but I paid it off last year.*

peel off

to remove (something) by pulling: *Joe peeled off his wet sweater. Sara's hat was covered in snow and she peeled it off.*

pencil in

to write (something) down in pencil, rather than in ink, because it may have to be changed, to write (something) down, knowing that it may have to be changed: *I'll pencil the appointment in for next Thursday and you can confirm or change it by phone. The committee secretary pencilled in a tentative date for the next meeting.*

We can easily change the date of the lunch, but I've pencilled it in for now.

pick on

to treat (someone) badly and unjustly, often doing so repeatedly: *The teacher started picking on Jean as soon as she joined the class. Jack is smaller than the other boys and they pick on him in the playground.*

pick out

to choose (someone or something): *May picked out a car she liked and took it for a test drive. The captains had to pick eleven people out to be members of their teams. We bought three skirts — Jane had picked them out.*

pick up

(of a car-driver, etc) to let a passenger into a vehicle in order to take him/her somewhere: *Alice is going to pick Laura up and take her to work. You could pick up Frances on your way home. The driver saw the hitchhiker, but did not pick him up. The bus will stop at the college gates to pick up all the students. I have to drive over to the next village to pick a friend up. Dad says that he'll pick us up outside the cinema.*

pile in/into

(of a group) to get into (a vehicle, room, etc) all together in an informal or disorganized way: *The students all piled into the hall to hear the concert. The children piled onto the train on their trip to the seaside. The bus is waiting — pile in!*

pin down

to make (someone) give a definite answer or opinion: *I tried to pin Fred down, but all he will say is that he will be here some time next week. The shop-owner spoke vaguely about offering me some work some time, but I couldn't pin him down about an exact date.*

pin up

to fix (a notice, poster etc) to a wall, notice-board, etc: *The teenagers pinned up posters of their favourite film stars on their bedroom walls. Could you pin this notice up on the shop wall? — it's advertising a charity jumble sale. Sean wrote out an ad for a flat and then pinned it up on the college notice-board.*

pit against

to put (someone or something) in competition with (someone else or something else): *In the tournament we were pitted against last year's champions. They pitted their superior skills against ours and won the quiz easily.*

plan on

to intend to (do something): *We're planning on taking an early holiday. John may end up taking early retirement, but he's not planning on it.*

play along

to pretend to accept or believe in (something): *We think that Alan's plan is useless, but we're playing along with it because we don't want to upset him. The boss has some strange ideas about sales techniques, and Mike plays along with these to flatter her.*

play down

to try to make (something) seem unimportant or less important, to minimize: *The police were trying to play down the danger in order to keep the crowd calm.*

play off against

to cause (people) to compete with (each other) or to argue with (each other) so that one gains some kind of advantage for oneself: *Tom played the two prospective buyers off against each other and got a very good price for his house. The children approached their parents separately about the possibility of getting a dog and tried to play one off against the other.*

plough into

(informal) to spend (a lot of money) on something, sometimes unprofitably: *The government is refusing to plough any more public money into the industry. The business failed despite the fact that all the partners ploughed huge sums of money into it.*

plump for

to choose (someone or something): *Pam and Beth were discussing holiday destinations and Pam plumped for Italy. You shouldn't criticize the party venue — you were the one who plumped for it.*

ply with

to keep giving (someone) supplies of (something): *They were generous hosts and plied their guests with excellent wine all evening.*

pop into

(informal) to visit (somewhere) briefly: *I'll just pop into the post office for some stamps. Olive popped into her friend's house for coffee.*

pounce on

to jump on (someone or something), to move towards and attack or grab (someone or something): *The cat pounced on the mouse. The school bully pounced on the younger child at the bus stop.*

pour out

to cause (something) to flow from a container, usually into another container, such as a cup or glass: *Would you please pour out some milk for the children? I'll pour the tea out later. The wine is over there — please pour it out.*

press ahead with

to continue (with something) in a determined way, despite difficulty, opposition, etc: *The protesters could not believe that the council were pressing ahead with the demolition of the old building. The project will be expensive, but we have decided to press ahead with it.*

prevail on

to persuade (someone) to do something although he/she may be reluctant: *We eventually prevailed on Toby to lend us his car. Ruby is very mean — I'm sure that you will not prevail on her to make a contribution to the charity.*

protect from

to try to (prevent someone or something) from harming or affecting (someone or something): *The hut protected the travellers from the wind and rain. The dog tried to protect his master from the attacker. There was danger out there and we were powerless to protect ourselves from it.*

pull in

to attract (people) to (an event, etc), often in large numbers: *If you don't advertise the concert, you won't pull in enough people to make a profit. The advertising posters certainly pulled the crowds in. There were crowds of people at the meeting and it was definitely the advertising campaign that had pulled them in.*

pull out of

not to continue with (something), to stop taking part in (something): *Our team has had to pull out of the football competition because of illness. There are not* many competitors in the race — several people pulled out of it at the last minute.

push around

to treat (someone) roughly and rudely and tell (him/her) what to do: *Stella is very ambitious and pushes the other workers around to get what she wants. Tom's elder brothers pushed him around when they were children.*

push for

to try very hard to achieve (something), for example by persuading others of its importance: *The parents are pushing for a new school and have contacted the local councillors and MP.*

push into

to force (someone) into (doing something): *The drama teacher pushed Celia into playing Ophelia in the college production of Hamlet although she was quite unsuitable. Val's father pushed her into studying medicine.*

push over

to push (someone or something) so that he/she/it falls to the ground: *Jack pushed the chair over when he was dancing. The boy did not even stop when he pushed over the old lady. The vase is broken — the dog pushed it over with his tail.*

put away

to put (something) tidily in its proper place, sometimes where it cannot be seen: *Their mother told the children to put their toys away in the cupboard before going to bed. The cookery books were lying on the kitchen table but I put them away on the shelf. I've put the Christmas tree away till next year. Could you put away the clean dishes, please? Pat lifted the box and put it away in the attic.*

put back

to put (something) back where it was before it was moved, to replace (something): *I wish that you would put books back on the shelves and not leave them lying on the floor. Tom was able to put back the money which he had borrowed from the till. Stella took all her dresses out of the wardrobe and put them back again.*

put behind one

to try to forget about (something) and not let it affect one any more: *Sara hopes to put her unhappy divorce behind her and make a new life for herself. Jake was involved in petty crime when he was young, but fortunately he has put it behind him now*

put down as

to regard (someone or something) as being of a particular type or kind although this is often not true: *Sheila had put Rod down as a respectable citizen, but she soon discovered that she had been quite wrong. Ron had put her down as a stupid person, but Sara was the brightest student in the class.*

put down to

to regard (something) as being caused by (something), to believe that (something) is a result of (something): *It is difficult to put the two burglaries down to coincidence. Jeff keeps getting headaches and his doctor puts them down to stress.*

put in

to put (something) in place, to install (something): *Our neighbours have put in a new central heating system. Beth's had a fitted kitchen put in. We've put an open fireplace in. That's a lovely window — when did you put it in?*

put in for

to apply for or ask to be considered for (a job, grant, etc): *Walter put in for the job of supervisor. There is a college bursary for overseas study and Sylvia has put in for it. Jim has put in for a job in a different department. Several jobs were advertised and hundreds of applicants put in for them.*

put off

to delay or postpone (something): *Because of illness we have decided to put off the meeting until next week. The club has put the match off until the end of the season. Jill hates cleaning the house and so she puts it off as long as possible.*

put on

to place (a piece of clothing) over part of the body and wear it: *It was cold and we all put on warm clothes. Since it was a lovely day, Pam put her best summer dress on. Rona carried a jacket, but did not put it on.*

put over

to place (something) so that it covers (something else): *Meg put a raincoat over her dress. She placed a hand over his.*

put through

to pay the expenses of (someone) who is studying, training etc: *Her parents put Sara through drama college although they wanted her to go to university. Jock is working part-time in a factory to put himself through college.*

put to

to present (something) to (someone), to bring (something) to (someone's attention) for his/her consideration: *Let us put the matter of truancy to the headmaster. The union put the workers' demands to management. This department does not deal with complaints — you will have to put them to the Customer Service Department.*

put together

to assemble (something), to join together (the parts of something) in order to produce it: *The doll's house was sold in a flat pack and Lucy's father and mother had to put the parts together. Colin bought a model aeroplane kit for his son, but could not put it together.*

put up

to assemble (the parts of something), to build (something), to erect (something): *They're putting up a new block of flats near our house. They put the new supermarket up in record time. The builders have finished the house — they put it up very quickly.*

put up

to provide (money) to pay for something: *The townspeople put up the money to build a war memorial. An anonymous benefactor put up half the cost of the new church. We collected quite a lot of money ourselves for the scheme, and the local council put up the rest.*

put up

to provide (someone) accommodation, usually temporarily and in one's home: *They put the homeless family up in a hotel. We can put up only one person. We can put you up for the night if you miss the last train.*

put up with

to tolerate (someone or something), to have to accept (someone or something) unpleasant or difficult: *The Millers can't put up with their noisy neighbours any longer and so they're moving house. Patsy hates the canteen food, but she has to put up with it because it's cheap.*

puzzle out

to think hard (about a problem) in order to find a solution: *We finally puzzled out why Vera was behaving in that weird way. Finding our way there will not be easy, but we're sure that Rick will puzzle it out.*

Q

quieten down

to make (someone) less noisy: *The police tried to quieten down the gang of youths. Her parents are trying to quieten the child down — she was over-excited. The children at the party were shouting and it was impossible to quieten them down.*

R

rake in

(informal) to make or earn a lot of (money) easily: *The company has been raking in excessive profits for years. The family have a lot of money — during the war they owned a munitions factory, which raked it in.*

ram into

to hit (something) very hard, often at great speed or with great force: *The van behind us was going too fast and rammed into our car as we slowed down. Leo lost his temper and rammed his fist into Dick's face. The gate closed as the lorry approached and it rammed into it.*

range against

to be opposed to (another person, side, etc): *We met several groups of protesters who were ranged against the government with regard to its economic policies. The council will find that many of the townspeople are ranged against them because of their decision.*

rank among

to have a place (in a particular group): *Fred's father ranks among the richest men in Britain. The inhabitants rank among the poorest people in the world.*

ration out

to give only small amounts of (something) to the members of a group of people because one does not have much of it: *Jane rationed out the children's weekly allowance so that they did not eat the sweets all at once. The hikers had not taken much drinking water with them and had to ration it out.*

rattle off

(*informal*) to say (something) very rapidly and without effort: *Peggy asked Jim if he knew of any plumbers in the area, and he rattled off a list of names. The tour guide rattled off a list of all the famous buildings in the city. The pupil knows the dates of all the battles — she rattled them off in a few minutes.*

read out

to say the words aloud as you read (something): *Could you read out the entry in the guidebook? The student read his whole essay out to the class. Jack received a letter from Freda and read it out.*

read through

to read the whole of (something): *The lecturer said that she had read through all the essays. The director read the report through and frowned. I gave Jo the letter and he read it through right away.*

reason with

to try to persuade (someone) to act in what one believes to be a sensible, reasonable way: *There's no point in trying to reason with Simon — he's made up his mind and he's very stubborn. Anne behaved far too hastily although we tried to reason with her.*

remark on

to say or write something about (something) which shows that you have noticed it for some reason, to comment on (something): *The teacher remarked on the high standard of the students' work. The skill of the player was so great that all the spectators remarked on it.*

rent out

to allow the use (of something) in return for money: *The farmer rents out one of his fields to the pony club. Phil has decided not to rent his flat out again. Rose inherited a cottage from her grandmother and now rents it out.*

resort to

to decide on or choose (some form of action) because all others have failed or are unsuitable, unavailable, etc: *The young men had to resort to sleeping on the streets when they had no money for rent. Murder is a serious crime and the young man did not have to resort to it.*

rest with

to be the responsibility of (someone or something): *The final decision rests with the planning committee. You must ask the head teacher about hiring the school hall — the decision rests with her.*

revert to

to return to a previous state or condition, often one that is thought less desirable in some way, to begin to use (something) again which one had used before, but stopped using: *Our central heating system's broken down and so we've had to revert to electric fires. For a while Jill seemed happy, but now she's reverted to her gloomy old self. Bob used to be a drug addict and I'd hate to think he would revert to that.*

revolve around/round

to be mainly concerned with (someone or something), to concentrate on (someone or something): *All their interests revolve round sport. The young couple's life revolves round their baby. The residents were worried about vandalism and their whole discussion revolved around it.*

ring round

to telephone (several people) in order to ask about or discuss something: *I'll ring round all my friends and ask them to help in the search for the dog. Here's a list of people who are interested — I've already rung round a few of them.*

ring up

to telephone (someone): *Jim rang up Lily to apologize. We've rung a few people up to get their opinions. Sara will know the answer — I'll ring her up right now.*

rinse out/off

to remove (something) by rinsing it with water: *I'm rinsing out the shampoo from my hair. Netta put a mudpack on her face and she's rinsing it off.*

root about/around

(*informal*) to search among (things), moving them around because one is looking for something, to rummage around: *Pat was rooting around the stuff in the attic when she found a valuable china vase. The dog is rooting about in the rubbish, looking for his bone.*

rough out

to draw or describe (something such as a plan or idea) roughly, and without much detail: *The architect has roughed out the plans for our new house. At the meeting a few people roughed out some ideas for raising money for repairs to the village hall.*

round up

to gather together (a group of people or animals): *Let's try to round up a group of volunteers to paint the village hall. We watched the dogs round the sheep up. Many prisoners have escaped and the prison authorities are trying to round them up.*

rub into/in

to apply something to (something) by rubbing: *The cleaner rubbed the polish into the chair. Put some of the cream on your cheeks and rub it in.*

rule out

not to consider (something) because it is regarded as being impossible or extremely unlikely: *The police have ruled out robbery as a motive for the murder. Suicide has been ruled out as a cause of death. The fire may have been a result of arson — the fire inspector has not ruled it out.*

run into

to meet (someone) unexpectedly: *The other day I ran into an old friend from my schooldays. We ran into each other when we were shopping.*

run over

(*of a vehicle or of the driver of a vehicle*) to knock down and possibly drive over (someone or something), often causing injury or damage: *We nearly ran over a cat as we drove off. The dog dashed out onto the road and a car ran it over. Watch you don't get run over as you cross the road!*

run up

to begin to be liable for, or to accumulate (debt, expenses, a bill, etc): *Tony has run up a huge credit card bill. You should not expect your parents to pay off these bills when it was you who ran them up.*

S

sail through

to pass or succeed at (something) very easily, to deal with (a situation) easily and successfully: *Dave sailed through his driving test at his first attempt. Polly just sails through life — she never seems to have any problems. Teresa was dreading her music exam, but she sailed through it.*

save up

to keep and collect (money) instead of spending it, often so that it can be spent later on something particular: *The children are saving up their pocket money to buy a present for their mother. We all save up a part of our salary each month. Don't spend your extra money — save it up!*

savour of

to suggest or seem like (something, usually something unpleasant): *Carl's actions savour of revenge. Marge's attitude towards her neighbours savours of envy.*

scare off

to make (someone or something) afraid so that he/she/it avoids one or runs off: *The farmer scared off the birds to protect his crops. Lara is so beautiful and elegant that she scares a lot of men off. A burglar tried to get into the house, but we scared him off.*

scout around

to look in several places for (something which one wants): *When we arrived in the town we scouted around for somewhere cheap to eat. They eventually found their ideal house but they had to scout around for it.*

scrape off

to remove (something) from (something) by rubbing it with something sharp, such as a knife: *We scraped the dried mud off the carpet. The cooker in the flat was filthy and the tenants had to scrape a lot of grease off it. There was dog dirt on the floor and we asked its owner to scrape it off.*

scrape through

to only just avoid failing or being unsuccessful at something), to pass (an exam, etc) with a very low mark: *Mark will have to study harder — he just scraped through last year's exams. Jenny thought that she had failed her driving test, but found that she had just scraped through it.*

scrape together

to get together or obtain with great difficulty (the amount or number which one needs): *Roy eventually scraped together a deposit on a flat. Can we scrape enough people together to hire a minivan? The monthly rent is high, but we usually manage to scrape it together.*

screw up

to twist and roll up (a piece of paper, etc): *Josh screwed the note up and threw it in the wastepaper basket. Did you screw up that piece of paper which was lying on my desk? Helen's phone number is on that piece of paper — don't screw it up.*

scrub off

to remove (something) from (something) by rubbing hard with a cloth or brush: *Joe scrubbed the wine marks off the carpet. Molly eventually managed to scrub the dirt off the kitchen floor. There is dried blood on the floor — someone will have to scrub it off.*

search for

to try to find (someone or something), to look for (someone or something): *The police are out searching for the missing child. We must start searching for somewhere to stay the night. I mislaid my notebook and spent hours searching for it.*

see over

to look at the various parts of (a house, etc): *We have seen over several houses, but didn't put an offer in for any of them. There is a flat to let in this street and I'm just going to see over it.*

see to

to go (somewhere) with (someone) to make sure that he/she gets there safely, to escort (someone) to (somewhere): *Elsie's escort saw her to the door of her flat. Bill didn't go in the taxi with is mother, but he saw her to it.*

seize on

to accept or grasp (something) enthusiastically: *Tim was desperate for volunteers for his project and he seized on Polly's offer of help. When Bob was offered a job overseas, he seized on the opportunity. It was an idea that would bring the company profit and they seized on it.*

send down

officially to ask (a student) to leave university because of bad behaviour: *Robert was sent down from his university for stealing money from other students. Anne's parents were very upset when she was sent down for attacking another student.*

send for

to ask (someone) to come, often in order to give some form of help: *Dad's ill — send for the doctor! There was nothing the police could do, but Bert still sent for them.*

send off

to tell (someone) to leave (a football pitch, etc) as a punishment: *The referee sent off three players in the first half of the match. It was difficult to see why the referee had sent so many players off.*

separate up

to separate (a group or quantity) into smaller groups or quantities: *This is a large class and we are going to separate the pupils up into groups of six. This is too large a group — we are going to have to separate it up.*

set aside

to ignore (something), to pay no attention to (something): *There's no point in complaining about the food — the restaurant management just sets any complaints aside. Try to set aside your worries — I'm sure the children will be quite safe. Many people raised objections to the scheme, but the council set these aside.*

set down

to record officially, to establish (a law, regulation, etc): *The school rules are set down by the head teacher and the school governors. They have broken the laws, which were set down to prevent cruelty to children.*

set off

to begin a journey: *The family had to set off at dawn to get to the airport in time for their flight.*

set up

to arrange (something), to fix up (something): *We have set up a committee of enquiry. When did you set the meeting up? An investigation is in progress, but we don't know who set it up.*

settle for

to accept (something) although it is not quite what you wanted. *I wanted to go to Europe, but I'll settle for a holiday anywhere.*

settle on

to decide on (something), to choose (something), after thinking about it or discussing it: *We settled on bright yellow curtains for the kitchen. We asked the baby's name, but the parents have not settled on one yet.*

shake off

to get rid of (something, such as a habit, reputation, etc): *I'm trying shake off the effects of a bad cold. Tom still smokes and says that he simply cannot shake the habit off. As a youth Mick got a reputation as the local bad boy, and he has never shaken it off.*

shell out

(informal) to pay (money) for something: *Tony's parents shelled out a great deal of money on his education, but he dropped out of college. The government has been asked to shell even more money out on the project. Paula is organizing a huge party and expecting her parents to shell out for it.*

shop around

to compare prices, quality, etc of something in various shops before purchasing (something): *If you shop around for a child's bike you'll find one much cheaper than that. We got a real bargain when we bought our new computer, but we had spent a lot of time shopping around for it.*

show around/round

to go to (somewhere) with someone in order to show him/her the main features of the place: *Bob showed his parents around the university. If you like I can show you round the town this aft...*

show up

to make (oneself or someone) feel embarrassed or humiliated by one's bad behaviour, mistakes, etc: *The child started screaming in the supermarket and really showed her mother up. Maggie should never have entered the dance tournament — she danced very badly and showed herself up.*

shut down

to close (a business, etc) completely so that it no longer operates: *The old man had to shut down his business when he became ill. The firm has decided to shut all their country branches down. The firm was losing money and the owners had to shut it down.*

side with

to have the same opinions as (someone), to support (someone) in an argument: *Victor said that he sided with Dave and thought that the rent for the flat was too high. I disagreed with Clara, but most people seemed to side with her.*

sift through

to examine (something) carefully and thoroughly, often because one is looking for something: *We sifted through all the replies to the job advertisement, but we did not find our ideal applicant. It will take Lorna a long time to sift through those historical documents for her research.*

single out

to treat (someone or something) differently from the others in a group, to select (someone or something) for special treatment: *Jackie was singled out as the most promising new team member. Sam was no more naughty than the other children in the class, but the teacher singled him out and punished him more.*

sketch out

to describe (something) roughly and without details: *Mother sketched out her plans for the party. Emma wanted an exercise programme, and her coach sketched one out for her.*

skimp on

to use less of (something) than is needed or desirable to make something satisfactory: *People complained that the caterers skimped on the wine for the reception. You will need a lot of material for that ball gown — you mustn't skimp on it.*

subject to

to cause (someone) to experience or undergo (something unpleasant or difficult): *The terrorists subjected their hostages to terrible torture. The police subjected the suspect to intense questioning.*

summon up

to try to get together enough (of something, such as strength, energy, etc) to do something: *I just cannot summon up enough enthusiasm to go swimming. Pete was so tired that he could scarcely summon up the strength to go home.*

swallow up

to use all of a supply of (money, resources, etc): *Phoning home from the payphone has swallowed up all my small change. Eating in expensive restaurants will soon swallow your allowance up. The student has a small grant but university textbooks swallow that up easily.*

swear by

to regard (something) as being very effective, reliable, etc: *Mum swears by this recipe for chocolate cake. This is a herbal remedy for headaches — June swears by it.*

sweep up

to remove (something) by sweeping with a broom or brush: *Anne dropped a cup and had to sweep up the pieces. The gardener was sweeping the leaves up from the lawn. There were crumbs all over the floor and the children were asked to sweep them up.*

switch off

to stop (an electrical device, etc) from working by pressing a switch: *Myra switched off the television when the programme finished. You can switch the engine off now. That radio's too loud — please switch it off!*

switch over

to change (from one person or thing) to another: *The factory used to use those machines, but we have these now — we switched over last year. There are two drivers on the coach — they switch over every four hours.*

swot up on

to study or read up as much as one can about (a subject), often for a test or exam: *I can't go out tonight because I'm swotting up on grammar for tomorrow's test.*

T

tag along

to accompany or go along with (someone) although one has not been invited and one may be unwanted: *Ellen is annoyed because Jack's young sister tags along whenever they go out on a date. If you're all going to the cinema, do you mind if I tag along?*

tail back

(of traffic, vehicles, etc) to form a long, very slow-moving or stationary queue, usually because of roadworks, an accident or a broken-down vehicle: *They are building a new roundabout, which means that traffic tails back during the rush hour. A lorry has overturned on the motorway and the traffic is tailing back for miles.*

take after

to resemble (someone) as regards appearance, character, etc: *Jill takes after her father in being a brilliant pianist. Willie is a lazy fellow and his son takes after him.*

take along to

to get (someone) to accompany you to (something or somewhere): *George went to the football match and took along two of his friends to it. I can take a guest to the reception and so I'm taking my daughter along to it. Meg is visiting me and so I'm taking her along to my dance class.*

take aside

to separate (someone) from other people because one wants to have a private conversation with him/her: *The lecturer took Paula aside and told her the news of her father's accident. The pupil was obviously upset and the teacher took him aside to find out what was wrong.*

take in

to understand and remember (something that is read, heard, etc): *I was too tired to take the information in properly. The pupils were restless and didn't take in what the teacher said. The lecturer gave an excellent description of the Middle Ages but few of the students took it in.*

take off

to remove (a piece of clothing) which one has been wearing: *Bill took off his wet clothes and put them on a* radiator to dry. The child was told to take all his dirty clothes off and have a bath. Janet's sweater was filthy and so she took it off and washed it.

take off

to remove (something) from (something) from where it was: *Meg took the wrapping off the meat. There were two pieces of wrapping paper round the present and we took off the outer one. There's a brown paper cover on the book — could you take it off, please?*

take on

to begin to compete against (someone or something): *Next week our team takes on the team which won the league last year. The firm, although small, is prepared to take the market leaders on. I would not take Toby on at chess — he's a brilliant player.*

take on

to begin to employ (someone): *The business is expanding and we have taken on new staff. The firm takes fewer people on in the winter months. We can't take you on just now as we have no vacancies.*

take out

to ask (someone) to accompany one to (something or somewhere), often paying for any expenses: *Ron took Judy out for a meal, but she insisted on paying her share. Matt took Pam out to the cinema. Paul likes Amy and we encouraged him to take her out.*

take out of

to make (someone) feel tired or weak: *Working such long hours has taken a great deal out of Tom. Anne needs a holiday — studying for exams has taken a lot out of her.*

take over

to gain control of (a company) by buying a majority of its shares: *Old Mr Massie does not want his family firm to be taken over, but his son wants to sell it. It was a multinational company that took over the local computer firm.*

take over

to take charge of (something), to become responsible for (something): *Ms Jones has taken over the running of the senior school. Mike's daughter will take over his role in the firm when he retires. Fred was in charge of the team, but Bert took it over when Fred retired.*

take up

to begin to be interested in or involved in (something), to start doing (something): *Fred was encouraged to take up a new hobby. Had you thought of taking teaching up as a career? Stella plays golf and Jo has decided to take it up. Jenny has decided to take up nursing as a career. In order to be good at ballet you really have to take it up when you are very young.*

take up on

to accept (someone's) offer, suggestion: *We decided to take George up on his offer to lend us his holiday cottage. I'll take you up on your offer of a cup of tea. You should take Malcolm up on his offer to pay for the damage. Paula suggested that she lend Bert some money, but he declined to take her up on it.*

talk into

to persuade (someone) to do something: *Harry talked his friends into joining him. We didn't want to go swimming, but Lucy talked us into it.*

talk over with

to discuss (something) with (someone): *We had a meeting to talk over our various experiences. The students were advised to talk their problems over with their teachers. We all have different ideas about the new sports centre — let's meet and talk them over.*

talk round

to persuade (someone): *It's easy to talk my mother round — she's now agreed to lend us the car. Jane's father said at first that she couldn't go on the college trip, but she eventually talked him round.*

taper off

gradually to become smaller in size, amount or quantity: *The number of tourists begins to taper off in late autumn. The side effects of the drug will start to taper off after a few days.*

tear up

to pull (something) into many small pieces: *Angrily Maggie tore the letter up and threw the pieces in the bin. We tore up old sheets to make dusters. None of the rest of us saw the boss's memo — Bill tore it up in a fit of temper.*

tell apart

to identify (which is which of two people or things that look alike) by recognizing the differences between them, to distinguish (someone from someone or something similar): *Few people other than their mother can tell the twin brothers apart. The painting and the copy are so similar that only experts can tell them apart.*

tell on

(*informal*) to report (someone) to someone in authority or in charge for having done something wrong: *The children next door saw Jerry break the window and told on him. Tina told the teacher on Pam when she tore her painting.*

tell on

to have a bad effect on (someone or something): *The long journey was beginning to tell on the old lady, and she looked exhausted. Sue wasn't sleeping properly and this began to tell on her work. Frank has been doing a great deal of overtime and it is beginning to tell on him — he looks ill.*

tend towards

to show more of (a certain quality, etc) than others: *Jan is very generous, but Tom tends towards meanness. I wouldn't actually accuse Derek of sexism, but he is tending towards it.*

think over

to think about (something) carefully before deciding: *Polly needs time to think things over before she decides about the job offer. I'm thinking over one or two ideas. That's the problem — please think it over.*

thrash out

to discuss (something) in detail to try to come to a decision or conclusion: *We have to thrash out the objections to the plans before we can proceed with the building. Government ministers are trying to thrash a new economic policy out.*

threw up

(*informal*) to vomit, to be sick: *The child got car sick and threw up all over the coats in the back seat.*

throw on

to put on (clothes) hurriedly and carelessly: *When she realized that she had overslept, Sue threw on jeans and a sweater and ran to catch the bus. It was cold and Jean threw a warm sweater over her summer dress. Look at his clothes — he must have thrown them on.*

throw up

(*informal*) to be sick, to vomit: *Bill drank too much wine and threw up all over Diana's new carpet. The food was so horrible that it made me want to throw up.*

thumb through

to turn over the pages (of a book, etc) and glance at them briefly: *I thumbed through the catalogue to see what the clothes were like. This book looks as though many people have thumbed through it.*

tick off

to put (a tick or other mark) beside an item in a list to indicate that the item has been dealt with: *Could you tick off the people who have accepted the invitation? I've made a list of the clothes which I'll need on holiday, and I'm ticking them off as I pack them.*

tidy up

to make (something) neat or neater: *I tidied up this room this morning, but it's in a mess again. Tidy up your desk before you go home. The garden had been neglected, but we tidied it up.*

tie back

to fasten (something such as hair) with a ribbon, string, etc so that it stays in place and does not get in one's way: *If you want to be a waitress, you'll have to tie your hair back. Amy looks pretty when she ties back her long hair. Jo's hair was getting in her eyes and she tied it back.*

tie down

to restrict (someone's) freedom: *Bill wants to marry Becky, but she feels that she is too young to tie herself down. Roger's mother is afraid that Lucy is trying to tie Roger down before he finishes his degree. Meg has postponed having children because she thinks that they would tie her down.*

tighten up

to make (something) tighter or stricter: *They've tightened up the school rules with regard to truancy. It is vital to tighten the security system up. The laws against speeding were rather vague, but they've tightened them up now.*

tinker with

to work at (something such as an engine), sometimes in an unskilled way, to try to make minor repairs or improvements to it: *Colin is an accountant, but he loves tinkering with motorbikes as a hobby. Henry offered to fix my car, but I'm not letting him tinker with it — he ruined the engine of his father's car.*

tire of

to become bored with or weary of (someone or something): *The children soon tired of their new toys and went back to their old favourites. I like sitting on the beach for a little while, but I soon tire of it.*

tow away

to move (a vehicle) by attaching it by a rope, etc to another vehicle and pulling it along: *The car had engine trouble and had to be towed away. Did the police tow away the car because they thought that it had been abandoned? The van broke down on the motorway and we had to get someone to tow it away.*

toy with

to consider (something) but not in a very serious way: *The Smiths are toying with the idea of buying a smaller house, but they haven't started looking for one yet.*

track down

to find (someone or something) after a long or difficult search: *Mel has just tracked down her father who left home when she was a baby. It took the police several years to track the murderer down. There are very few first editions of the book, but we eventually tracked one down.*

trade in

to give (something, such as a car) to a dealer etc in part exchange for a new model so that one gets this at a reduced price: *Bert traded in his old motorbike for a much more powerful one. I wonder if I can trade my computer in for a more modern version. Jill doesn't have her sports car any more — she traded it in for a family saloon.*

trap into

to trick or mislead (someone) into doing something: *His mother said that Alice had trapped Will into marrying her by pretending to be pregnant. Jill said that the police had trapped her into confessing to a crime which she did not commit.*

trigger off

to start (something), to cause (something): *The President's announcement triggered off a major rebellion in the country. The child's had an asthma attack, but we don't know what triggered it off.*

trip over

to knock one's foot against something and stumble and perhaps fall to the ground: *Watch that you don't trip over — those paving stones are loose. I tripped over a shopping bag in the shop doorway. There was brick lying in the path and the old man tripped over it.*

troop into

to go into (somewhere) in a large group: *We all trooped into the assembly hall to hear the results of our exams. The dance hall was ready, and all the students trooped into it.*

trot out

to put forward (the same excuse, argument, etc) repeatedly and without thinking about it: *The politician has nothing new to say — he just trots out the same old policies. We've heard Bert's ideas on economics many times, but that does not stop him trotting them out.*

trust to

to place one's hopes on (someone or something), to rely on (someone or something): *We shall have to trust to Polly's good judgement and hope that she makes the right decision. There is nothing else the team can do but trust to their superior strength.*

try on

to put on (an article of clothing) to see if it fits or is suitable: *Stella tried on three dresses, but didn't like any of them. Mark tried several pairs of trousers on. That's a lovely jacket — I'd like to try it on.*

try out

to test (something) by using it in order to see if it is suitable, reliable, etc: *I'm going to try out a new recipe. The firm is trying a new system out. If you're interested in the exercise bike you should try it out. The school is trying new truancy regulations out this term. Tim didn't like the motorbike when he tried it out.*

tuck into

(informal) to eat (something) with pleasure and enthusiasm: *The diners were tucking into juicy steaks. The children had never seen such food and they tucked into it right away.*

tune up

to adjust (a car engine, etc) so that it runs more efficiently or faster: *This car is going so much better since the mechanic tuned the engine up. You should get Mike to tune up your boat engine — it sounds a bit rough. Bill's sports car has been going a lot faster since he tuned it up.*

turf out

(informal) to throw (someone) out, to force (someone) to leave: *The barman turfed Craig out after he caused a fight. Ron is employed to turf out troublemakers from the club. Don't let the drunk annoy the customers — turf him out!*

turn down

to refuse, to say no to (someone or something): *We were surprised that the firm turned Sally down for the publicity job. The club has already turned down several applications for membership. Paul asked Sara to marry him, but she turned him down.*

turn into

to become (someone or something different): *It was a sunny morning but it turned into a stormy day. Nick was a charming child, but he turned into a really nasty young man.*

turn out

to empty (something, such as a room or cupboard): *We turned out the cupboard under the stairs and found lots of old bottles. It will be easier if we turn the bedrooms out one at a time. The kitchen cupboards are neat and tidy — we turned them out today.*

turn to

to ask (someone) for help, advice, support, etc: *Sally always turns to her elder brothers for advice. Roger's parents are elderly and poor — he cannot possibly turn to them for financial help.*

turn up

to be found or to appear, sometimes after being thought to be lost or to be unavailable: *The family thought that their cat was dead, but it turned up in the next village alive and well. Liz is unemployed but she's sure that the right job will turn up soon.*

U

use up

to use all of (something), to finish a supply of (something) so that there is none left: *We have used up all the milk — there is none left for tea. They've used most of the meat up, but there are plenty of vegetables left. There's no fuel left — we used it up last winter.*

V

veer off

suddenly to change direction: *Joe suddenly saw the exit sign and veered off the motorway. The police were chasing the thieves along the path when they suddenly veered off across the fields.*

verge on

to be very close or similar to, to border on: *Liz's laughter was verging on hysteria. They say that what Matt did was not an illegal act, but it was certainly verging on one.*

vie with

to compete with (someone or something), to try to do something better than (someone or something else): *Ella and Fay vied with each other for the English prize. It's difficult to predict who will win the golf trophy — several good players are vying for it.*

vouch for

to say that you can guarantee that (someone or something) is good, reliable, etc: *Tom is an honest worker — I can vouch for him. Rose said that she could vouch for Pat's skill as a nanny. The information is accurate — we can vouch for it.*

W

wade through

to read (a great deal of written material) with much time and effort: *I've got to wade through all these books for my research project. These documents contain new regulations and we've all got to wade through them.*

wait up for

not to go to bed because one is waiting until (someone) has returned to the house: *You don't have to wait up for Sue — she's an adult now. Jean wants to be back home before midnight because her parents insist on waiting up for her.*

wake up

to become conscious again after being asleep: *I woke up in the middle of the night, thinking that I had heard a noise downstairs. 'Wake up!' said Jane's mother, 'you'll be late for work!'*

wake up

to make (someone) more alert: *A walk by the sea might wake the children up. Having a cold shower certainly woke up Jenny. Harry said that he was going for a swim to wake himself up.*

wake up to

to become aware of (a situation, often a difficult or dangerous one): *George suddenly woke up to the fact that his firm was in financial difficulties. The troops soon woke up to the danger they were in.*

walk away from

not to try to deal with (a difficult or unpleasant situation), but to leave it or ignore it: *It was difficult for Jenny to walk away from the insults and jeers of her colleagues. The man in the pub challenged Pete to a fight, but he walked away from it.*

walk in on

to enter somewhere unexpectedly and see (someone or people) doing something private or something which one was not intended to see: *Ali walked in on the meeting that had been called to discuss sacking him from the firm.*

walk off with

to win (a prize, trophy, etc), especially easily: *Matt was the youngest competitor in the tournament, but he walked off with the first prize. The tennis championship trophy was shared last year, but this year Nell played so well that she walked off with it.*

wallow in

to choose to be in a state or situation, even although this is an unhappy one, as though you were enjoying it, to indulge in (something): *His friends were sorry when Tom lost his job, but he's been wallowing in self-pity ever since. Her husband caused Kate a lot of misery when he left — but she appears to be wallowing in it.*

warm to

to begin to like (someone or something), to become fond of (someone or something): *I didn't like Joe at first, but I warmed to him when he helped to fix my bike. The committee rejected the idea at first, but they are now warming to it.*

warm up

to heat up (cold food, etc) on a cooker, etc: *Molly warmed up the stew and served it with bread. Could you warm the soup up, please?*

warn off

to tell or advise (someone) not to do something because he/she might be punished or face other unpleasant consequences: *We warned the children off taking sweets from strangers. Jo has been warned off drinking too much. Acting is a very uncertain profession, and Lucy's parents tried to warn her off against it.*

wash down

to drink something after eating (food, etc) or while eating (food, etc): *The diners washed down the food with some excellent wines. They washed the sandwiches down with beer. Wilma took a sleeping tablet and washed it down with a glass of water.*

wash out

to remove (something) by washing: *Clive washed the dried mud out of his hair. Nita got paint on her shirt but managed to wash it out.*

wave off

to wave to (someone) as he/she leaves somewhere: *The children waved their father off to work. Your granny's leaving now — are you going to wave her off?*

weigh up

to consider (something) carefully, especially so as to come to a decision or make a choice: *We weighed the situation up and decided that we could not possibly win. Sheila weighed up the advantages and disadvantages of moving to the country, and decided to remain in the city. After weighing everything up, Charles decided to resign.*

while away

to spend (a period of time) without being bored, often because you have nothing else to do or because you are waiting for something: *We had an hour to wait for the bus, but we whiled away the time by walking in the park. You can while a few pleasant hours away watching the boats in the harbour. If you ever have an hour to spare try whiling it away at the local museum.*

whittle away at

gradually to make something smaller, weaker, etc: *Being unemployed for a time whittled away at Garry's savings. Various unsuccessful by-elections whittled away at the government's majority. A series of weak kings had whittled away at the power of the monarchy.*

win back

to win or get back (something which one has had before and lost): *Our hockey team had trained hard and won back the trophy which we lost last year. The government is campaigning hard to win disillusioned voters back before the next election.*

win over

to persuade (someone) to support or agree with one or one's point of view: *Paul tried to win his friends over to his way of thinking but failed. Val eventually got a new bike — she's good at winning her father over. At first Tina supported the rival candidate, but we eventually won her over to our side.*

wind up

to be in a place or situation, sometimes unpleasant, at the end of, and often as a result of, a series of events, to end up: *We were going to try a different holiday destination this year, but we wound up in the same old place again. If Pete does not take better care of himself, he will wind up in hospital.*

wipe off

to remove (something) by wiping it with a cloth, one's hand, etc: *You should wipe the sticky mess off the table. Did the cleaning agent wipe off the dirty mark? The child got dirt on her dress, but we wiped it off.*

wipe up

to remove (something such as dirt, liquid, etc) from a surface with a cloth, to clean (something) up: *The children were making dough on the kitchen table and it took a while to wipe up the mess. Please wipe up all that mess before you leave the kitchen. There's mud all over the carpet — I'll have to wipe it up.*

wolf down

to eat (something) quickly and greedily: *Teenage boys always seem to be starving — Beth's son's friends wolf down the contents of her fridge. The young man was very hungry and wolfed down a huge plate of food. Take time to enjoy your food — don't just wolf it down.*

work away at

to work hard and continuously at (something): *The research team worked away at the problem until they solved it. John must have nearly finished his thesis — he's been working away at it for months.*

work off

to get rid of (something), often by doing something energetic: *Mike worked off his weight increase by going to the gym. Ella's brother told her rudely to work some of her fat off by walking to work. Jock has a lot of stress at work and he works it off by swimming.*

work through

to deal with (something) gradually and thoroughly, in the hope of finding solutions to any problems: *It will take some time to work through all the objections to the proposal. Their marriage is experiencing difficulties, but they are prepared to work through these.*

work up

gradually to develop (something): *Have you worked up an appetite for dinner? Will couldn't work up the energy to go for a walk.*

worm out of

to obtain (information, a secret, etc) from (someone) slowly and gradually, usually after some persuasion: *Bill composed the questions for the quiz, but there's no point in trying to worm the answers out of him. Pam refused to give the name of the father of her baby, even though her parents tried to worm it out of her.*

wrap up

to cover (something) by folding paper, etc round it: *I'm just going to wrap up this wedding present. Barbara is just wrapping the gift up now. This is a valuable vase — I'll have to wrap it up carefully.*

wrap up

to be so involved with (someone or something) and spend so much time on him/her/it that one has little time for anyone else or anything else: *Jim was so wrapped up in his work that he spent hardly any time with his children. Jo and Annette are so wrapped up in each other that they rarely see their friends.*

wrestle with

to try with difficulty to deal with or solve (something), to struggle with (something): *Paul could not sleep because he was wrestling with his financial problems. I finally solved the problem after having wrestled with it for days.*

wriggle out of

to avoid doing something that one should, to dodge (something): *It was Anne's turn to do the washing-up, but she succeeded in wriggling out of it. You promised to deliver those leaflets — don't try to wriggle out of it now.*

write down

to record (something) in writing, using pen or pencil and paper: *I wrote down your telephone number, but I've lost it. She wrote several addresses down. I'll forget your address — please write it down!*

write off

to regard (someone or something) as being of no further use or value, or unimportant, unsuccessful, etc: *Don't write off the job which you've been offered without finding out more details. It would be foolish to write catering off as a career without knowing more about it.*

Y

yearn for

to want (something) very much, to long for (something): *It was mid-winter and we were all yearning for some sunshine. Sue finally achieved financial success, having yearned for it all her life.*

Answers

1. A Missing Passport

1 The burglar had **gone through** all the papers on my desk, looking for money.
2 The secretary was asked to **put** the documents **away** in the filing cabinet.
3 The police are **looking for** the murder weapon.
4 The student **asked for** more time to finish his essay.
5 We have to **hand in** the money for the college outing today.
6 Some people are off ill and so we are **putting off** the meeting until tomorrow.
7 The theatre trip has been **called off** — not enough people wanted to go.
8 We thought Don had left the area but he suddenly **turned up** in the pub last night.
9 I would like to **discuss** my career plans **with** my parents.
10 It had started to rain and Alice **had left** her umbrella **behind** on the bus.

2. A Street Accident

1 The delivery lorry **ran over** the little girl when she ran in front of it.
2 The burglar hit the old man on the head with a vase and **knocked** him **out**.
3 Tara **came round** in hospital after the attack on her.
4 We **ruled out** failure.
5 Mr Jackson is off ill and Mrs Cook is going to **act as** team coach until he recovers.
6 Tessa was only a student but she **made out** that she was an experienced teacher.
7 The referee **brushed aside** my protest and went on with the game.
8 Mike's account of the accident **agrees with** that of the other driver.
9 We always **keep** the children **in** their playroom if it is raining heavily.
10 The leading actor has a sore throat and has decided to **pull out of** the performance.

3. The Missing Directions

1 We haven't had time to **fix up** the annual meeting of the club yet.
2 Bert eventually **persuaded** his father and he was allowed to borrow the family car.
3 Jock has hired a minibus to take us to the football match and is going to **pick** us **up** at the college gates.
4 We **set out** at dawn.
5 'We've taken the wrong road,' **called out** Carol.

6 I wanted to find out exactly where Sydney was and so I **looked up** an atlas.
7 We had to stop **searching for** the missing child when night fell.
8 We simply cannot **take in** all the information that the teacher gives in one lecture.
9 My new desk arrived in a flat pack and I cannot **put** it **up**.
10 Mike had to take a reduction in salary when he moved jobs and now he has to **make do with** a poorer standard of living.

4. Childminding

1 Paul had been to a late-night party the night before and did not want to **get up**.
2 The childminder is paid to **look after** three young children.
3 The head of department is on study leave and her deputy is **standing in for** her
4 I was so tired that I could hardly **keep from** falling asleep.
5 Liz said that she divorced Alex because she could not **tolerate** his laziness.
6 It was a dull, wet morning but it **turned into** a beautiful day.
7 Fred drank too much beer at the party and **threw up** on the steps of the house.
8 The waitress **wiped up** the spilt coffee.
9 The patient is losing a lot of blood — she may not **last out** until the ambulance gets here.
10 The police **burst into** the nightclub to search for drugs.

5. A Change of Subject

1 The children **were heading for** the school when we met them.
2 Patrick has been advised to **give up** his present job as it is too stressful for him.
3 I have **got behind with** my ironing and all my clothes are creased.
4 Jo was a singer but he **dropped out of** the pop music some years ago.
5 Amy was a member of the Labour Party, but she **went over to** the Green Party some months ago.
6 Jack felt in need of a hobby and so he **took up** chess.
7 **get through to** someone.
8 We **put** her absence **down to** illness.
9 They didn't want to vote for us at first, but we eventually **won** them **over**.
10 No.

6. Waiting for a Job

1 Last night at the theatre I **ran into** my friend Bill.
2 John is going to ask the bank manager for a loan so that he can **start up** a sandwich bar.
3 Julie decided that it was best to **act on** her uncle's advice and get a mechanic to check the car before she bought it.
4 Kevin got really good marks in his exams and he is going to start **putting in for** a better job straight away.
5 I'm glad that I know how to type because it's something that I can always **fall back on** if I cannot find other work.
6 Ian was very upset when he realized that he would have to **close** his shop because it was not making any money.
7 Helen has already bought a car, so she is **banking on** passing her driving test.
8 Joe was devastated when he was **passed over** for promotion.
9 I tried to **pin** Jack **down** for an exact date for the wedding, but he did not give me one.
10 Carol was amazed that the bank agreed to **take** her **on** even though she had failed her exams.

7. Sunbathing Interrupted

1 I thought that it was very rude of Mrs Williams not to **ask us in** after we had done all her shopping for her.
2 The doctor advised Sharon that the best thing to do for her sore back was to **stretch out** on the floor.
3 David is really looking forward to his holiday; he plans to do nothing but **soak up** the sun for two weeks.
4 The glass of milk was on the edge of the table and when I stood up I **knocked** it **over**.
5 Daisy is going to make her chocolate cake for the bring-and-buy sale. It is delicious and is bound to get **snapped up** straight away.
6 Fred eventually **talked** Tina **into** going out on a date with him.
7 The waiter told us to **drink up** our wine and leave the restaurant as it was about to close.
8 I have to **put away** the laundry before I can make the dinner.
9 I don't take much care over my appearance; I tend to just **throw on** the first thing that I find in my wardrobe.
10 George is **saving up** all his coins in a jar.

8. Choosing a Present

1 Susan was delighted when she **found out** that her old friend had bought a flat in the street that she lived in.
2 Bob has gone to stay with his parents for a few days so that he can **think** things **over** and decide if he wants to get married or not.
3 I can't decide if I should accept the job offer; I think the best thing to do is to **sleep on** it.
4 Wendy had to **delay/postpone** her party because she was not well.
5 Steven was surprised to discover that the school had **done away with** exams and now all the students had to do was write essays.
6 Tracey asked an architect to **look over** the flat before she bought it.
7 On a Sunday Ruth likes to **while away** the time feeding the ducks.
8 Paul is going to **try out** the bike before he decides if he will buy it.
9 Mary reminded Lisa that she still had to **pay for** her share of the bill for the meal that they had last week.
10 I will be ready in a minute — I just need to **wrap** Andy's present **up**.

9. Burglary

1 Claire asked if I could **open up** the coffee shop in the morning as she had an appointment at the dentist.
2 Janice was very upset after the thieves **broke into** her house and stole her jewellery.
3 I had to **switch off** the computer because looking at the screen was giving me a sore head.
4 James had his phone disconnected because he had forgotten to pay his bill.
5 The teacher **sent for** George's parents because he had missed a lot of classes when he had been ill.
6 The flight was delayed and it was after midnight before we **reached** the holiday resort.
7 I had better **write down** this information in the files.
8 It took David a long time to **sweep up** the food that had been dropped on the floor at the party.
9 Carol did not agree with the manager's decision, but she felt that she had to **carry out** his instructions.
10 Peter was scared to go out at night after he had been **beaten up** by a complete stranger.

10. Dieting

1 Jill has decided to **give up** jogging because she finds that it hurts her knees.
2 When I was on holiday I practically **lived on** fruit and cheese.
3 Tracey could not **work up** any enthusiasm for her new job.
4 I hope that I can **get out of** going on holiday with Julie because I can't afford it.
5 The manager has **arranged** a meeting with the customer who made a complaint.
6 Robert is very reliable—once he makes a decision he **sticks to** it.

7 Wilma thinks that she will have to **do without** her car, because she has lost her job and can no longer afford to run it.

8 We had to spend a long time **clearing out** the house before we could sell it.

9 Sheila is **storing up** baby clothes in preparation for the birth of her grandchild.

10 The teacher warned the children to **keep off** the ice on the pond.

11. Gardening

1 Kevin is always moaning at me to **tidy up** the kitchen, but I don't make a mess — it's Fred.

2 Yvonne was very excited when she **dug up** a gold coin in her garden.

3 The local residents were very angry when the builders **chopped down** the woodland to make space for the new houses.

4 Keith has realized that he will have to **settle for** the place at the local college although he had really wanted to go to university.

5 Tina regretted asking the hairdresser to **cut off** her long hair.

6 Wendy got a terrible fright when she was **pounced on** by a stranger.

7 The football player had to be **carried off** the pitch.

8 We eventually **caught up with** the other cars after we found the right road.

9 We were **making for** the house, where the party was, but it started to snow so we decided to go home instead.

10 Pauline had to **stop** baking the cake when she realized that she did not have the right ingredients.

12. A Shopping Trip

1 Lesley decided that it was time to **look for** a new job.

2 I asked the driver to **drop** me **off** at the stop nearest the station.

3 The taxi is coming to **pick** you **up** at 8pm.

4 The police asked the protesters to **move on**.

5 Fiona will be able to tell me what has been happening while I've been away — she always manages to **nose out** the best gossip.

6 Colin took Rose to the jewellers and asked her to *choose* an engagement ring.

7 Anna was upset when she **tried on** her favourite dress and realized that it did not fit her any longer.

8 It was very cold outside so the teacher told the children to **put on** their hats and gloves.

9 Louise **covered up** the stain on the carpet with a rug.

10 I was too hot and so I removed my jumper.

13. A Surprise Test

1 It is a good idea to **pin up** a list of useful numbers on the wall by the phone.

2 My boss told me that I had better **get down to** the report.

3 Yvonne had to speak to the manager because she had **got behind with** her work after she had been off ill.

4 Rachel asked me to **pass on** her congratulations on passing your exams.

5 The teacher did not tell me that I had passed the exam, but she **hinted at** it.

6 I have to go to the library to **hand back** the books I took out last week.

7 Dave asked his girlfriend not to **get on at** him for not buying her expensive gifts.

8 Howard and Bob **worked away at** the decorating for hours.

9 George was embarrassed by all the attention that he received for saving the little girl and he tried to **play down** what he had done.

10 Ruth had hardly taken any driving lessons, but somehow she managed to **muddle through** it.

14. Organizing a Fete

1 Angela and Frank have not been getting on very well recently — I hope that they can **sort out** their problems.

2 The directors have been in a meeting all day trying to **thrash out** the take-over deal.

3 Tim finally decided to give up on his essay after he had been **wrestling with** it for days.

4 The flat-mates agreed to **divide up** the work that needed to be done.

5 If you give me a list of what we need from the supermarket, I can **tick** things **off** as I get them.

6 I phoned the hairdresser and asked him to **pencil in** an appointment for me on Tuesday.

7 The team **looked to** their captain to come up with a plan to save the game.

8 Susan is very pretty — she **takes after** her mother.

9 Wendy did not think the new restaurant was very good since they **skimped on** the portions.

10 The manager has decided that she is going to **tighten up** the security system after the shop was broken into.

15. A Dyeing Disaster

1 David and Joanna are **planning on** getting married in June, but they have not booked a church yet.

2 Tracey says that she can **vouch for** the new restaurant — she ate there last week and thought it was great.

3 I'm not sure about acupuncture, but Andy **swears by** it.

4 The teacher **read out** the list of names of children who had been chosen for the football team.

5 The doctor told Fred to **rub** the cream **into** his skin every morning.

6 Steven **put** a lid **over** the pot of soup.

7 The chef wanted to **use up** the cream because it would go off if it was left for another day.

8 Hilda tried to **wash out** the grass stain, but she had no success.

9 Jack carefully **peeled off** the plaster from his sore finger.

10 Richard **rinsed** the glass **out** before pouring his drink.

16. A Trip to the Seaside

1 The teachers **lined** the children **up** outside the cinema.

2 The teacher was asked to **quieten** the pupils **down** and get them to behave properly.

3 There were more guests than they had been expecting at the party, and so they had to **eke out** the wine.

4 Rupert loves desserts and he **tucked into** the chocolate mousse.

5 The family were glad to *reach* their hotel after a very long journey.

6 The sisters look very similar and it is hard to **tell** them **apart**.

7 Beverly dropped some butter on the carpet, but was able to **wipe** it **off**.

8 I always **tie** my hair **back** before I go swimming.

9 The helicopter was able to **land on** the roof of the building.

10 Peter is trying to **summon up** enough courage to ask Linda out on a date.

17. A Skiing Trip

1 Judy had to *cancel* her birthday party because she was not well.

2 I feel that I've **let** myself **down** by not studying hard enough for my exams.

3 The teacher had to go home early, and the head teacher said that he would **stand in for** her.

4 The police **called on** the local residents to come forward with any information that would help them to solve the crime.

5 Anna had to take her daughter to the hospital and she asked if I could **help out** by looking after the shop while she was gone.

6 Ian would love to go on holiday, but he feels that it is a lot of money to **part with** for two weeks in the sun.

7 Bobby was **turfed out** of the club for refusing to pay for his drink.

8 Lynne is desperate, but she can't think of anyone that she can **turn to**.

9 The family decided to go for a walk to **work off** the big meal.

10 You would get indigestion if you **wolfed down** your meal.

18. The Perfect Cottage

1 Dennis was surprised to notice that it was getting dark and that he had **idled** the whole day **away**.

2 Trevor spent a long time looking at flats before he bought one, but eventually **decided on** one near his work.

3 Donna thought that the house was worth the asking price, but she asked her father to **see over** it before making an offer.

4 Julie **noted down** the details of some holidays that she saw in the travel agent's window.

5 I **telephoned** Paul and asked him to come to the party but he was not in the mood.

6 Evelyn made an appointment for the estate agent to **show** her **round** the flat.

7 Donald searched in his rucksack and eventually **fished out** his passport.

8 The police **impressed on** the children the dangers of playing on thin ice.

9 The successful candidate had to **beat off** a lot of stiff competition to get the job.

10 Alison decided to **take** Robert **up on** his offer of a job at the coffee shop.

19. An Important Invitation

1 Rachael **popped into** her granny's house on her way home from work.

2 Simon regretted **letting in** the salesman, who refused to go away until he had delivered his entire sales pitch.

3 The waiter **poured out** the wine for the wedding guests.

4 John **cooked up** some excuse about not being well but I did not believe him.

5 Philip has not studied for the exam and he is trying to **duck out of** sitting it by saying that he is ill.

6 William wants Helen to marry him, but he realizes that there is no point in trying to **force** her **into** it.

7 The couple decided to **leave aside** the details of the menu until they knew how many people would be coming.

8 Roger is upset that his daughter has again **foisted** her dog **on** him while she goes away on holiday.

9 The manager **sided with** the customer and said that Mary had been in the wrong.

10 John has decided to leave university — his parents have tried to **reason with** him but he will not change his mind.

20. A Stress Test

1 The students were **herded into** the hall and told where to sit for the exam.

2 Sam is trying to **bear up**, but he is finding it difficult to cope with his new job.

3 Walter has told Elaine that it is her responsibility to **deal with** staff who are late for work.

4 Sarah says that she has **heard of** a new restaurant that is meant to serve excellent food.

5 Sid **hit on** the idea of selling coffee outside the new office block.

6 The children were **separated up** into three teams for the relay race.

7 The protesters were distributing leaflets outside the nuclear plant.

8 Karen tried hard to **fit into** the flat, but she found her flat-mates annoying.

9 Lydia was invited to join in the game, but she refused to **enter into** it.

10 It took Terry several hours to **hammer out** his essay but he finished it on time.

21. A Car Accident

1 Trevor plans to **meet up with** some old school friends when he is in town.

2 Diane set a fast pace in the race and soon the other runners were **lagging behind**.

3 The traffic got **snarled up** when a flock of sheep wandered onto the road and could not be moved.

4 Rona wished that she had **listened to** her teacher and studied harder for her exams.

5 Veronica was so annoyed with her husband that she **smashed up** the set of antique plates which he had given her as a present.

6 The car skidded on the ice and **rammed into** the wall.

7 The family decided to **leave** their dog **behind** when they went on holiday.

8 I had to phone the police and ask them to **tow away** the car that was blocking my driveway.

9 The firm **ploughed** a great deal of money **into** the new venture, but it did not work out.

10 The bank manager suggested that I take out a loan to buy a car, but I don't think that I could afford to **pay** it **off**.

22. A Football Camp

1 The council **set down** strict guidelines for the design of new houses.

2 You will be asked to leave if you cannot **abide by** the rules.

3 Joseph decided to leave university because he did not feel that his results **measured up to** the level he needed to get a good degree.

4 Janice is not very popular because she tends to **look down on** other girls who are not as pretty as she is.

5 Susan was annoyed that the boss had **singled** her **out** for criticism when she thought that the whole staff team had been at fault.

6 The security guard refused to **let** anyone **through** to see the film star.

7 The members of the audience all **remarked on** how well the actress had played her part.

8 The celebrity tried to **fend off** the attention of the press.

9 Andrea had been working very hard on her essay, but she was finding it difficult to maintain that level of study.

10 The referee **sent** Ian **off** for swearing.

23. In Financial Difficulties

1 Bill and Suzanne have finally **faced up to** the fact that their marriage is over.

2 It suddenly **dawned on** Tina that Steve had been seeing someone else behind her back.

3 I don't know how Jenny is going to **cope with** working full-time and looking after the children on her own.

4 Charlotte **frittered away** all her money and could not afford to pay her rent.

5 Paying for the repairs to her car after the accident really **ate into** Kate's savings.

6 The young man was so hungry that he **resorted to** stealing a sandwich from the shop.

7 Keith had to admit he was having an affair because he could not **explain away** the lipstick mark on his shirt.

8 Jonathan is going to move out of his flat because he keeps **falling out** with his flat-mate.

9 The manager is refusing to **cough up** for the overtime that I worked last week.

10 Sheila **coaxed** Ruth **into** going on holiday with her.

24. The Winners

1 The team had been playing very well all season, and they felt they had a good chance of **walking off with** the cup.

2 Christine warned John that he was not to **show** her **up** at the office party by flirting with other women.

3 Darren **levelled** his criticism **at** the doctor for not diagnosing the illness sooner.

4 Jeff is doing his best to **win back** his girlfriend's affection.

5 Our team may not have a chance of getting through the next round — we are **pitted against** last year's champions.

6 Steve has made an appointment with the bank manager so that he can **rough out** the plans for his new business.

7 Lynne went to watch the race so that she could **cheer on** her friend.

8 I'm too busy to organize the holiday and so I am going to **trust to** Pam to do it.

9 William is **banking on** getting good enough marks to get into university.

10 Tim was annoyed that Fred **carried off** the prize for the best player of the match.

25. A Would-be Actor

1 The soldier was **hailed as** a hero when he returned to his home town.
2 Lucy is determined to **carve out** a career as lawyer.
3 If Gerry gets a good degree, it will **open up** a wide range of opportunities for him.
4 Tina **disagreed with** the way the company treated its customers.
5 Bob was looking at rings in the jewellers, and Helen suspected that he was **leading up to** proposing to her.
6 Dom tried to **argue** Jane **out of** calling off the engagement.
7 Chris was late for the meeting because he had not **allowed for** getting stuck in a traffic jam.
8 If Russell and Pauline do not stop arguing all the time, I think they will **wind up** getting divorced.
9 The children get bored because the teacher just **trots out** the same lesson every day.
10 Since Caroline had missed so many classes through being ill, it would be best to **opt out of** her college course and start again at the beginning of the year.

26. Buying a Car

1 Trevor has been **flicking through** holiday brochures for days, but he has not booked anything.
2 Sarah **shopped around** and got a really good deal on her new stereo.
3 Dawn has asked me to give her back the book that she lent me and so I am going to have to **hunt** it **out**.
4 The parents **hit out at** the head teacher for not making sure that the climbing frame in the playground was secure.
5 I would like to see the film that all the critics have been **enthusing over**.
6 Our plan to go on holiday **fell through** because I fell and broke my leg the day before we were due to leave.
7 Sue has rushed down to the clothes shop because she heard that they had **marked down** the designer clothes.
8 Jennifer is going to **try out** renting a cottage in the country for a few months before she decides if she will buy a house there.
9 The television was working fine until Andrew started to **tinker with** it.
10 The car doesn't seem to be running very well — I think that it probably needs to be **tuned up**.

27. A Health Scare

1 The teacher threatened to **keep** the children **in** at lunchtime if they did not behave.
2 Susan was a bright pupil and naturally **fell into** the group that was expected to go to university.
3 The teacher warned the pupil that if he did not behave, he would **end up** in the principal's office.

4 Robert promised to take me on holiday, but now he is trying to **wriggle out of** it.
5 The salesman **frightened** Jane **into** buying a burglar alarm by saying that there had been a lot of break-ins in the area.
6 When I go on holiday, I always try to **guard against** pickpockets.
7 Michelle **woke up to** the fact that her husband was unfaithful when she saw him kissing another woman.
8 George **warned** Fred **off** eating in the canteen because it was horrible.
9 Tracey made an appointment with the bank manager to **sketch out** her plans for a new business venture.
10 The editor has **imposed** a very tight deadline **on** all of his staff.

28. Planning a Night Out

1 The manager had to **ring round** all the staff about the missing keys.
2 Tom wanted a rare copy of an old record, and I eventually **tracked** it **down** in a charity shop.
3 It was a very cold winter and granny **ran up** a huge heating bill.
4 Jean's parents do not **approve of** her boyfriend.
5 Roger and Julie were looking forward to getting married, but his parents kept **interfering with** their plans for the wedding.
6 Can I **call** you **back** in half an hour? I'm just washing my hair.
7 Ruth explained to the customer that she could not help him, but he **hung up** before she finished talking.
8 The jumble sale would be very busy, and so Lisa tried to **round up** as many helpers as possible.
9 Keith offered to **put** me **up** for a couple of nights while my flat was being decorated.
10 I asked John not to **wait up for** me, but he was still awake when I got back after the party.

29. Room-cleaning

1 The children were **hoarding up** sweets for a midnight feast.
2 Frank said that it made a huge difference to his heating bill since he had his house **fitted up with** central heating.
3 Vera had to **empty out** the rabbit hutch so that she could clean it properly.
4 I asked Dave to **fill up** the bath with piping hot water.
5 No-one would admit to stealing the money, and so the teacher asked all of the children to **turn out** their pockets.
6 The vase looked as good as new once it had been **dusted down**.

7 The security guard told the thief that if he replaced the items that he had stolen he would not call the police.

8 James is a very messy cook — he manages to **clutter up** every surface, even when he is making a simple meal.

9 Tricia **derives** a great deal of pleasure **from** telling other people that they are wrong.

10 Now that the meeting is over, I can **file away** the report.

30. A Broken Leg

1 Kevin is going to have to **do without** an assistant in the shop because he cannot afford to pay any more wages.

2 Louise **dispensed with** her lawyer because he was useless and expensive.

3 Susan had to go to hospital after she **fell over** and banged her head.

4 I twisted my ankle when I **tripped over** the curb.

5 It did not **occur to** Jane that she could just ask for a pay rise.

6 The soldiers were ordered to **stand up** when the officer entered the room.

7 The librarian **lifted up** the pile of books and took them over to the shelves.

8 The police **carted** the protesters **off** to the station for questioning.

9 Ruth ruined the plan to have a surprise party for Tom by telling him all about it.

10 Peter does not think that the job will pay enough money for him to **live off**.

31. Making a Job Move

1 Lorraine bought the dress straight away — it was just what she had been **looking out for**.

2 Fiona said that she would have to **mull over** the proposal that she move to another city to get a better job.

3 Wendy somehow managed to **muster up** the courage to ask her boss for a promotion.

4 I **came across** the advert in the local newspaper yesterday.

5 The girl said that she had stolen the sweets from the shop because she had been **egged on** by her brother.

6 Paul complained that heating his flat was **swallowing up** his wages.

7 I cannot **fathom out** why James left university — he always got excellent marks.

8 The manager was very pleased with Robert for **coming up with** the idea of going on a team-building course.

9 Dave is trying to **gear** himself **up** to sell his house.

10 The editor told the journalist that she would need to **flesh** her article **out** a bit.

32. The Exam Aftermath

1 Ivy does not like her new teacher — she **tends towards** strictness.

2 Fred was trying to keep a straight face when the policeman was talking to him, but he was **verging on** laughing the whole time.

3 Trudy has **written off** her relationship with Peter because he refuses to talk about getting married.

4 Tom is going to spend the day **brushing up on** general knowledge in preparation for the quiz.

5 Tony will have to **swot up on** algebra if he wants to do well in the test.

6 Trevor and William have been **vying with** each other for the attention of the new girl at work.

7 Liam did not run a very good race and was relieved that he managed to **scrape through** to the next round.

8 My essay was a bit short, but I managed to **pad it out** with some quotes.

9 Julie was very nervous about her job interview, but she **sailed through** it.

10 Philip keeps **brooding over** the accident he had last week, but it was not his fault.

33. A Winter Holiday

1 The children **huddled round** the teacher while she told them the ghost story.

2 The local residents **prevailed on** the council to change their mind about closing the school.

3 Helen is furious at Ruth for **backing out of** going on holiday with her.

4 I was sick last night and did not **feel up to** going into work this morning.

5 After studying the menu for a long time, Bob eventually chose the chocolate mousse.

6 We should get someone else to move in to share the cost of the rent, and I am hoping that she will **fall in with** the plan.

7 I have a lot of outstanding bills to pay and I am going to **attend to** them when I get paid at the end of the month.

8 I'm not surprised that Yvonne has dropped out of university — her father **pushed** her **into** going.

9 Peter needs a cup of strong black coffee in the morning to **wake** him **up** before he starts work.

10 Caroline **called in at** the office where she used to work, to see her old colleagues.

34. Sudden Illness

1 Aileen switched on the indicator to show that she was about to **move off**.

2 The police asked the crowd not to **cluster round** the cyclist, who had an accident.

3 I saw Paul at the party last night and he was **asking for** you.

4 The boxer had to be taken to hospital after he **blacked out** at the end of the fight.

5 Roger could not stop sneezing and he hoped he was not **coming down with** a cold.

6 Crowds of fans **descended on** the hotel where the band were staying.

7 Sheila's mother is **buzzing around**, trying to finalize the arrangements for the wedding on Saturday.

8 The manager **took** Fiona **aside** and warned her not to be late again.

9 The doctor said that the only way that I will be able to use my arm again is to **operate on** it.

10 Lucy enjoyed climbing the mountain, but it **took** a lot **out of** her.

35. Market Research

1 I feel sorry for Derek, but he should have known what he was **letting** himself **in for** when he married Joan — she has a terrible temper.

2 The train journey passed quickly after I **struck up** a conversation with the woman sitting beside me.

3 Keith **jotted down** the date of the concert.

4 The family **loaded up** the car with all the things that they need.

5 Julie was worried that Kevin would **fly into** a rage when he realized that she had crashed the car.

6 The children soon **cast aside** their favourite toys when their mother brought home a computer for them to play with.

7 George decided to stop for a rest after he had **clocked up** eight hours of driving on the motorway.

8 Joanna is a very shy girl and does not like to **engage in** social gatherings.

9 Tracey got a terrible fright when the youth **leapt out at** her from behind.

10 Monica was telling her friend about the surprise she had planned for her husband's birthday, but had to **break off** when he walked in.

36. Amateur Dramatics

1 I am going to ask Jane to take me shopping with her — she always manages to **ferret out** the best bargains.

2 Peter has been **thumbing through** the property guide, but he has not seen a house which he likes.

3 The teacher asked Jenny to **hand round** the books for the afternoon's lesson.

4 There was a lot of work to do before they could set up camp and so the friends **parcelled out** the various jobs.

5 I agree that the team played well last year, but I still think that they can **improve on** their tactics.

6 The referee told the football player to stop **hamming up** his injury and to get on with playing the game.

7 I cannot **shake off** the feeling that someone has been going through my belongings.

8 Charles finally managed to **scrape together** enough money to pay for the bill.

9 The manager fired Elaine because she was always **stirring up** trouble in the office.

10 Wilma **stuck up for** Jean when the manager accused her of being useless at her job.

37. Auditions

1 After we got off the train, we decided to **scout around** for a place to stay.

2 Ruth asked if she could have time to **weigh up** the pros and cons of accepting the offer of a new job in another city.

3 Steve **ranks among** the fastest sprinters in the country.

4 Tony's parents were **brimming over with** pride as they watched him receive his award for bravery.

5 The sale of the house **hinges on** the couple, who want to buy it, being able to sell their own house.

6 Needles **bring out** the coward in me — they just make me want to run away from the clinic.

7 Lorraine resigned from the residents' committee because she was tired of **getting bogged down in** petty arguments.

8 The children **trooped into** the dining hall to get their lunch.

9 I think that we will have to **partition off** part of the lounge to use as an extra bedroom.

10 Getting turned down for so many jobs has really **whittled away at** Emma's confidence.

38. Bullying

1 The doctor told Jane not to worry about her son sucking his thumb, and that he would soon **grow out of** it.

2 Suzanne was delighted when the other children asked her to **join in** their game of chase.

3 I bet the treasurer is relieved that the scandal about the missing money seems to have **blown over**.

4 Trudy complained to her manager that Donald had been **picking on** her.

5 The teacher gave the children a scolding for **ganging up on** the boy.

6 Peter is a very strong character and does not let anyone **push** him **around**.

7 Jessica decided that she would **tell on** Robert for cheating in the test.

8 Thomas was trying to pick an argument with me all morning, but I just **walked away from** it.

9 Darren's father told him that he should have **hit** the other boy **back** when he punched him.

10 Stealing money from the till **went beyond** the usual schoolboy pranks.

39. A Breakdown

1 We decided that it would be nice to go down and **camp out** at the beach.

2 If we all **club together,** we can probably afford to buy Diana a necklace.

3 Rachel's friends all **chipped in** to buy her a birthday present.

4 Alex is going to **rent out** his flat while he is working abroad.

5 The tourists all **piled into** the open-topped bus that would take them on a sightseeing tour of the city.

6 The dog was chasing the cat along the street when it **veered off** up an alley.

7 Hurry up, I don't want to miss my train and end up having to **hang around** at the station.

8 We are running low on food — we are going to have to **ration out** what we have got left.

9 You will get indigestion if you **gulp down** your food.

10 William tried to **make up for** forgetting Hannah's birthday by buying her an expensive pair of earrings.

40. A Visit to the Zoo

1 Ruth decided that she would **take** her boss **up on** his offer of a promotion.

2 Ella was looking forward to the party because Suzie had said that she would try and **pair** her **off** with her cousin who was very handsome.

3 Rose **held onto** the handrail as she descended the steep stairs.

4 The friends **gathered round** the bonfire as it began to get cooler after the sun went down.

5 The thief grabbed Mavis's bag, and then **hared off** down the street.

6 Our friends **went round** the exhibition last week.

7 The police had to **barge through** the crowd of onlookers in order to get to the scene of the accident.

8 I **hosed down** the windows but they are still dirty.

9 Tom told Helen that he planned to **slip away** before anyone made a fuss and insisted that he stay at the party.

10 I think that we should **head back** — it looks like the weather is going to turn nasty.

41. A Surprise Goes Wrong

1 Katie was so **wrapped up** in studying that she forgot to eat her dinner.

2 Martin **clammed up** when the manager started quizzing him about where he had been all morning.

3 Roger **crossed out** the items on the shopping list as he put them in the trolley.

4 Anna **screwed up** the letter telling her that she had failed her exams and threw it on the fire.

5 At first I was pleased that Frank had won the race but he keeps **harping on** about it and it is getting on my nerves.

6 No-one knows the name of Ben's new girlfriend but Jean is determined to **worm** it **out of** him.

7 Ian **bluffed** his boss **into** believing that he had been working hard.

8 Yvonne could not stand to keep it a secret any longer and she **blurted out** the name of the father of her baby.

9 Sometimes I get the feeling that Howard is just **playing along** with Lily's plan to get married next year.

10 Sharon **cried out** for help after the man snatched her handbag.

42. A Murder Investigation

1 The hockey player **keeled over** after the ball hit her head.

2 The animals had been **subjected to** years of neglect.

3 The company was **snowed under** with complaints after it failed to honour its promise to give each customer a free gift.

4 I am going to spend the weekend **sifting through** the replies to my ad for a second-hand bike.

5 Fiona spent hours **keying in** the statistics for the annual report, but forgot to save her work.

6 We are going to that new restaurant tonight and you are welcome to **tag along**.

7 The manager **genned** his staff **up on** what had happened at the directors' meeting.

8 Fred expects that he will **take over** as manager when Paul retires.

9 Fiona was making a good job of her presentation to the committee, but Sam **horned in on** it and ruined it.

10 The judges have **narrowed down** the number of contestants to three for the final round.

43. A Wedding Invitation

1 Steve decided that he was going to buy his own flat because he was sick of **forking out** for rent.

2 Dave wanted Sheila to forgive him and **plied** her **with** gifts, but she would not speak to him.

3 Trisha felt that an early marriage would **tie** her **down**.

4 When Emma suggested that Louise could move into her spare room, she **seized on** the idea.

5 Nervous tension was **mounting up** amongst the students as the week of the exams drew closer.

6 Lydia resented **shelling out** money for a meal that had been almost inedible.

7 Phil admitted that he needed to **pare down** his book collection because it was taking up the whole of his front room.

8 Oliver wanted to live abroad for a year, but Trudy **was opposed to** the idea.

9 Pamela has been on a diet for a week, and she is **yearning for** some chocolate.

10 Simon and Mandy have **settled on** May 6th as the date for their wedding.

44. The Missing Tickets

1 We really need a bigger house, but I can't bear to **go through** the ordeal of selling this one.
2 Tom **marked down** the name of the hotel where he was going to be staying and gave it to his parents.
3 The waiter **checked** our names **against** his booking list, but could not find our reservation.
4 Yvonne had a wonderful holiday, **lolling about** in the sun and reading her book.
5 The baby was just about to **drift off** when somebody slammed a door and woke it up.
6 I did not **wake up** until the alarm went off.
7 The teacher **announced** the names of the pupils who had been chosen for the school football team.
8 Phillip has **come up with** a brilliant plan for Samantha's birthday.
9 The actor **tore up** the article that criticized his performance in the play.
10 Freddy **believes in** astrology, and won't go anywhere without reading his stars.

45. Lost Love

1 The airport official studied Jenny's passport before **handing** it **back** to her.
2 The manager is hoping that the technical difficulties with the new computer have finally been **solved/overcome**.
3 It took several hours to **straighten out** the house after it had been broken into and vandalized.
4 James is determined to **work through** the problems that he has been having with his flat-mates.
5 Anne **stormed off** without saying goodbye when she saw Tony kissing another woman at the party.
6 Al and Vera **split up** after they realized that they did not love each other any more.
7 Carol should spend more time studying, and less time **mooning about** thinking about boyfriends.
8 Karen is **toying with** the idea of going back to work after the children start school.
9 Walter has been **wallowing in** self-pity since Jackie left him.
10 Oliver thinks that it was eating the shellfish that **caused/started** his food poisoning.

46. Hard Work Rewarded

1 It was no surprise that John got **sent down** for cheating in his exams.
2 Pat tried to **juggle** studying **with** working full-time.
3 At school Hannah was often **put down as** stupid because she had difficulty spelling.
4 Andrew wants to **dissociate** himself **from** the crowd that he used to hang around with because they are always causing trouble.
5 The children were warned to **stay away from** the derelict factory because it was not a safe place to play.

6 Next year I am going to **centre** my attention **on** studying for my exams.
7 Fiona **confided in** her father that she was having second thoughts about getting married to Terry.
8 Hugh decided that it was time that he **put in for** a promotion.
9 The outcome of the court case **rests with** the jury.
10 Drew was **debarred from** the tennis club after he swore at the umpire.

47. A Proposal with a Difference

1 Jane's parents think that the man that she has **fallen for** is likely to cause her trouble.
2 Penny's enthusiasm for her new job was **damped down** when she got a new boss.
3 Ernie discovered that Gina had just been **stringing** him **along** by saying that she would go into business with him.
4 Samantha is **buttering up** her boss before she asks if she can have three weeks off.
5 Donna promised to go to the cinema with Jake tonight, but now she is trying to **get out of** it.
6 Ralph was **turned down** for a job with the police because he was too short.
7 Paula had been **trapped into** accepting the blame for the missing money.
8 I lost my job because my employers **delved into** my past and found out that I did not have the qualifications.
9 Heather **stumbled on** the advert for the holiday.
10 It was a difficult decision, but Yvette and Paul decided to **go through** with their divorce.

48. Permission for a Party

1 Debbie had been expecting her father to buy her a new car, but he **palmed** her **off with** an old banger.
2 Pauline was only just able to **choke back** her anger as her manager informed her that she was expected to work all weekend while he played golf.
3 The residents were **ranged against** the plan to dig up the trees to build new houses.
4 Ivy is going to **press ahead with** her plan to start her own business.
5 Don't forget that Des and Mary have **invited** us **over** for dinner tonight.
6 Irene is having her grandchildren to stay for the weekend and has **stocked up on** their favourite food.
7 Dave decided to **jazz up** the table by putting out some candles and flowers.
8 Kevin's father offered to **lay on** the transport to take people home after the party.
9 Sharon's face **lit up** when Sean asked her to marry him.
10 Robert **launched into** a string of excuses when the manager asked him why he was late for work.

49. A Family Trip

1 The bus was full but the driver let me **squeeze into** it because it was pouring with rain and I was soaking wet.
2 Everyone **marvelled at** Julia's performance in the play.
3 The inspector waited patiently while Ruth **dug into** her bag to find her ticket.
4 The teacher asked Veronica to **dish out** the books for the lesson to the children.
5 The taxi driver would not set off until he knew that everyone was **strapped into** their seats.
6 Sarah felt like crying as she **waved** her brother **off** when he left home to go to university.
7 Tracey was watching a film on television, but it was boring and she **switched over** to watch a comedy show instead.
8 The traffic always **tails back** on this stretch of road at the weekends.
9 Ian tried to **jolly** everyone **along**, but they were bored and wanted to go home.
10 Travelling by bus always makes me **sick/vomit**.

50. A Successful Take-over Bid

1 Ron has been **raking in** huge wages.
2 The old church is in a bad state of repair — it's **crying out for** a new roof.
3 It is sad that the large supermarkets have **taken over** the small, local shops.
4 The teacher **deferred** the decision regarding Hamish's future at the school **to** the head teacher.
5 Fiona's parents **put up** the deposit of her house.
6 It is difficult for small businesses to compete with the large companies who **cream off** the best workers.
7 Elaine was **divested of** her position as a local councillor after she was charged for corruption.
8 Claire has two boyfriends and she is always **playing** them **off against** each other.
9 Charlotte had to **pass up** the offer of a free holiday because she could not get any time off work to go.
10 I won't be able to come with you to the theatre tonight because an emergency has **happened/occurred** at work.

51. Assembling Furniture

1 Martin could not **put** the shelves **together** because he did not have a screwdriver.
2 May and Bob were going to get divorced, but they decided not to bother when they realized that they would both have to **lay out** a fortune on legal fees.
3 Amy reminded Douglas to **add in** a tip for the waitress when he paid the bill.
4 Dennis has been trying to **laugh off** the fact that he did not get the job that he applied for.
5 Tracey's childminder let her down at the last minute, but Nicola was able to **bail** her **out** by agreeing to watch the children while she was at work.
6 I am going to spend the evening **mugging up on** the Highway Code before my driving test.
7 The salesman wanted $5,000 for the car, but I **beat** it **down** to $4,000.
8 The librarian **took** the book **off** the shelf and gave it to the customer.
9 The lawyer **read through** the case notes before meeting his client.
10 We had to find an alternative hotel because the travel agent had **muddled up** our booking.

52. The College Prize

1 Gail's employers are going to **put** her **through** a computer course.
2 The lawyer is going to **wade through** past case reports to see if she can find any instances of similar cases being dropped.
3 The exercise class is **geared towards** people who are already quite fit.
4 The doctor told Des to **ease up on** his jogging because of his age.
5 The stress of bringing up two children on her own is beginning to **tell on** Colette.
6 The manager said that she had expected sales to **taper off** after the Christmas rush.
7 Ruth **warmed towards** her new teacher from the first day they met.
8 I don't like my new boss — his manner **savours of** bullying.
9 The sprinter was **gaining on** the leader when he fell and twisted his ankle.
10 I would not like to **take** John **on** in an argument — he has a fierce temper.

53. A Skating Trip Goes Wrong

1 Just because the water has **frozen over** does not mean that it is safe to walk on.
2 The windscreen of the car had **iced over** during the night.
3 The manager **ignored** his staff's concerns about having to work at weekends.
4 Please lower the volume of your music — I'm **listening out for** the phone ringing.
5 Hal **opted out of** the holiday at the last minute.
6 Marion phoned the police when the youths tried to **muscle in on** her party.
7 Melanie was helpless as she watched the thief **make off with** her bag.
8 Sarah **stowed** the presents **away** under the bed so that the children would not find them.

9   Charlie was **rooting about** in the garden shed looking for his old tennis racket.

10 The car was **jutting out of** the driveway and got hit by a bus.

54. A City Attack

1   Ian had to **dip into** his rent money to pay the electricity bill.

2   The manager **drummed into** his staff the importance of treating customers well.

3   Rick and Fay are trying to **protect** their children **from** the effects of the divorce.

4   The hotel used to be beautiful, but it has **fallen into** disrepair.

5   The drunk man **grabbed at** his drink before he was thrown out of the pub.

6   Julie decided to turn round and **face down** the man that was following her.

7   The little girl **cut into** her birthday cake with delight.

8   The first-aid team were able to **bring** the player **round** before the ambulance arrived.

9   Phil was relieved that he had **got away with** lying to his girlfriend.

10 The stray cat **answered to** the description of the cat that Jack had lost.

55. Locked Out

1   Wilma is worried about going to the hospital and so she is going to **take along** her brother **to** the appointment.

2   I asked Tom what sort of music he liked and he **rattled off** a long list of bands that he listened to.

3   Offering free wine certainly helped to **pull** the crowds **in**.

4   The nurse **saw** the patient **to** the ambulance.

5   The teacher told the children to **put away** their books and get ready for gym class.

6   Janet was furious with Jim for being late — so she **locked** him **out** of their flat.

7   It is **getting on for** 2am and I think that we should go home.

8   The secretary finally managed to **puzzle out** what had happened to the missing cash.

9   Helen promised to **look out** the recipe for me.

10 Tim could not sleep and so he **warmed up** some milk and made himself a cup of cocoa.

56. Party Clean-up

1   Victoria **washed down** the nuts with a glass of juice.

2   Yvonne **pursued/followed** the customer suspected of stealing from the shop.

3   Sid looked at his watch as Fred **held forth** about his holiday in Spain.

4   Tracey **gathered up** the dirty clothes and put them in the washing machine.

5   Nicola could not **get** the grass stain **off** her jeans.

6   Before we could begin to decorate, we had to **scrape off** the old wallpaper.

7   It took a long time to **scrub off** the grease from the cooker.

8   At the end of the argument, Bob lost his temper and **pushed** Howard **over**.

9   Wendy said that she would try to **patch up** the old dress, but that Jane would need to buy a new one soon.

10 You had better **slap on** some sunscreen before we go to the beach.

57. No Sea View

1   George's parents **insisted on** him going to university but he would have preferred to get a job.

2   Sue happily **fell in with** her friend's plan to get a flat together.

3   Greg **put** his complaint about the new development **to** his local councillor.

4   It was a bad connection and I could not **understand** what Don was trying to say.

5   Gavin **lashed out at** Grant for damaging his computer.

6   Robbie **laid** his proposal **before** the directors.

7   I suspect that he is guilty of stealing the money, but I think that we should **hear** him **out** before we decide what to do.

8   Mary is **pushing for** a pay rise and, if she does not get it, she will look for another job.

9   My washing machine was leaking and I had to **get** a plumber **in** to fix it.

10 It takes a lot of money to **keep up** these old buildings.

58. Work Comes to a Halt

1   The Browns had an alarm system **put in** after their next-door neighbour's house was broken into.

2   I **went by** the recipe, but the cake turned out to be inedible.

3   Paul had given up drinking, but he **reverted to** it after his wife left him.

4   I **traded in** my old car and bought a brand new one.

5   Dave managed to **stave off** his hunger by eating a banana.

6   Frank left his last job because he had a manager who **was** always **doing** him **down.**

7   News about the assault soon **got around** the small community.

8   Mavis has asked her daughter to try and **keep down** the cost of the wedding reception.

9   My mother always advised me to **invest in** a good pair of walking shoes.

10 I had to hand wash all my clothes when the washing machine **broke down**.